What teens and others are saying about
Secrets G

"As media and commercial cult
on girls to conform to standards that
and their relationships with others, Secrets Girls Keep gives teenage
girls down-to-earth, practical, heartfelt advice that will empower them
to resist the pressure and take care of themselves and others in these
hard-to-grow-up times. Parents will thank Carrie Silver-Stock for giving them this book to give to and discuss with their daughters."

—Diane Levin, Ph.D.
professor of education, Wheelock College,
and author of *So Sexy So Soon*

"The key to happiness is getting real and finding a way to be okay
with who we are . . . our authentic selves. How great would it be to
learn how to tap into this honest and open place as a teenager? When
girls follow Carrie's guidelines for shedding their secrets and taking
charge of their lives, the world has no choice but to be a better place!"

—Deborah Reber
teen advocate, speaker, and author

"*Secrets Girls Keep* is compelling in its honesty, openness, and just
plain good sense. Written for teenage girls who face pressures that are
almost impossible to imagine, it models getting beneath the silence
and shame that all too often accompany life problems (loss, sex, abuse,
eating problems, mood disorder) and actively engages them in self-
exploration and disclosure. A vitally important book."

—Stephen Hinshaw, Ph.D.
professor and chair, department of psychology,
UC Berkeley, author of *The Triple Bind:
Saving Our Teenage Girls from Today's Pressures*

"I loved *Secrets Girls Keep* because it helped me figure out a lot
about myself. The book was very inspiring. I also loved the book
because it helps me to talk to my friends better and even my mom."

—Tierra B., 14

Secrets Girls Keep

What Girls Hide (& Why) and How to Break the Stress of Silence

Carrie Silver-Stock, M.S.W., L.C.S.W.

HCI TEENS™

Health Communications, Inc.
Deerfield Beach, Florida

www.hcibooks.com

Library of Congress Cataloging-in-Publication Data

Silver-Stock, Carrie.
    Secrets girls keep / Carrie Silver-Stock.
        p. cm.
    Includes bibliographical references and index.
    ISBN-13: 978-0-7573-1369-1
    ISBN-10: 0-7573-1369-8
    1. Girls—Psychology.   2. Girls—Social networks.   I. Title.
HQ777.S55 2009
155.5'33—dc22

                                             2009023433

Publisher: Health Communications, Inc.
          3201 S.W. 15th Street
          Deerfield Beach, FL 33442–8190

Cover design by Andrea Perrine Brower
Interior design and formatting by Lawna Patterson Oldfield

For every girl with a secret . . .

Too many of us think we're the only ones dealing with a problem, or if we share something personal, we'll be judged, ridiculed, or looked down upon. On the contrary, it is only by sharing our experiences (and our secrets) that real progress begins and hope is born.

My deepest thanks to every girl who courageously shared her life stories, secrets, lessons, and ideas. Your resilience, hope, and courage inspire me.

The stories in this book are written by real girls. In some cases, the stories are composites and names, ages, and other identifying information have been changed.

Contents

Why I Wrote This Book xi

How to Use This Book xix

Introduction: Seven Tips Every Girl Needs
  to Deal with Any Problem..1

What Type of Secret Keeper Are You? 2

The Seven Tips Every Girl Needs to Deal with Any Problem.........3

Chapter 1: Beauty Is a Beast 23

Secrets Girls Keep About Beauty 24

Beauty Lies 25

Taking Care of Yourself 31

How Can You Feel More Beautiful?...40

Seven Tips Every Girl Needs to Build Her Beauty Confidence 43

Chapter 2: Boys, Boys, Boys 50

Secrets Girls Keep About Boys 50

Common Questions About Dating..53

Dating Stuff 56

Guy-Related Things Teens Need to Know 60

Common Dating Problems 67

What If I'm Not Attracted to Boys? 81

Seven Tips Every Girl Needs to Deal with Boys..........................86

Chapter 3: Best of Friends or Worst of Enemies? 96

Secrets Girls Keep from Their Friends 97

Good Friends Bring Out the Best in You 98

Problems with Friends 100

Mean Girls and Bullies 110

Keeping Friends...116

Seven Tips Every Girl Needs to Deal with Friends 119

Chapter 4: Funky Family Stuff 125

Secrets Girls Keep About Family 126

Common Sibling Problems..127

Common Parent Problems 131

Seven Tips Every Girl Needs to Deal with Funky Family Stuff..150

Chapter 5: Dealing with School, Now and Beyond..............157

Secrets Girls Keep About School...157

Teachers 158

Grades 160

The Social Scene..162

What If You're Too Involved?..164

Money . . . Never Enough!...166

Big Blows 170

Life Beyond High School 172

Seven Tips Every Girl Needs to Deal with School,
Now and Beyond 176

Chapter 6: Are You Cyber Savvy? 184
Secrets Girls Keep About Cyberspace 184
Is the Internet Good for You? 185
Cyber Bullying 187
Meeting Guys and Friends Online 191
Downloads and File Sharing 196
Communication Mishaps 197
Seven Tips Every Girl Needs to Be Cyber Savvy 201

Chapter 7: Dealing with the Tough Stuff 207
Secrets Girls Keep About Tough Stuff 208
Depression 210
Suicide 212
Drugs and Alcohol 217
Eating Disorders 222
Dating Violence 227
Sexual Abuse 230
Teen Pregnancy 232
Sexually Transmitted Diseases (STDs) 233
Self-Harming Behaviors 237
Dealing with Grief and Loss 241
Seven Tips Every Girl Needs to Deal with Tough Stuff ...245

Chapter 8: What's Your Secret? 253

A Few Final Things to Think About 254

Acknowledgments 257

Share Your Secret..259

References 260

Resources...262

Index 264

Meet Carrie 268

Why I Wrote This Book

This book is for every girl with a secret. That makes all of us, doesn't it? Our secrets . . . they help us, hurt us, and seem to be part of our rite of passage into, through, and beyond the teen years. I think most teenage girls have secrets; some cement our friendships, others come in the form of hiding behind a fake smile to please a teacher, laughing at something even when we don't think it's funny, or pretending not to have an eating disorder, addiction, or some other problem.

I don't want girls to have to fake it anymore. I don't want girls to hide their fears, their pain, or their despair. I want us to be able to tell our truths, share our secrets and stories, and give each other the strength and courage we need to be ourselves and follow our dreams. It is by opening up and sharing that we take steps toward our best lives. In a world that is changing and opening up with more opportunities for girls and women, don't we all want to put our best foot forward to embrace these possibilities?

After all, you are amazing, courageous, intelligent, unique, and beautiful! Can you accept that? Or are you going to let society brand you with one of its labels? Unfortunately, you know labels get put on people all of the time. For teen girls, you know what the list contains: the popular girl, the pretty girl, the jock, the book nerd, the prep, the Goth, and the list goes on.

This book is about dropping the labels we've given ourselves and the labels we've given one another. This book is about celebrating being girls and sharing the ideas and secrets that connect all of us. I'm tired of all of us buying into what society tells us we need to be in order to be accepted, pretty, and successful. It's based on the premise that we're never beautiful enough, never good enough, and worse, we better knock each other down to get to the top. I don't believe it needs to be that way. I want to start a movement where girls push back the stereotypes, false labels, and images that surround us. I want to create a safe place where girls create and own their biggest dreams, a place where we can support each other, and a place where we take action in our own lives and the world around us.

Unfortunately, so many of us block our own progress. One of our biggest challenges is our secrets. Yes, secrets are a part of girlhood and the basis for many of our friendships. Yet there are certain secrets we never want to share, secrets about our eating disorders, sexuality, parent problems, insecurities, and more. We fear shame by sharing them and worry we won't be accepted, liked, or understood.

If you're a teen girl, this book contains the secrets to success, but you will have to figure out your own formula. There's no magic recipe that works the same for each person, but I hope that by reading the stories I've collected from other girls, and by applying the seven tips every girl needs, you'll start to figure out what you need on your journey. If you haven't been able to dream or think about what you really want in life, I hope this book will get you started! We all deserve to have dreams.

The bottom line is this: I wrote this book because I'm tired of watching young girls turn into teens only to lose that strong spirit that once roared within them. I'm tired of watching girls walking with their heads down, losing their hopes, putting down other girls, or never holding on to a dream. I'm tired of watching girls ruin their lives with the secrets they keep about their bodies, low self-esteem, sexuality, addictions, and suicide.

I've been a teen, watched teens, listened to teens, and talked to teens. I'm alarmed by how many girls, including myself, have been caught up in the whirlwind of media frenzy and societal pressures that tell girls what they are supposed to be when what they want to be is often something quite different. I know because I struggled with this problem.

Many people, and the images bombarding us on a daily basis, convince girls that they have to be the perfect size, wear the perfect clothes, date the perfect guy, make the perfect grades, get into the perfect college, and so on. This is both tiring and overwhelming. How are girls supposed to be themselves when there is such immense pressure to be perfect? So much pressure to fit in? So much pressure to be sexy? *The theme is universal with every girl I talk to: girls just want to be themselves.*

Many girls—and sometimes their parents—wonder what happened to that little girl who used to not think twice about trying something new. What happened to the little girl who would sing in front of a big crowd without fear? Where is the girl who came home proud of the grades on her report card? What happened to the girl who used to shake off negative comments made about her?

But then again, what about the girl who never could shake off hurtful comments? What about the girl who never stood up for herself? What about the girl who always did her best to blend in and not be noticed? What were her dreams, and whatever happened to her, anyway?

The fact is that many of us compare ourselves to images we see in the media, listen to the wrong people, and listen to negative comments said by ourselves and others. Whether it's trying to look like the airbrushed supermodel (yes, computer alterations distort the real image) or listening to the boyfriend who tells us he hates our outfit, the parent who says we're too fat, the best friend who tells us she doesn't like our new haircut, the music teacher who says we can't sing, or our own thoughts about how ugly we are, the messages about our imperfections are always present. Because most of us believe what we see and take what others say at face value, if we can't live up to images in magazines and on TV, or if someone makes the tiniest comment that plays on an insecurity of ours, the balloon that represents our confidence can completely deflate.

The secrets I kept

If you want to know why I feel so strongly about helping teen girls, I need to take you back a ways. I want to tell you about the secrets I kept. On the outside, I looked happy and successful. I had good grades, was a good singer, played soccer, was involved in school activities, and had friends. I had a good family, and I lived with both of my parents and my younger brother. But there were secrets I kept. Some of them I told·my best friend, Kathryn, but others I thought were too ugly even to talk about. I was embarrassed, ashamed, and confused.

When I was in middle school, I had some friends and was probably liked by most kids, but I didn't feel that way. One of the worst memories I have was about some teasing that started after I got a new haircut. It's almost funny now, but it was devastating then. It was a chant that went "Bushy woop, bushy woop, waaay woop." It became a song most kids chimed in on whenever this particular boy started singing. I tried to blow it off and outwardly would just laugh, but deep down this ripped my self-esteem to shreds. I'm lucky we didn't have cell phones back then; can you imagine how fast the humiliation would have spread?

Though I had friends, I felt really alone. I certainly didn't feel pretty. Disliking myself and my body was just the beginning of a serious problem: starving myself. I don't remember how my obsession with my weight started. I think it was a combination of many things, including a growing dislike of my body, depression, low self-esteem, comparisons I'd make between myself and other girls and the images around me, and a desire to be liked and loved by others. As I started getting thinner, I enjoyed being able to control my weight, unlike so many of the other uncontrollable things going on around me.

Ultimately, I found myself dealing with an eating disorder, depression, loneliness, suicidal thoughts, boy problems, and the stress of trying to be perfect with grades and everything else. Oddly enough, the more skilled I became at hiding this very sad and depressed side of myself, the bigger my problems became. My parents even confronted me about not eating after they received a call from a teacher, but I held tight to my secrets and just lied to everyone about what I was eating. I didn't know how to tell them about my problems. I was embarrassed about how I felt, so I just pushed my parents away.

I started feeling depressed and sank deeper into depression until I felt that the only way to end the pain might be suicide. I didn't know and couldn't see how much the depression was impacting my life and emotions. I thought about suicide a lot, but I never tried it. I didn't want to talk to anyone about it because I thought no one would understand. Now I can see I needed professional help, but I was too embarrassed to seek it.

Then there were my relationships with boys. These experiences are still hard for me to talk about. I didn't like the way I depended on them to make me feel good about myself. My first dating experience was awful. I looked up to a boy who was very popular and older than me, but he took advantage of me in a way I didn't know how to deal with. To make things worse, I stayed friends with him because I thought his friendship was helping me. In reality, it was doing just the opposite. Looking back, I bought into this idea that I could only value myself if boys liked me.

What helped me

The good news is that I overcame my problems, but the stress and hard times I mentioned didn't just magically disappear. Many different things helped, and I can't single out any one thing because they all worked together.

In middle school, I remember talking to the school counselor. I didn't tell her everything I was feeling, but our talks were important, and I needed to know she was on my side.

My friends, like Kathryn, were there for me as best as they knew how and as much as I would let them. I had a strong bond with Kathryn, Izzi, and Karen. It might sound cheesy, but we called ourselves KICK because it started with all of our initials. We were different in many ways, but it was like having our own sisterhood. These types of friendship circles in our lives are so important that I want you to be able to start your own! (You can find out more about how you can do this at www.girlswithdreams.com.)

I had a strong faith in God. I prayed about my life and my worries, and I never gave up. I went to church, and some of my best memories come from the time I spent at a church camp that I started going to in the fourth grade.

Then there was my family. Even though I didn't tell them about everything I was dealing with, I loved my parents and brother, and I knew they loved me. Also, there was what I would call my nonbiological family. These were teens and adults I met along the way who I really looked up to and considered to be family and role models. I also remained involved in activities and stayed determined. Even though I didn't have a lot of what I would consider close friends, I was friendly with a lot of people I'd met through the many activities I was involved in at school.

I tried to stay positive. When I didn't make the extremely competitive soccer team my senior year in high school, I was devastated, so I started coaching my little brother's soccer team, and I had a blast. I also lost a school election for class president, but I went on to become vice president of the student government instead.

In college, I went on to play Division 3 soccer. I was really proud of this since I hadn't made the team during my senior year in high school. I started to learn about some of the reasons I had been so challenged as a teenage girl. I dealt with the issues that had followed me, and I also learned how the media and our everyday lives sometimes give us unrealistic examples to live up to. My parents wanted me to study engineering in college because I was good at math, but I was drawn to sociology, and ultimately I pursued my master's degree in social work and went on to work with young people.

Eventually I uncovered my real purpose and passion—empowering teen girls. Once I discovered this and allowed myself to follow this dream, I saw how all of my past experiences, including the negative and the positive, led me to where I am today.

My dream

My dream was this: What if I could create a global movement where girls discover their power, passion, and big dreams? A space where girls could just be girls? Where girls could put their differences aside and share their ideas, stories, and, yes, their secrets?

What if we could help millions of girls feel confident? That's what the Girls with Dreams community and this book are all about—creating a place where girls can see that it's okay to mess up and that other girls deal with this stuff too. The fact is that we can all help each other get to where we're going and where we want to go. We can all help each other build our best lives and be a positive force for good in our own lives and the world.

There are many reasons girls hesitate to share their secrets and ideas with one another, and that's ultimately why I created www.girlswithdreams.com and community. Girls all over the world are dealing with the same basic problems, and the website and this book provide a safe forum in which you can find other girls you feel comfortable with, as well as inspiration and ideas for dealing with your own challenges.

I invite you to find us on Facebook and visit www.girlswith dreams.com as often as you like and contribute to it if you are so inspired. A free and secure site, it features real stories, ideas, advice, and everything teen girls are looking for. You can even sign up to receive insider tips, create your own profile, and be one of the first to know about exciting news. Send us your questions at info@girls withdreams.com. On page 259, you can see a complete list of all the places to find us online.

My real hope

Girls will continue to have challenges. They are an inevitable part of growing and learning. They are even good for us—usually. My hope is that this book will help you learn strategies that will make the challenges less painful and more productive. I want the stories in this book to remind you that you are never alone. It is my intention that these stories, ideas, and tips ultimately help you live a life that is true for you, based on your big dreams, because when that's the case, you will feel marvelous, powerful, radiant, confident, strong, and ready to make a significant contribution to the world. Now that's amazing!

HOW TO USE THIS BOOK

I hope you can pick up this book when you're having a specific problem, and read a page or two, or you can read it from cover to cover. The chapters cover just about any problem teen girls come across: Beauty, Boys, Friends, Family, School (Now and Beyond), Cyber Savvy, and Tough Stuff. The introduction shares with you the Seven Tips Every Girl Needs to Deal with Any Problem. These are words to live by! Master these and you'll have the tools to handle any challenge that comes your way.

More important, the advice isn't just from me; there are tons of stories and tips from girls just like you. Quizzes are sprinkled throughout the book, and at the end of every chapter are fun, hands-on exercises, questions, and tips. You can use these to challenge yourself, get more information, write about in your journal, talk about in your own Girls with Dreams Friend Circle, discuss at a book club, or use at school. Finally, we'd love to hear how you're using the book! Write us a note on Facebook (www.facebook.com/pages/Girls-With-Dreams/18595557863) or send us an e-mail at info@girlswithdreams.com.

Introduction

Seven Tips Every Girl Needs to Deal with Any Problem

Secrets. Every girl has them. Girls keep secrets about the way they feel about themselves, their eating disorders, their hook-ups, their insecurities, and even their successes. What secrets do you keep? Do you realize when girls keep their secrets, most feel more alone and in trouble?

This is one of the reasons I wrote this book—*so you can see that you are not alone.* When it comes to secrets, where do you keep your biggest secrets? What type of secret keeper do you think you are? Figuring this out is key to learning how to open up. Take the quiz to find out!

> Life is a succession of moments. To live each one is to succeed.
>
> —Corita Kent

I

Quiz   What Type of Secret Keeper Are You?

Read each of the scenarios below. Which one sounds like you most of the time? You might change from time to time, but most likely you will identify with one of these the most.

- **You share your secrets with the wrong people.** You always seem to tell the wrong friend, who then blurts your most private issues, exposing you to several or hundreds of people. This really hurts!

- **You keep up a perfect image when things are really falling apart.** So many girls fall into this trap of trying to be perfect. Many girls are naturally people pleasers, but it's not easy to live a lie. Outwardly you look like you have it all together, but really you are dealing with a lot of pain. This was the kind of secret keeper I usually was. I was so afraid to tell people about my insecurities, my hatred of myself, my feelings of depression and suicide. Keeping these secrets only prolonged the problems and made them worse.

- **You totally fall apart, but deny anything is wrong.** Your secrets have almost ruined your life. At this point, you're engaging in self-destructive behaviors. It might be drinking, cutting, suicidal thoughts, not eating, or binge eating, just to name a few. Whatever it is, people can tell something is wrong, but when they confront you, you continue to deny anything is wrong.

- **You find the right friend and adult to tell.** You realize no one is perfect and everyone makes mistakes and goes through stuff, so you go to your friend and she helps you talk to an adult you trust. This might seem like the hardest secret keeper to be, but we all need to try to be more like this. If we could learn to tell our secrets to the right people, we could deal with the stuff that is holding us back from living our best life.

Now that you know your secret-keeping profile, you can do something about your secrets if you need to. If you're feeling stuck, or feeling like you want to hold tight to your secrets, that's okay for now. Keep reading, and you'll be sure to find just what you need.

Now I'll let you in on the biggest secret: the seven tips every girl needs to know to deal with any problem. Some girls use all seven tips in dealing with challenges. Some girls use just a few of them. Wouldn't it be amazing if we all had access to these strategies at every point in our lives? The good news is we do! Here are the seven tips I have discovered through listening, talking

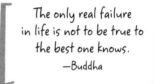

> The only real failure in life is not to be true to the best one knows.
> —Buddha

to, and watching girls. When you apply these ideas to the genuine challenges you face, life can be so much better!

The Seven Tips Every Girl Needs to Deal with Any Problem

Tip One: You Gotta Use Your Gut

Our gut, our intuition, is that little voice inside of us that protects and helps us—if we listen to it. When we listen to our gut, we make choices that are in line with who we are.

> I started dating Lewis, but after a few weeks I broke it off. He was surprised, but deep down something told me he wasn't the right guy for me. I was starting to have a hard time holding him back. Kissing wasn't enough for him, and I just didn't want to have to fight him all the time. He's a nice guy, but he's not for me. We're just on different paths.
>
> ♥ *Melanie, 15*

So often we don't listen to our own instincts. We doubt ourselves, ignore ourselves, follow the crowd, or put others' opinions and thoughts above our own.

> "I think it's always best to be who you are."
> —Halle Berry

It's so easy to be swayed these days, whether by images that bombard us on television and in magazines, by friends, or even by family. These influences fight against our gut feelings, and it is really confusing to know what to listen to.

When is it hardest for you to hear your inner voice? What is happening? Who are you with? Are you afraid? Under pressure? Handling stress? Having fun?

The problem with not listening to our gut is that it makes us go against ourselves. Every time we don't listen to ourselves, it chips away at more of who we really are. And sometimes, not listening to our instincts has devastating results.

❝ I shouldn't have gone driving with Tonya and Carissa. They'd both been drinking, but they said they could handle it. My parents always said, 'When in doubt, call us,' but I didn't do it.

The accident happened so fast. One minute we were just cruising along, and the next minute we were wrapped around a telephone pole. I will never forget the feeling of the car spinning out of control or of Carissa sobbing in the front seat. I can't believe Tonya is dead. How could this have happened? It could so easily have been me. ❞

♥ *Ava, 16*

Then again, listening to our gut can really pay off sometimes.

❝ It was kind of cool how I got my internship at a reputable law office. I was interviewing for a summer internship, and I felt like I was on the verge of something big. At the same time, something told me they didn't quite know if I was a fit. My gut told me I needed to explain to them my dream of becoming a lawyer and how important this position was to me.

A few days later, I found out I got the internship. They told me they don't usually take high school students, but they were impressed with my interview. I was really glad I listened to myself! ❞

♥ *Tina, 18*

How Strong Are Your Instincts?

Quiz

a. I know when my instinct or gut is talking to me.
b. I'm good at making my own decisions.
c. I listen to my gut, and I'm not afraid to tell my friends.
d. I use my instincts on a daily basis.

If you answered yes to three or more of these statements, congratulations. You're a natural at listening to your intuition. If you need help, use the five ideas you just read about to develop your intuition. For more fun quizzes, visit www.girlswithdreams.com.

Remember: No matter what, your intuition is your best friend! If you learn to listen to it, you'll be amazed at the results. Take the quiz above to see how strong your instincts are.

Tip Two: Discover Your Strengths and Use Them

Know your strengths and make sure you capitalize on them. I'm talking about all kinds of strengths, including social strengths, emotional strengths, spiritual strengths, academic strengths, and physical strengths.

I always felt kind of lost. My big brother was a basketball star and my

> Our deepest wishes are whispers of our authentic selves. We must learn to respect them. We must learn to listen.
> —Sarah Ban Breathnach

younger sister a gymnast. Then, in ninth grade, I discovered the flute. I loved the way it sounded. I loved playing it, and guess what? I was really good at it!

♥ Jenny, 15

There are many reasons why girls don't always know or use their strengths. Sometimes we just don't think about them, sometimes we haven't been taught how to look for them, and sometimes we feel embarrassed to claim bragging rights. Whatever the reason, not using or knowing our strengths can have devastating consequences.

What if you were the first to discover a new element on the moon, the first to discover a cure for cancer, or the fastest person to climb Mount Everest, but you never entertained such ideas because you had no idea what your strengths were?

By the same token, not using our strengths can make us feel dumb or awkward. Maybe you've been having problems in school. Part of it could be that you haven't learned how to use what you're good at to be successful.

" I was really struggling in my math class. I was talking to my teacher after class one day, and she had an idea. She knew I was a great reader and that Margie was really good at math. She set us up and had us tutor each other. It's kind of funny because I never thought of myself as good at reading because I was always so focused on how bad I was at math. This idea worked great! Both of our grades came up, and it felt really good to help someone else. "

♥ *Sabrina, 14*

The other problem is that even when we know what our strengths are, we often overlook them. Think about it: How many times have you put yourself down today? How many times have you doubted yourself? How many times have you gotten mad about a grade? How many times have you beaten yourself up for not doing something well?

Just imagine: what if we all started to recognize our gifts and

Quiz

How Well Do You Know Your Strengths and Use Them?

1. I rarely put myself down.
2. I have used an assessment to identify my strengths.
3. I can list seven things I am good at.
4. I make an effort to use my strengths daily.

If you said yes to three or more of these statements, you're on your way! Make sure you continue to discover them. If you said yes to fewer than two statements, start figuring out how you can find and use your strengths more. You'll be in awe of the results.

were able to use them? One way to get started is to talk to a teacher or parent, and/or go online. Stop by www.girlswithdreams.com for more quizzes and tips.

When you identify your strengths and use them, you will have incredible results! However, finding your strengths doesn't give you permission to take a backseat when you're not sure whether you can do something. You still have to work hard and take risks! Take the above quiz to see how well you know your strengths and use them.

Tip Three: Choose the Right Friends and Respect Them

Friends are important! Whether you feel like you have no real friends or too many friends, friends support us, lift us up, laugh with us, cry with us, and play a big role in our everyday lives. However, it doesn't matter how many you have if you haven't picked the right ones.

Many of us get caught up with the wrong friends for a variety of reasons. Maybe they were right at first, but now one of you has changed. Or maybe you are still friends and know you will be forever.

❝ Colby and I have been friends since the third grade. We've had our ups and downs, but we've always been there for each other. Like the time she got her tonsils out, I was the first one to visit her in the hospital, or the day I found out my parents were getting a divorce, and she was there to cheer me up. We've laughed together, cried together, and even yelled at each other, but Colby is like a sister to me, and I can't imagine not being friends forever. ❞

♥ Lizzie, 15

> Each friend represents a world in us, a world possibly not born until they arrive, and it is only by this meeting that a new world is born.
> —Anaïs Nin

The friends you pick have a huge impact on you. Are your friends going in the same direction as you? We've all heard the expression "You are what you eat." It's also true that you are who you hang out with. Your friends influence who you become. Look around and ask yourself a couple of questions. Do your friends make you feel good? Are they nice to you? Do you have similar goals? You don't have to be cookie-cutter replicas of each other, but it does help to have some basic things in common. For instance, you might want to be a doctor and your friend a teacher. Among other things, this means you both want to go to college.

Friends are so important that I've been working on something new called Girls with Dreams Friend Circles. You'll read about this online and later on in the book. And I've dedicated a whole chapter to talking about friends, but in the meantime, take the following quiz to see how well you choose and respect your friends.

Quiz

How Well Do You Choose and Respect Your Friends?

1. I make an effort to meet new people.
2. I have at least one friend I can trust.
3. My friends make me feel good about myself.
4. I treat my friends respectfully, and they do the same for me.

If you said yes to all four statements, congratulations! You're a star friend and know how to pick them right. If you said yes to fewer than four statements, make sure you read more friendship tips in Chapter 3, "Best of Friends or Worst of Enemies?"

Tip Four: Be Courageous and Confident

Courage and confidence are huge issues. When I've talked to teen girls, it's apparent that this is an issue for almost everyone! Because so many women of all ages continue to struggle with these areas, it's clear that we're not learning what we need to as young girls.

Why don't we have courage and confidence? Because we listen to put-downs and allow our inner critic to take over. We all want to be accepted, liked by others, and fit in somewhere. Beyond a shadow of a doubt, the consequences are frightening: we take fewer risks, we act small, we talk with little voices, and we miss opportunities we're qualified for. In other words, we shrink. Too many of us stay stuck, fail to try things, and ultimately stop believing in who we are.

> Always be a first-rate version of
> yourself, instead of a second-rate
> version of somebody else.
> —Judy Garland

The classic dictionary definition of "courage" is the ability to face danger, difficulty, uncertainty, or pain without being overcome by fear or being deflected from a chosen course of action.

Kelly didn't want to go to school. It had been a really bad week. The teasing had gotten way out of control, and she wasn't sure she could face another day of it. Her dad told her to just brush it off, but she wasn't sure she could do that, either. Nonetheless, she didn't want the bullies to ruin her day or her grades.

Kelly decided to go to school anyway. When she arrived, the teasing started again, but this time Kelly spoke up for herself, and some other kids backed her up. Wow. Kelly was shocked. It hadn't been easy, but she was glad she'd gone to school after all.

Confidence is the belief in your ability to succeed; it's believing that you are good enough. It's believing in your own worthiness. When you are confident, you are able to hold your head up, and you know your value.

Confidence is the belief in your ability to succeed. It's believing that you are good enough.

Why do so many of the young girls I meet lack courage and confidence? Why don't they see how they have been courageous or confident? Many of us don't see the things we're good at. What's more is that we don't always support each other as girls. Finally, we believe our own criticism and the intentional and unintentional comments of others.

Oddly enough, sometimes we have courage without confidence.

You may know you have to do something, such as moving to a new town and starting a new school, but you're terrified to do it. You continue forward even though you may not be sure how you're going to do it. Though you have no confidence, you have the courage to do what must be done.

Here are some courageous acts:

- Trying out for something new
- Going to a new school
- Standing up for what is right, even if it's not popular
- Getting a new haircut
- Making a new friend
- Quitting a bad habit
- Being honest when you've made a mistake

Here are some confident acts:

- Having faith in your abilities to complete a task
- Standing up to your self-doubt and the doubt of others
- Holding your head high and walking with good posture
- Looking directly into people's eyes when you speak to them
- Thinking for yourself
- Not needing other people's opinions to build you up
- Holding the conviction that you are worthy, just because

Most of us have confidence issues. Whether we question our size, looks, ability to speak, grades, athletic performance, or anything else, we all occasionally suffer from a lack of confidence. This causes dramatic ripple effects that influence every aspect of our lives, from how we dress, to where we decide to go to college, to plans for our future. But take heart: you can be more confident.

How Courageous and Confident Are You?

Take another look at the list of what confidence and courage look like. Can you say you do at least four of these things regularly? (If you have something you want to add, you can count that too.) If your answer is yes pick one more to work on. If your answer is no, work your way up to four by working on one new point each week.

- Think back to any situation in which you've expressed courage and confidence. What did you learn from that situation? How can you repeat it? Remind yourself of your success.
- Support your girlfriends and don't expect anything less from them. We can all be successful. We don't need to put each other down or deflate each other's confidence to get ahead.
- Pick role models who are courageous and confident. Follow their example and don't be afraid to ask how they do it.

As a culture, we need to work on this. We need to work on ourselves and help each other out. At Girls with Dreams we believe in friends collaborating. Let's start working together and stop competing in a mean way and see what we can accomplish. Sometimes we are toughest on other girls, but trust me, this isn't something to be proud of.

Tip Five: Be Fit and Stay Fit

Staying healthy and fit on all levels, physically, mentally, and emotionally, not only helps you deal with stress, but it will help you live longer and stay happier. The most immediate benefits, though, can help you get through stress you may feel every day.

There is not a teenage girl anywhere in the world who doesn't experience stress. It's something we all seem to have, and some teens suffer more or less of it depending on their personal circumstances and how well they cope. Taking tests at school, managing friendship problems, overcoming issues with parents, dealing with boys, and adjusting to a sudden move can result in a significant amount of stress.

Too much stress affects us physically, emotionally, and mentally and usually leads to unhealthy or unsafe coping strategies. To avoid this, we need to practice staying fit.

❝ I wasn't very athletic until the eighth grade, when my mom suggested I try out for the track team. I decided to give it a try, and I loved it. I loved the feeling of running and the high it gave me. ❞

♥ Janine, 14

What do you do when you get stressed? Do you exercise? Do you talk to friends, siblings, parents, or other adults you trust? Do you make a plan for dealing with your stress and follow through with it? Do you try to get more sleep? These are all good strategies.

> A sound mind in a sound body is a short but full description of a happy state in this world.
> —John Locke

Physical fitness

Getting physical is a great idea. Exercise reduces stress, increases serotonin levels (serotonins are natural chemicals that help your body handle stress and keep your brain happy), burns fat, and gives you a healthy appetite. Exercise can also help to lower depression and improve your health. Whether you run, play sports, Rollerblade, or hike, do something! If you don't like to exercise, start slowly. Go for a bike ride, take a walk, ask a friend to go with you, or even try something new. Just get moving!

Getting sufficient sleep is also a big part of staying fit and dealing with stress. Ever notice how dull or even grumpy you are when you don't get enough sleep? In our informal surveys, we found high numbers of teens are getting fewer than six hours of sleep per night, but experts say teens need eight or more hours of sleep every single night!

You need to eat properly, too, because food affects stress. Most people tend to overeat or undereat during stressful times. To combat this tendency, eat breakfast every day. This habit gets your body going and gives your brain and body important nutrients. Then make sure you drink plenty of water and eat your fruits and veggies. In our soda-crazed culture, water isn't always fun to drink, but it sure is good for you. It hydrates your system, boosts your energy level, and removes toxins from your body.

Emotional and mental fitness

As we all know, stress affects our emotions and mental state greatly. If we yell at those around us because we're stressed, we only draw them into our bad mood. What's more is that sooner or later we have to deal with the chaos we've created.

Instead of becoming angry or irritated, surround yourself with good things and good thoughts and use positive self-talk. If your attitude isn't positive, deliberately alter it. For example, ask yourself, "On a scale of 1 to 10, how difficult is this problem or situation?"

It can also help to find good role models. Look at others who take their stress in stride, and copy what they do.

❝ I can always tell when I'm getting in a bad mood. To combat it, I do a couple of things. First, I tell my friends I'm feeling bad. Then I go to my room and listen to music. Third, if the weather is decent and I can go outside, I take my dog for a walk. ❞

♥ *Mira, 15*

You can increase your emotional and mental fitness by taking quiet time to renew your spirit. Try taking a minimum of ten to fifteen minutes every day just to relax, meditate, drink a glass of fresh juice, lie down on the couch and daydream, lose yourself in a book you enjoy, listen to your favorite music . . . the list could go on forever!

> My relaxation list: take a hot shower, get a pedicure, read a good magazine, lie in my hammock.

Also try your best to set aside at least two hours each week in which you can relax and not think about what's stressing you out.

❝ Saturday morning is my time. I like to sleep in until 10:00 AM, and then I do something fun for myself, like paint my toenails, or go shopping, or go to breakfast with my dad. ❞

♥ *Dena, 15*

Tip Six: Dream Big

"Dream big" sounds like a cliché, but it is so much more than that!

Dreaming big means pushing yourself to the next level. It means thinking out-

> [We can do anything we want if we stick to it long enough.
> —Helen Keller]

side of the box, wanting a bigger life for yourself, and daydreaming about your wishes.

Here are some big dreams:

I want to work for *Elle* magazine.
I want to be a veterinarian.
I want to be an art teacher.
I want to be an international chef.
I want to be a soccer player.
I want to open a foster home.
I want to travel all around the world.

❝ At the age of five, I wanted to become a rock star. I was going to become the rocking-out drummer of an all-girl band and live the life of fame. Hollywood, here I come!

It all started when I went to my older sister's first band concert. Seeing people play the drum set was amazing, and it became my goal, my destiny. In the fifth grade, I followed my dream of becoming a great percussionist.

I'm not the drummer of an all-girl band yet, but I have acquired many percussion skills that have brought me great things in life. I have played in jazz bands, marching bands, and concert bands, and I have played for my church—all because I had a dream. It takes patience, persistence, courage, and lots of practice, but the road to achieving the dream makes it all the more glorious when you get there. ❞

♥ *Mo, 18*

Unfortunately, many girls are not dreaming big. This happens for a ton of reasons. Perhaps they've never been shown how to dream big, perhaps they have too much to face, or perhaps they just haven't thought about it. The problem with not dreaming big is that it causes you to sell yourself short.

When you dream big, you open up the world to thousands of

possibilities. You stretch yourself, your mind, and your actions. Some of your dreams may not come true or they may change, but just the fact that you have dreams gives you bigger possibilities.

> *"Your regrets aren't what you did, but what you didn't do. So I take every opportunity."*
> —Cameron Diaz

No one thought I could do it. They didn't think I could make it to college because no one else in my family had. I almost believed them, but I met an amazing teacher in ninth grade, Mrs. Pearl. She believed in me and encouraged me to work toward college. It wasn't easy. I had to stay after school a lot for extra help, and I had to apply for financial assistance, but I made it, and I'll be graduating in three years.

♥ *Nera, 19*

Dreams don't cost anything, so you might as well go for the biggest dream possible.

When I think about my future, I think about the Peace Corps. I have had this infatuation with South Africa ever since a Rotary exchange student named Lance came to our high school for my sophomore year. I was gripped by his stories about his home. I hope to travel there during college and eventually work there.

♥ *Tanya, 17*

Have you ever had a goal that seemed very hard to achieve? You may have wanted to climb Mount Everest or go to Princeton, but you gave up hope because you thought it was impossible. I have also had one of these dreams. I always wanted to be in a movie, but I didn't think I would be. When I was in sixth grade, I was an extra in the movie *Alice Upside Down*, starring Alyson Stoner and Lucas Grabeel. I am now in the eighth grade, and the movie recently came out on DVD. I didn't have a speaking role, but I can be seen in several scenes. I had a lot of fun and I learned a valuable lesson. Don't give up on a dream you really want to come true. If you reach for the stars, you may actually touch them! 🍃🍃

♥ *Audrey, 12*

Quiz

Are You a Big Dreamer?

1. When you get a new idea, do you remember to ask yourself, "What else? How can this be bigger?"
2. When the words "I can't" pop into your head, do you automatically change them to "How can I?" or "I can"?
3. Have you written down your dreams in a journal or notebook?
4. Do you talk about your future and plans?

Give yourself one point for every yes. If you scored four points, you're dreaming big. Encourage your friends to dream big, too, and stay open to new possibilities. If you scored three points or fewer, that's okay. There is still time to dream, and you can start today!

Tip Seven: Get Outside of Yourself

Hmm . . . get outside of yourself. Doesn't this contradict what I've been saying?

Not exactly. You can be true to yourself and give back to others, and there are many good reasons to do so.

Think about the last time you helped someone. Maybe you volunteered for a school project or just helped a woman who dropped her groceries all over the ground. *Doing the right thing and helping someone just plain feels good.*

Becca took a trip to Haiti and was so moved by the plight of the people she met that when she returned, she started her own social justice business called Prints for Peace. Not even in college yet, Becca decided to start making bags and selling them to help the people of Haiti. She felt a connection to the people, especially the children, and wanted to help them with their education and impoverished homeland.

I'm not saying you should forget about your needs or always put others first. Just make sure that when you're helping others, you don't forget to take care of your needs, too.

> One of the secrets of life is that all that is really worth the doing is what we do for others.
> —Lewis Carroll

Why don't we always get outside ourselves? There are many reasons, but some of them might be that we just don't think about it, or we haven't been taught how to do it, or our own problems seem too big to think about anyone else's.

It's important to get outside of ourselves, because not only do we improve the community, help others, and make them feel good, but it also has many rewards for us, such as improving our mood to providing perspective about our own lives. This is so important to me that part of the purpose of the Girls With Dreams Friend Circle is to help each other find ways to give back.

There are essentially four parts to getting outside of yourself:

1. Make sure you laugh at yourself

Sometimes we get so caught up in our own world and everything going on that we forget to take a step back, breathe, and, yes, laugh at ourselves. When we are able to do this, it breaks things up and helps us see there is a world outside of our worries and concerns.

Elise took herself so seriously. She had to get the best grades and have her hair perfect every day. One day she got caught in the rain, and she walked into school soaked, with her mascara running down her cheeks and her hair plastered to her skull. She looked like a fright, but rather than be upset about the situation, Elise was amused. She took one look at herself and started laughing, and she actually had a terrific day.

2. Give back and volunteer

There are countless examples of teens giving back and volunteering. Did you know some teens are giving up their spring breaks to go on volunteer trips with their churches or to help organizations like Habitat for Humanity? Also some schools are making volunteer work or service learning part of their curriculum. Giving back means thinking about both our local and global community.

❝ We had a service project to do for school. We decided to create a mural for a local battered women's shelter. We talked with the moms and the kids about what they wanted to see and then started creating. It was amazing to see their faces light up with this new mural. I think it brightened their day each time they saw it. ❞

♥ *Amy, 15*

If you're interested in finding more ways you can give back to your community or the world, be sure to check out the following sites: www.oambassadors.org, www.metowe.com, www.global leadprogram.org, and www.volunteermatch.org.

3. Pay it forward

Years ago a book by Catherine Ryan Hyde, *Pay It Forward*, and the movie version of it, started a new movement. The idea is that if you receive an act of kindness, you are to pay it forward in some way. What can you do to "pay it forward" in your own life? Here are a few things girls have told us that they have tried:

- shoveling their neighbor's driveway after a big snow
- donating to a prom dress drive so other girls can go to prom
- buying a cookie for the next person in the lunch line
- surprising their teacher with breakfast

4. Care about our world and planet

Caring about the world environment can help you get outside of yourself, too. This means paying attention to what is going on in the rest of the world, noticing our interconnectedness, and caring about our neighbors across the street and around the globe.

> *"I don't think you ever stop giving. I really don't. I think it's an ongoing process. And it's not just about being able to write a check. It's being able to touch somebody's life."*
> —Oprah Winfrey

One way to start making an immediate impact in the global community is to begin solving the worldwide energy crisis right now and be more green. There are many great ideas shared at this website: http://www.earthday.net/greentips.

If you want to take a fun quiz and find out how much you are personally impacting the environment, visit www.earthday.net/ecofootprint. For more great ideas, look online or read books like *MySpace/OurPlanet: Change Is Possible* by MySpace Community, Jeca Taudte, and Dan Santat. Then tell us how you're going green and giving back at www.girlswithdreams.com.

Quiz

Are You Getting Outside of Yourself?

1. Do you volunteer in your community a few times a year?
2. Do you think about how you can help others and act on it?
3. Do you try to do your part to help the environment, like turning off lights, carpooling, or hanging laundry on the line instead of putting it in the dryer?
4. Do you laugh at yourself at least once a week?

Give yourself a point for every yes. If you have four points, you are a pro at getting outside of yourself. If you have three or fewer points, keep working on it.

As you can see, all of the seven tips can be employed to meet the challenges teen girls face (and they work for teen boys and adults, too). Because these tips can be customized to individual problems, you will meet them again and again in the following pages.

What's more, as you have hopefully realized by now, you are never truly alone. If you are dealing with a challenge, other teens are dealing with it, too! You don't have to keep it a secret anymore. If you're interested in meeting other girls like you, visit www.girls withdreams.com, and think about starting your own Girls with Dreams Friend Circle. We'd love to hear what you're up to! Just e-mail us at info@girlswithdreams.com. For a list of all the places you can find us online, look on page 259.

In the meantime, this book holds the simple secrets to living your best life and to being savvy, smart, and successful. Come on! There are girls to meet, problems to face, and life to embrace. Read on!

1

Beauty Is a Beast!

Beauty is a beast! Some of us have days when we love how we look, and other days we dread every glance in the mirror. Some of us never really care for the way we look, and others feel beautiful one week and the next week like something that escaped from a freak show!

Why wouldn't we feel this way, when

> Remove those "I want you to like me" stickers from your forehead, and instead place them where they truly will do the most good—on your mirror!
>
> —Susan Jeffers

each week the media gives us a new diet, a new fad, a new style, or a new beauty tip to try? It's overwhelming! On top of that, your body is in a major state of change when you're a teenager. Lovely puberty has made her debut, and you will never be the same again.

> ❝ I stood in front of the mirror, and it was almost like I didn't recognize who I saw. I felt so pretty yesterday. How could one pimple ruin everything? ❞
>
> ♥ *Clarissa, 13*

23

SECRETS GIRLS KEEP ABOUT BEAUTY

One might argue that the secrets girls keep about their beauty might be some of the most tightly kept. Our perception and feeling of our own beauty is often tied to how we value ourselves, our worth, and our relationship to the world around us. So, what are the beauty secrets you are keeping to yourself? See if any of these sound familiar:

I have an eating disorder.

I hate the way I look.

I have big, ugly toes.

I have a scar I don't want anyone to see.

I'm jealous of how great my best friend looks.

I'm way too fat.

Maybe if I use more makeup no one will see what's underneath.

I'm just not as pretty as other girls.

So, maybe you're not alone. Did you see your secret on the list? When we are feeling beautiful, we are feeling on top of the world. On the other hand, when we're not feeling beautiful, it's easy to find fault in others or put them down. In some cases, this gives some girls a temporary feeling of power or beauty, in a backward kind of way.

Ultimately, our conflicting feelings about our looks are tied to our love of ourselves and our place in the world. It can feel impossible to be satisfied with our own beauty because too often the images presented to us on TV, in magazines, and on the Internet are those of girls who are thin and tall with perfect skin, teeth, and bones.

Here's the problem in a nutshell: we realize that not everyone can look like a supermodel, but we continue to compare ourselves with every supermodel we see. How crazy is that? Worse, we compare ourselves to our best friends and the girls around us. This competition between girls is sometimes silent but often spoken. It shows up in mean comments, put-downs, eating disorders, school, and between friends. One of the ways we can start to change this troubling pattern is by dumping some of the beauty lies we routinely believe.

"When I lay my head on the pillow at night I can say I was a decent person today. That's when I feel beautiful."

—Drew Barrymore

BEAUTY LIES

Lie No. 1: "Pretty" is a tall, thin, supermodel type

Sure, some girls fit this description, but that leaves more than 2.5 billion girls and women who don't. Who gets to decide what beauty really is? You do! Every person in the world has his or her own version of beautiful, and fortunately they're all different.

Sometimes you might feel like boys are attracted to only one type of girl or to only one body type, but that just isn't true. Many of them see through the supermodels, TV ads, and MTV. While some boys are attracted to the images our culture promotes as sexy, you don't have to buy into this, and neither do they. We all know that stereotypes don't always hold true. This doesn't mean your chances of finding the right boyfriend are zilch, as Kaitlin discovered below.

❝ I always hated being short. I was self-conscious about it and felt like I was never going to have a boyfriend because boys only liked girls with long legs. Was I wrong! When I was a junior, I met this guy who fell for me head over heels. He didn't care how tall I was. In fact, it worked out better that I was short because he was only 5 feet 6 inches himself. 🙖 🙖

♥ *Kaitlin, 17*

The world would truly be a boring place if we were all the same, and fortunately that's not possible. Beauty really is in the eye of the beholder, which is why people routinely disagree about whether a certain model or actress is beautiful.

Even though our own common sense tells us that it doesn't really matter what boys think, it is still hard to accept when we haven't yet found that special boyfriend who appreciates us for who we are. This is especially tough when you like someone and he doesn't like you, but we'll save that for a different chapter.

In the meantime, take comfort: if you can be patient and be yourself, you will eventually find someone who will like you for who you are.

Lie No. 2: You can't eat if you want to be pretty

Girls believe this lie all of the time. On the contrary, it's important to eat a healthy, balanced diet. No one should be too thin. Your body is still growing, and it's essential to eat enough fruits, veggies, whole grains, and proteins to ensure your health.

Candace battled this lie all of the time. She thought that if she ate three meals a day, she'd gain weight and might not look as good. Her parents realized she wasn't eating a healthy diet, and they became worried and made her start eating a balanced meal three times a day.

Candace was shocked at the results. She didn't gain weight, but she did have more energy in the morning, and she felt better. She was also surprised to find she was less irritable than before.

If you eat three balanced meals a day, you will be a healthy—and therefore a truly beautiful—weight.

Lie No. 3: Mirrors tell the truth

Many girls have distorted views of themselves. When they look into a mirror, they honestly think they see a fat person. Such girls may be experiencing disordered eating or may even be on the verge of an eating disorder like anorexia nervosa. Girls with this problem need professional help.

Ruth's problems were a little different, but they grew out of the same basic problem: her perception of her own looks.

> Ruth was lonely. She was a freshman in high school, and she was extremely self-conscious about her enormous nose. At least to her it looked enormous. Every time she looked in the mirror, it practically jumped out at her. She was sure her nose was the reason she didn't have a boyfriend or many friends. She was sure people were looking at it every time they glanced in her direction. It made her so self-conscious that she was beginning to look away any time someone approached her—a habit that, unwittingly, was making people feel she wasn't interested in them.

Dove soap has created several video ads that appear as part of its Campaign for Real Beauty. One reveals the hundreds of things that must be done to a fashion model in order to get her to look the way she does. In the video, you see not only all the makeup and primping but also how the computer distorts the image to make the girl look perfect. Talk about a lie every time we look at a supermodel!

The truth is, like supermodels, the ideals we seek are often distorted, airbrushed versions of the truth. All of us could be supermodels if we had a team of people working on us and a computer that concealed our so-called "flaws"!

Lie No. 4: Other girls are prettier than me

Rather than value who they are and what they have to offer, teen girls often compare themselves to other girls. It happens fast, but that jealous twinge doesn't feel good, nor does it go away very quickly.

It may be part of human nature to compare ourselves to others, but it's not a very helpful part, at least when it comes to our looks. Next time you notice yourself starting to compare yourself to other girls or becoming jealous, stop. Instead, focus on the things you like about yourself.

> Lisa felt jealous whenever she saw Catherine. This long-legged beauty with vibrant blue eyes seemed to have it all: long, flowing hair, a beautiful face, a drop-dead gorgeous figure, and good grades, too.
>
> Lisa wasn't bad herself, but she sure didn't have Catherine's gorgeous features. Her eyes were a little too narrow, and they were kind of a washed-out shade of green. Still, Lisa was grateful for her pretty smile and can-do attitude. As her mom always said, "What can't be cured must be endured."

Endured *cheerfully*, Lisa's mom might have said. We can't control our looks beyond the most basic of changes unless we're thinking of plastic surgery, but we can always control our attitudes.

Lie No. 5: You need to spend two hours getting ready in order to be beautiful

Wow. How many of us believe this? I was never one to spend long hours in the bathroom, but many girls do.

Are you one of them? Think about how much time you spend getting ready each day. Is it too much or just right? If it's too much, look at it this way: wouldn't you rather sleep in, hang out with friends, read, play the guitar, or do something else during this time? Two hours a day adds up to fourteen hours a week!

Start small and see whether you can cut back. Try to reduce the time it takes you to get ready each day by fifteen minutes the first week and work down from there.

Jill was proud of herself! She was overcoming what she privately thought of as her addiction to the bathroom mirror. For almost two years, she had washed and styled her hair at least twice every morning, getting up forty-five minutes earlier than any other member of her family in order to have sufficient time alone in the bathroom.

Her mom finally talked to Jill about how much time she was spending on her hair, and she and Jill agreed that Jill would limit herself to styling it once a day from now on. This gave Jill extra time in the morning to sleep, catch up on homework, or just relax before school started. Occasionally she still felt the urge to wash and style her hair for a second time, but she just shut her eyes for a moment and walked out of the bathroom. Enough was enough.

Lie No. 6: You're only pretty if you have a boyfriend

Let's get one thing clear—you don't become more beautiful through the number of guys you date. If you're starting to buy into this, stop yourself. It's an easy trap to fall into, but as Carmen recognized, it's a dangerous one.

❝ I couldn't see it when I was in high school, but I depended on guys to make me feel good about myself. It was like I couldn't recognize my own value or beauty. Instead, I needed their interest in me to validate myself. I was in a lot of dumb relationships because of this, and some of them were only one-night stands. I wish I had started with more belief in myself. **" "**

♥ Carmen, 17

Here's another take on recognizing your own beauty as Megan learned.

" " Like many teenage girls, I was shy, awkward, and convinced that I was alone in my mutant appearance amid a sea of beautiful peers. Perhaps I was also lacking in the self-esteem department.

I found my niche in the drama department and hung out at a local coffeehouse. At this time I also lusted after Scott, who worked at Video Unlimited. He remains the demigod of unrequited lust. Scott was beautiful.

So it really wasn't stalkerish at all when a friend and I made a detour to Video Unlimited en route to the coffeehouse from the theater. The two shops were across the street from each other, and there might have been a movie we really wanted to see. It was unlikely Scott would be working, since we knew he worked the last two nights and rarely worked three nights in a row.

We went in. Scott was working. We ogled shamelessly. The highlight of that interlude was when Scott turned just in time to catch me worshipping him. I broke eye contact and picked up the first movie at hand, feigning interest in renting whatever I discovered. Unknown to me, I had wandered into the porn section and found myself face-to-full-frontal with *Milady's Court*.

Even my friend and I were uncomfortable, so we crossed the street to more familiar ground. The coffeehouse was staffed by tattooed college boys whom I regarded as being too cool to converse with, speakers played bands that were too cool for me to recognize, and the menu boasted fancy coffee drinks that were too cool for me to pronounce. I don't remember what we talked about, but I do remember when we stopped talking. Scott was crossing the street, and my friend watched him enter the shop. I have no memory of what I was discussing so animatedly, just the moment that I realized Scott had come over to us and was handing us something.

'I believe this is yours.' I forced my most gracious adult smile and assumed I had dropped something. Scott handed me a folded brown napkin. I was still holding the napkin after he left, puzzled about when I had dropped it. My friend squealed, 'Open it!' Inside, written in orange marker, was 'You are one of the most naturally beautiful women I have ever seen and I did not think it should go unrecognized.' Again, I can't recall much of what happened next. I don't remember her reaction, what we talked about, or what happened to Scott.

From then to now, I have received the occasional poor grade and made an awkward mess out of myself. Nevertheless, I know that at least two people believe I am one of the most naturally beautiful women ever seen, and such a fact should never go unrecognized. One of these people is Scott, and the other one is myself. 🙲🙲

♥ *Megan H., 23*

TAKING CARE OF YOURSELF

Your body

It sounds simple, but teenagers don't always take good care of their bodies. Take the following true-or-false quiz to see how well you do.

Quiz

How Well Do You Take Care of Yourself?

1. I sleep 8 to 10 hours a night.   ○ T ○ F

2. I exercise for 30 minutes a day, five times a week.   ○ T ○ F

3. I eat breakfast every day.   ○ T ○ F

4. I eat at least three meals a day.   ○ T ○ F

5. I eat a balanced diet, including fruits, vegetables, and whole grains.   ○ T ○ F

6. I rarely eat fast food.   ○ T ○ F

7. I drink at least eight glasses of water a day.   ○ T ○ F

8. I use kind words with myself and try not to put myself down.   ○ T ○ F

Give yourself one point for every answer you marked T and add up your points. If you have six to seven points, magnificent job. You are committed to taking care of yourself! If you have four to five points, try to improve your care quotient by one point. Pick one thing to improve on and keep building on it. If you scored three points or fewer, watch out! You might be jeopardizing your health. Start to take better care of yourself by picking the easiest thing for you to change. Some might find it's easiest to start eating breakfast every morning, while others nearly throw up at the thought and will have to work up to such a goal.

Work with your strengths to overcome your weaknesses and take better care of yourself, but be wary of anything that sounds too good to be true. It's the "tried-and-true" methods that provide benefits over the long haul, as Kate explains next.

" It seems like a new diet is introduced every minute, each one promising amazing results. At what cost, though? Counting calories and cutting carbs doesn't sound like fun to me, even if it means losing a few pounds. In fact, flip-flopping from fad diet to fad diet might do more harm to your body than good.

My philosophy is simple: everything in moderation (including carbohydrates and sweets). If you never allow yourself a few indulgences, you will be more likely to binge on whatever food you're depriving yourself of.

The most effective way to lose weight and keep it off is to change your lifestyle, and your diet is just one aspect of how you live your life. Take a step back and examine other areas that contribute to your well-being.

Do you tend to watch TV all day or hike in the park with a group of friends? Do you drive around the parking lot just to get a spot close to the door, or do you intentionally park farther away so you have an excuse to walk for a few minutes? Do you use the elevator even if you need to go up only a few flights?

You also need to pay attention to your body. Before you grab that bag of chips, ask yourself whether you're really hungry. Some people develop emotional attachments to food, so eating makes them feel better. Others simply eat because they're bored.

Also, take your time when you eat. Eating meals slowly gives your body enough time to let you know when you're full. The most important thing to remember is that your body needs a well-rounded dose of nutrients.

This is especially true in the teenage years, when your body is still developing. So go ahead and fix yourself that bowl of ice cream, but only after eating a salad, of course. "

♥ *Kate, 23*

Your hormones

Did you know hormones will play tricks on you? Starting any-where between the age of eight to thirteen, you will undergo major changes as your body goes through puberty for two to three years. During that time, major chemical changes from hormones are under way in your body. It's important to understand how you might be feeling and how things might be changing so you can better under-stand what you're dealing with. Here are a few things that will be happening to you:

- Major emotional changes (you might have feelings ranging any-where from confused, moody, anxious, angry, sad, or easily upset to major mood swings).
- Your body will be growing in length, your breasts will develop, and you will start your period.
- You might notice more acne, body odor, or growth of body hair.
- As your interest in boys grows, you might have confusing feelings about sex.
- Keep in mind that everyone grows differently and on their own timetable.

I always felt a little behind everyone else because I didn't develop as early as most of my friends. I was really self-conscious about my body, and I had to learn to get over this. It wasn't easy, but I talked to my mom and she reminded me that there is so much more to people than just their looks. She was right! I started focusing on other things I was good at and accepted that my body was on its own timeline.

♥ *Hannah, 15*

Whatever your experience is during puberty, take heart, because all girls experience it one way or another. One of the best ways to get support during this time is to talk to an adult you can trust who can give you answers to your questions.

Your hair

Hair is a huge part of our identity. Some of us change our hairstyle every couple of months, while others keep the same look for years. The fact is, our hair is important. Ever notice how a bad hair day sometimes has a huge impact on your emotions and attitude?

❝ I have naturally curly hair, and recently I got a new haircut and had it straightened. I don't know what it is, but I couldn't live with my curly hair anymore. I honestly have a better day when I can straighten my hair. ❞

♥ Emma, 13

Here are a few tips for keeping your hair under control, literally as well as figuratively:

- Ask your friends and hairstylist what kind of haircut would look good on you.
- Don't be afraid to try new styles. Computer programs can help you experiment without cutting.
- Take an example of the look you want to your hairstylist.
- Take pride in your hair, but don't obsess over it.
- Keep it simple. You want a look you can primp but also a style that's easy to manage on those days when you're running late.
- Remember: it grows back!

Don't let your hair become a burden for you and the ones closest to you. For too many girls, it's all that and more, as Melissa finally discovered.

    I'm ashamed to admit all the times I screamed at my mother or father or little brother and then burst into tears because of my hair. I absolutely hated it. It was flat and limp, and nothing I did made it look nice. Believe me—I spent hours trying. I hated wearing bangs, and I hated the way my hair hung when I didn't have bangs. I was out of high school before I found a hairstylist who could really work with my hair.

    I still have a 'bad hair day' once in a while, but it doesn't take over like it used to. I guess maybe I had to grow up a little and realize my hair isn't the most important thing in life.

♥ Melissa, 19

Your skin

When our skin looks good, we feel better about ourselves, but hormones during the teen years fluctuate. Did you know they can affect the way your face and skin look?

Sometimes we have bad acne even when we do all the right things. In that case, it's probably time to see a dermatologist. You'll be amazed at how much a professional can help.

Also be careful about what you put on your skin in terms of cleanser, moisturizer, sunscreen, and so on. Do your research. Some products are good for you but bad for the environment or for animals. Some products contain chemicals or oils that can actually make acne worse. Take a look at the resources section at the end of the book to find out more.

Finally, drink a lot of water because it hydrates your skin and helps your body get rid of impurities.

    Ellie felt really self-conscious about her acne. She had large pores, blackheads, and pimples, and somehow it all got worse right around her period each month. She knew some acne was normal, but this was ridiculous. Those creams you could buy at the drugstore didn't help. She'd tried them all. She was getting really depressed about her skin, even though she tried to eat healthy and drink lots of water.

She finally asked her mom whether she could go to a dermatologist. She was so relieved when her mom said yes!

The doctor said her acne did require treatment, and Ellie could hardly wait to start taking medication. It was going to be a huge relief not to walk around looking like a pepperoni pizza anymore.

What if you have a skin condition that won't go away?

❝ Looking back on my baby pictures, in every single one I look like I had two huge red dots on my face. It hurts to even look at or show them to my friends. When I was in kindergarten, the other little kids in my class would ask me, 'What's wrong with your face?' My first instinct was to just ignore it. Then in about third grade when all the other girls started getting crushes, all I could think about was 'no boys are going to like me because I have big red splotchy patches on my face.' In sixth grade everything went downhill. My classes were harder, my friends were changing, gossip was ridiculous, and then my face got even worse. My mom took me to the dermatologist to finally figure out once and for all what was going on with my cheeks and chin, and they told me I had keratosis pilaris rubra faceii (it looks like a really irritated rash that never goes away and is ridiculously red).

In middle school, everybody started wearing makeup; some girls were touching up the blemishes or pimples while I was covering my whole face with makeup so no one could tell I had red cheeks. To make things worse, the immature guys in my grade would make remarks like, 'Your face is orange. Why do you wear so much makeup? It looks weird.'

It was the summer before eighth grade and everyone was having pool parties, and I was scared out of my mind to go swimming with the other kids because I didn't want them to see my makeup come off. I had to beg my friends not to dunk me. I was embarrassed to tell them why. It ruined everything. I made myself think that hiding my face would fix everything. Freshman year of high school—OH BOY—I was meeting people I had never ever seen in my life. I thought the first impression of me in their minds was that I had pounds of makeup on my face. Later on, I realized it was my secret that I wanted to keep from everyone forever.

Nobody really knows how bad it really is because the only people who have seen it to this day are my family. I am only fifteen and I have my whole life ahead of me. I have tons of hopes and dreams I want to accomplish. I can't let my cherry cheeks get in my way anymore. 🙰

♥ *Alex, 15*

Your clothes

Clothes accentuate our positive attributes as well as our more negative ones. Choose your clothes carefully so you feel good in what you are wearing. In addition, take note of these timeless fashion tips:

- Just because something is "in" doesn't mean it will look good on you. Make sure you match your looks with the right clothes.
- Figure out what your style is. Do you like preppy clothes? Vintage clothes? Are sporty or casual clothes your style?
- It doesn't have to be expensive. You can find nice clothes that are very costly or nice clothes that are affordable at places like Target, H&M, Delia's, Old Navy, and Wal-Mart. If you just have to have the more expensive clothes, consider getting a job to pay for them or shopping at resale stores.
- Look at magazines for ideas. If you see something you like, cut it out and shop around to find a similar piece that fits your budget.
- Don't feel embarrassed if you don't have designer labels. Look for

knockoffs and read the suggestion below for an idea on how to stretch your wardrobe economically.

" Would you like to have a whole new wardrobe for the new school year but lack the money to stock up on different pieces? Have a clothing swap party before school starts!

You and your friends probably have similar tastes in clothing, so you'll be able to score a lot of clothes that you'll get a lot of use out of. Plus, this might be your chance to nab that sweater your best friend is tired of but you've been eyeing since she bought it. All you have to do is gather the clothes you haven't worn in a while or won't wear again and invite your friends to do the same.

After everyone arrives, it's time to shop around! You can either keep track and swap a piece of your clothing for a piece of your friend's or keep things flexible by just picking an item or two from every pile. To top it all off, tell each of your friends to bring a snack and a movie. You'll be able to munch, mingle, and meander through the piles of clothing.

After you've finished your shopping spree, you and your friends can either plan a trip to Goodwill to donate your clothes or go to Plato's Closet or any thrift store to make a few bucks to put toward completing your back-to-school collection. " "

♥ *Kate, 23*

Your makeup

When you're ready to start wearing makeup, you might want to talk to your mom or another woman you trust about what would look good on you and which of your features you'd like to enhance.

Remember, less is more. This means the less makeup you use, the more your natural beauty will shine through. You should be using makeup to complement your features, not cover them up.

(Besides, I've heard from a lot of guys that they don't like it when girls wear gobs of makeup.)

You probably don't need foundation at this age, but if you decide to wear it, consider light alternatives like mineral powder foundation or a tinted moisturizer. If you want more great makeup ideas, look at Bobbi Brown's book in the resource section. Be careful what you put on your face. Go to a website like www.safecosmetics.org to check the ingredients in your makeup. Many beauty products have been found to contain harmful chemicals.

    I guess I'm the middle girl in our family for a reason: I'm in the middle on everything, including makeup! My older sister wears a ton of makeup every day. Yuck. You'd hardly recognize her if you saw her first thing in the morning. She almost looks like a clown after she puts her makeup on.

My younger sister is fourteen and doesn't wear any makeup. She doesn't really need to. She's got really pretty skin and everything.

I wear just a little makeup. Just some mascara and eye shadow and some lip gloss. I don't want to look fake, but I like to have a little color. The middle way feels good to me!

♥ *Debi, 15*

HOW CAN YOU FEEL MORE BEAUTIFUL?

No one is going to be able to make you feel beautiful until you feel it yourself, and you can't expect to feel good, much less beautiful, if you can't do two things: appreciate the parts of yourself that you do like and stop comparing yourself to others.

    Don't criticize yourself too harshly. Some people are harder on themselves than they are on other people. That is a big mistake.

Oftentimes you can leave yourself feeling upset or depressed. This can hurt your self-image in the long run. Be patient and take it one day at a time. 〃〃

♥ *Rukiya, 16*

As soon as we begin to compare ourselves to anyone—our best friend, a girl on the other team, or someone in a fashion magazine—we have immediately said, "I'm not pretty."

〃〃 When was the last time you heard your girlfriends describe themselves as beautiful? Are the expressions 'I'm beautiful' or 'I love myself just how I am' something you hear every day? Or do you tend to hear more of 'I'm too fat . . . or too skinny . . . I hate my nose, thighs, arms, or stomach . . . I wish I could be more . . . tall, short, or skinny.' Have you noticed how we have let others define what and who is considered beautiful? What happened to celebrating uniqueness, radiating self-confidence, and realizing how beautiful we REALLY are? 〃〃

♥ *Maria, 21*

Every one of us also needs to work on building our confidence, as Patty explains.

〃〃 Self-esteem and confidence are close companions, and we need them both. Since everything starts with a first step, including gaining more confidence, here is step one: dress to your preference. Believe it or not, if you dress the way that feels right to you instead of like everyone else, you will gain more confidence. And walk with your head up and your shoulders back, like you own the world. If you do this, you'll already look more confident.

Now that you look confident, you need to feel more confident, so here is step two: don't be scared to be different, whether you decide to dress differently or live in a dream world. If you can just be yourself, you'll find that more people will respect you and be your friend.

Now you're well on your way to showing others your newfound confidence. 🙶🙶

♥ Patty, 16

Take the true-or-false quiz below to find out how high your beauty confidence is.

How High Is Your Beauty Confidence?

1. I spend less than an hour getting ready for school every day.   ○ T   ○ F

2. I am proud of at least two features of my body.   ○ T   ○ F

3. I generally feel good about how I look.   ○ T   ○ F

4. I don't spend much time thinking about my appearance.   ○ T   ○ F

5. I don't need guys to tell me I'm pretty. I know I am.   ○ T   ○ F

6. I rarely compare myself to other people.   ○ T   ○ F

Give yourself one point for every answer you scored T. If you scored five or six points, congratulations! You know your beauty inside and out. If you scored three or four points, you need just a little more confidence. Look at the areas you scored F and apply our tips.

If you scored two points or under, you need a beauty confidence boost. Read our "Seven Tips" and the "Try It!" sections at the end of the chapter. Pick two things you can start doing every day. Take the quiz again in a couple of weeks and see whether you've improved your score.

Here's the bottom line: if beauty is a beast for you, use the seven tips below to give yourself a beauty boost.

Seven Tips Every Girl Needs to Build Her Beauty Confidence

Tip One: You Gotta Use Your Gut

What is that little voice inside of you telling you about beauty and about your unique beauty in particular? When do you feel most beautiful? Who are you with, and what clothes are you wearing?

On the flip side, if that little voice inside of you is telling you you're not beautiful, ignore it. No one is perfect. The important thing is to accept ourselves and not let our appearance keep us from achieving our dreams.

> " I have good days and bad days. Sometimes I think I look really good, and other days I wonder who that ugly girl in the mirror is.
>
> I know I shouldn't think like that, so I've started to turn things around. Every time I start to feel ugly or hear my negative voice, I tell myself to stop. I try to remind myself to think about the things I like about myself. It's like working from the inside out. I have to change my view on the inside so I can feel beautiful on the outside. "
>
> ♥ Emily, 14

Tip Two: Discover Your Strengths and Use Them

We all have personal features we like better than others. Some of us are fortunate enough to have bouncy, shiny hair, some of us have attractive eyes, and others have brilliant smiles.

What are your personal strengths in the beauty department? Identify and make the most of them, as the girls below decided to do.

❝ We just got tired of each others' complaints. I always complained about my height, Maggie her hair, Shira her flat chest, and Francine how heavy she felt. So we made a pact to help each other remember our good stuff. Any time we started to complain, we'd stop and tell each other the thing we all just loved. ❞

♥ *Stella, 15*

Join Stella and her friends and stop the fat talk in your friend circles and focus on your strengths instead. Check out the resources at the end of the book for more great ways to get support.

Tip Three: **Choose the Right Friends and Respect Them**

The fact is, good friends like us and support us no matter what we look like, but they're also willing to help us make the most of ourselves and even help us figure out what we've got to make the most of!

Like the girls above, good friends also help us understand when we're overreacting to a feature we don't like.

Ask yourself: Are you hanging out with the right friends? Do they make you feel beautiful? Do you make them feel beautiful?

❝ Even though I thought Kristin was prettier than me, she thought the same about me! We were great friends. When I got upset about my acne, Kristin would make me laugh about something or remind me of what a great runner I was. When Kristin stressed out about her hair, I could usually get her to smile by reminding her that we all have those days, and we'd start laughing about it. It's good to know you have someone to make you feel good when you're having a hard time feeling it yourself. ❞

♥ *Lakita, 14*

Tip Four: Be Courageous and Confident

Being totally confident in your own beauty is hard, but if you're determined, you can do it! So what if you don't think your hair looks very nice? Probably no one else thinks that, but even if someone does, so what? What difference does it make? Should someone else's opinion—or your own—be enough to keep you at home and hiding in the closet, or should you just march on out there and get to work, get the business done, and start having fun anyway?

❝ It can be hard to be confident. Models in magazines make you think appearance is the only form of beauty and that you're not beautiful unless you look like them and wear the same clothes they wear. Certain people at school might be mean to you because you're a unique individual who's not afraid to stand up for your own beliefs.

Instead of allowing other people to shape your identity, focus on developing and strengthening your own sense of self. It's easy to pick apart every detail about what you don't like about yourself, but instead of worrying about the outside so much, start working on yourself from the inside. Celebrate the qualities you're proud of.

Discover your skills by joining different extracurricular activities at school or organizations in your community. Be open-minded and branch out. Check out a tae kwon do class or contribute to your school's literary magazine. The rest will come naturally because your confidence and beauty will shine through. ❞

♥ *Kate, 23*

Marissa has similar ideas.

❝ There is a lot of pressure to be beautiful in this world, especially if you're female! In order to achieve inner and outer beauty, you must first have confidence in yourself.

When I'm not feeling pretty, I point out the things I like about myself. I also try to remember compliments people have given me in the past. Even if I'm not feeling pretty on the outside, I know I'm a good person, and that gets me through the days when I'm not feeling my best.

It's best not to compare yourself to others; just be yourself! Don't talk down to yourself or allow others to talk down to you, either. I have days when I don't feel pretty, but they always pass. If you believe you are beautiful on the inside, that inner beauty will be seen from the outside. 🍏🍏

♥ *Marissa, 16*

Tip Five: Be Fit and Stay Fit

There is absolutely no question about it: when you're fit, you feel better, and when you feel better, you look better. No, that's not accurate: when you're fit, you glow. Being fit from the inside out is what true beauty is all about, so take care of yourself. Exercise appropriately, eat nutritious meals, and avoid foods that aren't good for you.

This is a good time to remind you again of how unrealistic the images of beauty are that surround us. The reason models in pictures are airbrushed to perfection is because real perfection simply doesn't exist! Keeping this in mind will go a long way toward maintaining your mental and emotional fitness.

🍏🍏 Sometimes I don't think I'm very pretty, and whenever I feel self-conscious about my looks or unhappy with my hair, I find myself feeling really down. I decided since volleyball season had ended for the year and I wasn't getting much exercise, I'd start running a couple of days a week.

I couldn't believe how much better I felt after about two weeks of running! My skin looked better, I was sleeping better at night, and I just plain felt better. Somehow, I wasn't as concerned about my hair as before either. I'm going to keep running! 🍏🍏

♥ *Sherri, 15*

Tip Six: Dream Big

❝ My dream is a little different from most girls' . . . I dream of graduating from high school and never again being stuck in a situation in which I'm constantly judged on the basis of my looks. I've stopped wearing makeup altogether because I'm tired of having to conform to some standard of beauty I don't even agree with. I want to find a boyfriend who feels the way I do about natural beauty and health and eating right. I guess I'm looking for someone with real maturity. It's okay. I'm willing to wait for him. ❞

♥ *Lauren, 18*

Lauren really got out of the box when it comes to dreaming big! What's your big dream when it comes to beauty? Can you allow yourself to create something other than what appears in most magazines? When it comes to loving your own beauty, how can you dream bigger? Maybe you go out on a limb and try a new hairstyle, get a new outfit, or like Lauren, decide to not wear makeup. Once you decide, tell us your big dreams for beauty at www.girlswith dreams.com.

Tip Seven: Get Outside of Yourself

Where beauty is concerned, this really adds a dose of perspective. Just look around you. Most people are not beautiful by modern cultural standards, and yet they lead happy, fulfilled, productive lives. Look at all the happily married couples you know who aren't celebrity knockouts! The truth is, most of us aren't.

There's another element to this, too: when we think about others, we are less inclined to think about ourselves and wallow in our own misery. Think about how you can give your friends a beauty boost. Maybe you give them a compliment, help them find just the right outfit, or decide to be workout buddies together. The list is endless. Or try giving someone a compliment and watch his or her face light up. Yours will too!

You can also think about green beauty products. This is not only good for you, but the environment too. Stores like Whole Foods Market carry these products, but you can also visit websites like www.safecosmetics.org or www.gengreenlife.com for more ideas.

❝ I didn't want to do it, but my parents signed our entire family up to help serve meals to the homeless this past Thanksgiving. I couldn't believe this was how we were going to spend the holiday, but I have to say it was one of the best experiences I've ever had. Some of these people had nothing. One woman had a dirty baby in her arms. It needed its face washed, and it was crying, and she looked so miserable and tired. I held her baby while she ate, and the baby stopped crying.

I've been thinking a lot about that woman and wondering what will happen to her and the baby. There's a whole world out there struggling to make it, and somehow I want to help. It just makes my focus on my appearance less important than it used to be. I've got to come to terms with myself, and I'm closer to doing that now. There are more important things to think about. ❞

♥ *Kayla, 17*

Think about it . . .

- How can you redefine beauty for yourself? Next time you start thinking that beauty is what you see on television and in magazines, stop and think about how you want to redefine beauty.
- What beauty secrets are you keeping? Are you willing to open up?
- Put a sticky note in your room with a beauty boost for yourself such as "I love my eyes" or "My hair color is pretty."
- Who are you competing with? Stop! Remind yourself that it's not

fair to compare. There are billions of people on the planet, and not one of us is the same.

- Who are you listening to in the beauty department? Do these people make sense, or do they feed your insecurities?
- How much time do you spend thinking about your weight or your looks? Are you okay with this?
- How easy/hard would it be to not put yourself down?
- How can you be a better friend when it comes to beauty?

Try it!

- Work from the inside out and the outside in. Sometimes it's our inner confidence about beauty that needs a boost. Maybe we have the cute hairstyle, but our own doubts make us feel less than beautiful. On the other hand, sometimes we need to start with the outside. A new outfit or a hip haircut can give us the confidence we need to work on the inside and face our fears.
- Go for a day without makeup. How does it feel?
- Go for one day without looking in the mirror. Can you do it?
- Tell yourself the truth! Reverse the beauty lies at the beginning of the chapter and write them down.
- Tell yourself three times a day for one week "I am beautiful!"
- Eliminate negative self-talk. No more "I'm fat," "I'm ugly," or "I hate my butt." You know what I'm getting at.
- Pick your favorite body part and remind yourself how great it is!
- Do your best to appreciate your least favorite part.

66 I hated my thighs, so I did my best to focus on my smile. I have a great smile. Every time I got mad about my thighs, I would just remind myself that I didn't need to be so harsh. I've got a lot of beauty, even if I get mad at my thighs. Maybe you hate your thighs, too. 99

♥ Nat, 17

2

Boys, Boys, Boys

Whether you are dating, thinking about dating, or haven't really been interested in dating, boys are everywhere. They go to school with us, they are at the mall, and they are in our magazines and on our TV shows. There's no way around it: boys are a huge part of our lives.

> True love doesn't come to you, it has to be inside you.
> —Julia Roberts

It's weird going from a time in grade school when we were interested only in our friends to now having to sort through why we might be having feelings for guys. Or maybe you don't understand why your best friend can't stop thinking about them. Or maybe you're thinking to yourself as you read this, "I can't ever imagine being with a boy!"

SECRETS GIRLS KEEP ABOUT BOYS

What secrets do you have about guys? Read on to see some of the secrets girls told me about:

I have a crush.

He hit me.

I went too far.

I think I have an STD.

He called me an awful name.

I'm so jealous.

I'm not pretty enough.

He told me he loves me.

In some ways, our secrets about boys might be some of the hardest to share, but by keeping our crushes, questions, hurts, and thoughts a secret, we often put ourselves in more danger. It may keep us from respecting ourselves and having the knowledge and information to make better decisions for ourselves.

> Whatever way you look at it, I challenge you to rethink the story you've been buying into.

While talking to girls, I have heard many stories and questions. One of the hardest things about figuring out guys is that we are all fed false notions of dating, romance, and intimacy in movies, TV, and our culture. Whatever way you look at it, I challenge you to rethink the story you've been buying into. I hope this chapter will address some of your biggest uncertainties and give you some tips to help navigate the crazy world of dating. Even if it's not new to you, it can be pretty confusing!

Quiz

What Kind of a Dater Are You?

Read through each scene and decide which one you relate to most.

Scene 1: He adores you and is kind, sweet, and funny, but you don't feel like you have much in common with him or feel energized when you're with him. You like him, but not as much as he likes you. You definitely don't love him and don't see a future with him.

Scene 2: Guys? What? Why would I be interested in them? I'm too busy—and, honestly, a little scared. I can't ever imagine having a boyfriend.

Scene 3: He mostly treats you like crap, but you can't see it. You are crazy about him, but you don't feel beautiful. You hold on to the good days with him and try to forget about the bad ones.

Scene 4: You are good friends. You have fun together. He supports you, and you support him. You feel good when you are with him, and you appreciate the fact that he doesn't pressure you to have sex.

Scene 5: You are more than good friends. In fact, you love each other very much. You think you have a future together, and you certainly hope so. He is responsible, caring, hardworking, and thoughtful.

Scene 6: You don't have a boyfriend. Sometimes it seems like you're the only girl in school who doesn't, but you're glad you don't have a boyfriend. There's time for that later. Right now, you want to focus on your grades and putting money away for college.

Scene 7: This boyfriend is just the latest in a whole string of them. You don't like to keep them around for very long, but you sure enjoy them while they last! You don't have a problem being sexually active. It just feels good.

Quiz

Scene 8: You are desperate for a boyfriend. All your friends have one, and you are taking certain measures to get one, too, like wearing more revealing clothing and more makeup and flirting really heavily. As far as you're concerned, if you don't have a boyfriend, you aren't cool. You'll do anything to get a boyfriend. In fact, it's become an obsession, and you're now spending hours each day looking online for the right guy.

Scene 9: You really like your boyfriend, and he likes you. In fact, he's started talking about sex, but you don't want to have sex until you're married. You're sure of it. You're starting to wonder whether he's still going to want to date you if you don't want to have sex.

As you can see, when it comes to boys, we're all different. Visit www.girlswithdreams.com if you'd like more information on how to deal with your particular scene.

COMMON QUESTIONS ABOUT DATING

? Can boys "just be friends"?

Yes. Boys can just be friends, and a lot of girls really like having guys who are "just friends."

❝ My closest and best friends are four guys. They are pretty much my entire social life. Each of them has different qualities you often see in different cliques at school. James is the smart one. If we ever need school help, he's the one we turn to. Ari is laid back and more of a ladies' man.

John is the funny one. No matter what, he is cracking a joke. Ricky is the crazy one. He has all of the ideas.

There is one thing these guys love, and that is cars, whether it's watching cars wreck on the Internet, racing cars, or fixing up their own cars. Me too. It's like having brothers with one sister hanging around.

It's so much better having guys as friends. They always laugh at you, and there's no competition between us and no drama. 🙰

♥ *Kylie, 17*

❓ What is dating really like?

It's certainly not what it looks like on TV and in the movies. Girls get this romanticized version of love. Girls want to be swept off their feet, rescued from the castle, and then live in a picture-perfect world. Yes, love can be great. It's just important to look for real-life examples versus only what is seen in the media. When you find real-life, quality relationships, don't be afraid to ask those individuals for advice. Then get clear about what you want in your relationships. How good is your friendship? Do you respect each other? Do you help each other out? With one in ten girls being physically hurt in a relationship (according to www.cdc.gov/injury), it's important to point out love is not supposed to hurt (verbally, emotionally, or physically). Real-life dating and love are about respecting each other and not being put down. Take a stand for respect and encourage your friends to do the same.

❓ Are all guys jerks?

No, of course not, but sometimes it feels that way. If this is the case for you, think about who you're hanging around with. If the guys all seem like jerks, maybe it's time to find some new friends.

? Do they only like our bodies?

Just like girls have struggles right now, so do guys. They're dealing with hormones, too, which is why some of them may seem like they're obsessed only with your body and with what you look like. This can put tremendous pressure on you, but you don't have to buy in to it. Stay calm and try not to obsess too much about your looks. Don't you want him to like you because you're smart and funny, too? This is hard for girls to figure out because so often our culture sends mixed messages to boys and girls. It starts when we're young, with everything from toys and dolls we might play with to pictures we see on TV, in magazines, and in books. Many of the images tell girls in a subtle way and sometimes not-so-subtle way that you have to look "hot" to be liked. Don't be afraid to stand against this. If we all stand up together, things will change!

? Do they only want sex?

This is true for certain boys, but it's not true for every boy. At the same time you're trying to figure out how your hormones are affecting your body, boys are going through a similar experience. Their hormones make them attracted to girls, just like you are very attracted to guys at times.

If you think your boyfriend is interested in sex, talk to him. Tell him how you feel about it. Make sure you figure out what you want before you get into the heat of the moment. This is a really big decision to sort through. Make sure you read later on in this chapter more questions to help you out with this. When you are with your boyfriend and the emotion or passion of the moment flares, you might not be able to make a clear decision or you might let your feelings or hormones take over. Many of the girls we talked to said when they let their emotions overrule their common sense, they felt used and upset that they let things go further than they really wanted.

? What if boys aren't really attracted to me?

For starters, you are attractive, even if you've never heard it from anyone! This is something I dealt with personally.

It is really hard to cope with the feeling that boys aren't attracted to you, but you don't have to feel this way forever. Just because boys don't seem interested in you now doesn't mean you aren't fun to be with or that you aren't beautiful. It could mean a hundred different things. Maybe . . .

> . . . you're so confident that boys are intimidated.
> . . . you haven't learned how to feel pretty.
> . . . you haven't found the right guy.
> . . . your unique beauty is unappreciated as of yet.
> . . . you haven't come into your own beauty yet.

The best way to deal with this feeling is to stop focusing on it and start appreciating your good stuff, whether you love your hair or how great you are as a friend.

DATING STUFF

Whether you are already dating or are thinking about it, I hope this section will help answer your biggest questions about dating.

For starters, here are some of the top reasons girls date:

- Because it feels good.
- It's all about image.
- To feel pretty.
- It's what girls do.
- To fit in.
- Because the guy "paid attention to me."

Do you have a different reason?

When should I start dating?

One question to ask yourself is do you have a strong sense of yourself? By this I mean, can you stand on your own? Are you looking to this guy to complete you or make you feel loved or good enough? If that's the angle you're coming from, you're setting both of you up for failure. As you start sorting through all of this, don't try to do it on your own. Talk to someone you trust, like a parent. If you don't have a good talking relationship with your parents, then find an adult you trust. Dating has different meanings for different people. Here are a few things to think about before you go to your parents: (1) Why do you want to start dating? (2) What does it mean to you? (3) What are you not sure about? (4) What does it mean to have self-respect toward yourself and your body? (5) What questions do you still have about sex and your body? (6) What makes your nervous, scared, or excited?

How do I know what kind of guy to date?

This may take a little time to figure out. You might want to start by thinking of all the things you like to do. For example, perhaps you like to watch movies, paint, play field hockey, ski, hang out with friends, or sing.

Now write down some of your best qualities, such as being friendly, optimistic, hardworking, and so on. Get the idea?

[In order that she may be able to give her hand with dignity, she must be able to stand alone.
—Margaret Fuller]

I want my guy to be . . . smart, kind, have a desire to go to college

_____

_____

_____

Start thinking about what kind of guy you want to be with. Is he funny? Smart? Athletic? You might even want to write down some of these qualities.

Now compare your lists. Do they complement each other? Just because you write down your perfect match doesn't mean it will necessarily turn out that way. You might find a wonderful boyfriend who isn't athletic, but you like him anyway.

At the same time, get clear about qualities you want to avoid, such as someone who puts you down, someone who is interested only in sports, a guy who calls you names, and so on. Be clear about this, and don't back down from your expectations.

The teen years are a great time to get to know guys, but this doesn't mean you have to date every one of your friends. Relating to guys can be like learning a new language or visiting a foreign country. Take your time and get to know different types of guys so you'll be able to pick out the right guy when he comes along.

How do I find a boyfriend?

This will be different for everyone. There are no hard-and-fast rules, but here are a few ideas to help you find him.

- Don't be afraid to be just friends with guys.
- If you want to start a conversation with someone, talk about something you might have in common or offer to help them.
- Give the guy you're interested in a genuine compliment.
- Be patient. Sometimes if you're looking too hard, you might miss out on a lot that's going on around you.
- Know what you want. Know where you're willing to be flexible and where you're not.
- Do something with a group of guys and girls. This can be a less intimidating way of getting to know someone.

Maybe you don't need to look after all, as Thu learned.

" Since elementary school, I've wanted a bouquet of red roses, a gold necklace, and a huge teddy bear. We all dream of the perfect guy, and I've found mine. My boyfriend is the Romeo who comes to my window, takes me out to dinner, and sings me his favorite songs.

However, I didn't find this perfect guy. He found me when I least expected it. Too many girls pass up on friends who are interested in them, because they're not sure if they'll like them. How will anyone know their 'type' if they don't give people a chance? The people I'm worried about are the girls who act catty and fight over the same guy. Or the ones who say they can't find the right guy, the girls who overlook the freedom to make their own rules of dating, might miss out.

I'm Vietnamese, sixteen, and there are more obstacles in my life than I can count. I never imagined I'd be with my boyfriend, but he's shown me you can be with anyone as long as you give people a chance to make you happy. Girls need to look deeper and discover everything someone has to offer. My boyfriend's the closest thing to perfection, and I never expected him to be the guy I would feel so strongly about. I've experienced months of pure happiness by not worrying about if he's right for me or not. The next time someone asks you out and you hesitate, I hope you know that he could be the person you've been looking for all along. 〞 〞

♥ *Thu, 16*

GUY-RELATED THINGS TEENS NEED TO KNOW

Here are the things I wish had been spelled out for me when I was a teen.

Expect respect

One of the things that tugs at my heart the most is when I hear stories of girls who are disrespected by boys, or hurt in a relationship by going too far, or not taking a stand to respect themselves. Part of this hurt comes from a place of me being there when I was a young girl, and I wish I had been able to figure things out before I made several mistakes. Statistics from www.cdc.gov/injury tell us at least one in four girls will actually face some form of dating violence (whether it's physical, emotional, or sexual) just like Julia in this next story. Here's how she learned a tough lesson about self-respect the hard way.

〝 'Slut!' I heard him yell down the hall as he laughed and pointed me out. It started six months earlier. I just moved and was a freshman without friends. It didn't take me long to make new friends, and I was looking forward to homecoming, especially for the chance to dance with my crush. He was outgoing and sweet, someone fun who I thought I could depend on. Sadly, it was just an image, an ego he was trying to maintain, but that didn't stop me from falling hard.

Things got rough. He started smoking weed all the time. It changed him, and I was his scapegoat. Things went downhill so fast, I didn't see it. I thought I loved him and needed him, but I was completely blind to his abuse. His anger was out of control. He would call me a bitch and say things about my image that tore me down. At his worst, he occasionally hit me. He would grab me with a violent grip and anger so fierce in his eyes, that I hid the bruises he left under my T-shirts. He broke promises and lied constantly, but he would somehow make it okay with the 'Baby, I love you, I'm so sorry' and his heart-melting sweet talk. I felt so small, so helpless.

I became depressed and even resorted to cutting. I felt I had nowhere else to go. I was losing my family and friends, even my two lifelong best friends, at only fifteen—and over a boy. I was lying to them, and I argued when my best friends tried to show me what was happening. I hated what I was becoming.

A short time after I lost my virginity with him, he ended it. People were saying things like he banged me and dumped me, while he went around calling me a slut. He would literally yell it in the hallway! I was hurting so unbelievably bad. It was the worst pain I ever felt. With the help of my best friends, I healed and moved on. Although it destroyed my confidence, made me always blame myself, and created major trust issues, what I went through made me stronger. It changed me for the better. I learned that I need to listen to my family and friends and not go against my gut. I still struggle sometimes and hate the things that are habit now, but I am not ashamed of myself. Any person—friend, family, boyfriend, whoever—should treat you with respect. No matter who you are, or what you've done, you deserve that much.

♥ *Julia, 18*

What Julia didn't realize is that in addition to her friends, there are places to help with verbally and physically abusive relationships. These are complicated situations. Look at the resources at the end of this book and read more about violence in relationships later in this chapter.

You don't have to be dating someone to be somebody

This is so, so true, but not every girl realizes it.

❝ I felt like my status would go up if I dated Jake, one of the most popular guys at school. We were just friends for a long time, and then we did start dating. I thought this would make me feel different, more special. It didn't, and I realized how dumb it was to think that by dating Jake I would be cooler. Why couldn't I be more popular just because of who I was? ❞

♥ *Candy, 14*

Amanda realized it, but wished her friend would too.

❝ For years I watched my best friend doubt herself, and give up on herself, all over boys. There would be times when she was so upset about something a guy did (or didn't do), I really got worried about her. A lot of her stress came from wishing she had a guy to be upset about. But that's just it, guys aren't everything. Sure, I love having a boyfriend who is there for me. However, I would never want to lose sight of who I was or who other people are in my life for one. After living through my own mistakes and watching her get depressed over her, I really began to believe that guys shouldn't be that important to a girl. They are certainly not worth ruining your life over. It is far more important to focus on what you already have. For most of us, that's great friends, a loving family, a roof over our heads and food on our plate. I have done everything I can to help her understand this so she can be the happy. I hope she takes it to heart and that every girl can understand that guys shouldn't be able to make or break your life.

With guys come fun, excitement, trust, mystery, disappointment and heartbreak, and no matter whatever stage you are in, you just have to accept it and move through it, good or bad. In the end you can become a better person, a better woman. 🙂🙂

💜 *Amanda, 17*

Hormones will play tricks on you

During your teen years, hormones are all over the place. They can make you have feelings for boys, and they can also make you have mood swings and feel depressed.

🙂🙂 My mom was always really open with me about my body and stuff. I was really glad we talked about hormones because I started to be in sync with my body. I noticed when my mood swings came and went. Sometimes it was close to my period. This helped me understand when my hormones were affecting me more than my head. When my emotions feel out of control, it's nice to know there's a reason for it. 🙂🙂

💜 *Emma, 17*

Did you know that researchers have found that the "in love" feeling releases chemicals in our bodies that are similar to what addicts feel? More on this later . . .

Our families influence our choice in boys

One thing I wish I had known when I was a teenager is how much our families influence our choices in boys. Some theories about relationships suggest that we date people who remind us of our family or of things we need to work out.

For example, perhaps you have a dad who doesn't pay attention to you. You may consequently pick a boy who also doesn't pay attention to you. Or maybe you've witnessed a lot of arguing and fighting between your parents. You might be attracted to a guy who also yells at you a lot or who you argue with. Do we always pick someone who repeats our family's problems? No, of course not. There are so many factors that go into why we date people. In fact, sometimes our experiences in our families show us exactly what we don't want, and we are able to see that and not repeat unhealthy patterns.

Our boyfriends may offer a big clue about how we feel about ourselves

This means we should pay attention to a couple of things. First, how does he treat you? If you keep dating guys who put you down, somewhere down the line you start to believe it is okay to put yourself down. This means you don't value yourself enough to get out of the relationship or ask for this abuse to stop. Remember, no one has the right to put you down verbally or hurt you physically. If you're in a situation like this, don't put yourself down for being here; it can happen to anyone. If this is you, look for more tips later in this chapter.

Second, how do you feel about yourself when you're with him? Does he respect you? Does he make you feel good about yourself? Can you feel good about yourself without him?

Don't rely on guys to bring you happiness or boost your self-esteem

Too many girls do this. I've done this. It seems almost normal that we wait for that guy in our lives to cheer us up or make us feel better, but it's dangerous to be dependent on someone else for our own happiness. It encourages us to stay in bad relationships, forces us to miss out on new opportunities, isolates us from our friends, and lessens our chances of being able to find true happiness.

❝ Once I was depressed and didn't realize it. My friend Jarod invited some friends over, and I was having a good time. A bunch of people were spending the night, and I ended up outside in a camper with my friend Autumn and these two guys we just met. We were just hanging out, and the guys had a little bit to drink. Before I knew it, we were both hooking up with these guys. When I woke up, I felt used and sick to my stomach. The guy I was with didn't have any interest in seeing me again. I mistakenly believed this hook-up would make me feel good about myself. That couldn't have been further from the truth. ❞

♥ *Monica, 16*

You are always in control of your body

No one has the right to touch you without your permission.

❝ Nelson was a senior; I was a freshman. I loved how he paid attention to me and wanted to be friends. On my birthday, we went to a movie and things got weird. He put his hands down my pants, and I didn't know what to do. We hadn't even kissed yet.

This was my first real experience with a boy. Was this how it was supposed to be? Later at his house, he kissed me. It was strange and exciting all at the same time because it was my first kiss. This wasn't a healthy relationship. Nelson took advantage of me and our friendship. I was so thrilled that a guy was paying attention to me, but I shouldn't have let him touch me in a way that made me uncomfortable. We continued to 'do stuff' on and off for the next year, though we never dated. I'm so glad we never had sex, but even so, the way he took advantage of our friendship wasn't right. I should have stopped him, but I was too shocked. He was very well respected in the community, but didn't respect girls. I regret that I didn't have the courage to speak up. ❞

♥ *Corrine, 18*

When you date a boy, how would you label your behavior? Take the quiz on the next page to find out.

Which One Are You?

- **The clinger.** You want to spend every waking moment with your guy. If you haven't gotten a text message from him before first hour, you're devastated. Each weekend is planned out, and he'd better check with you first before making plans with his friends.

- **The idolizer.** You adore your boyfriend to the point that he can do no wrong. You are constantly telling him how amazing he is.

- **The I-always-put-myself-last type.** He wants to go to batting cages on dates, and you say okay, even though you hate baseball. He is worried about flunking his biology test, so you help him for three hours, even though it means you don't finish your own homework.

- **The pusher-awayer.** He is just perfect for you. He's funny, smart, and kind. But every time he reaches out to you, you push him away.

- **Just right.** You like your boyfriend but know he's one of many friends. You take care of your own responsibilities first, and there is balance in your life. You have fun together and really like each other or maybe even love each other.

Okay, let's figure out your answers:

- **If you're a clinger,** loosen up a little and give your guy some space. Make sure you focus on things that are important to you as well as to him.

- **If you're an idolizer,** think about putting yourself on a pedestal. Think about what you've accomplished that you can be proud of.

- **If you always put yourself last,** try putting yourself first for a change. Speak up next time when you're deciding what to do, and tell him the truth.

- **If you're a pusher-awayer**, ask yourself a couple of questions: Is this about you or him? Is there something about him that's telling you you're not in the right relationship? Or is it usually hard for you to trust people? If that's the case, think about why it is hard for you to trust others.

- **If you're someone who's just right**, congratulations! You've figured out how to be in a relationship and still hold on to yourself and your friends.

  Which dating type do you want to be? You have the power to decide.

COMMON DATING PROBLEMS

I want to date, but my parents won't let me

Some girls are allowed to date at twelve or thirteen, while other parents won't let their daughters date until they're sixteen or older. Try to see it from your parents' perspective. For starters, how old are you? Are you responsible? Do you give your parents reasons not to trust you? If in all honesty, you have to answer yes, there's a reason they are reluctant to let you date. If you can honestly answer "no," then perhaps it's time to talk calmly and truthfully with your parents about their reasons and then go from there.

My best friend and I like the same guy

This doesn't have to be a deal breaker. It might seem hard sometimes, but try to always put your girlfriends first. Most of the girls who do this told me they never regret it. (Look for more advice on this in Chapter 3.)

Boys put me down

This is never okay, even if it's in a joking and teasing way. To make things even worse, sometimes guys try to convince you it's your fault they're teasing you or talking to you disrespectfully, whether it's talking about one of your physical features, making fun of your outfit, or teasing you about your relationship with someone. The fact is, when guys put you down, this could be a big warning sign of an unhealthy relationship. If this is someone you're dating or thinking about dating, you should think twice. No matter what, you don't deserve to be put down. Read more about this later in this chapter.

I don't have a boyfriend

Does that mean you are weird? Not pretty? Not good enough? That you have a purple nose? No way. Some of the coolest girls I know don't have boyfriends. If you feel you must have a boyfriend to be cool or accepted, then you will either date the wrong guy in hopes of being cool or feel miserable and really down on yourself because the right guy hasn't yet come along. This sets you up for failure from the very beginning. Remind yourself often—you don't need to have a boyfriend to be cool or accepted!

❝ Who says you have to have a boyfriend, anyway? The magazines you read and the TV shows you watch might make it seem like teenage girls are supposed to have boyfriends, but why? It seems like some girls go from boyfriend to boyfriend just for the sake of having a boyfriend.

Take me, for example. I never had a boyfriend throughout high school. Although this was frustrating at the time, it allowed me to develop a strong sense of self. I wouldn't be the independent, self-confident person I am today if I had been constantly trying to impress a boy. While some girls worried about whether they said 'I love you' back before hanging up the phone, I was busy having fun with my friends, exploring St. Louis, and developing skills and interests.

If that pep talk doesn't help, ask yourself why you even want a boyfriend in the first place. Is it because all of your friends have one and you feel left out? Do you want to be like the characters in your favorite chick flick? If all else fails and you're still desperate for a boyfriend, stop thinking about it. Everything will fall into place when you stop obsessing about boys. I don't mean to bash all boyfriends, though. If you've found a great guy who respects and appreciates you for who you are, great!

But while you're waiting for Mr. Right, focus on doing well in school and your activities. This will allow your true personality to shine through, which is your most attractive quality. 🙶 🙶

🤍 *Kate, 23*

Why do I feel so crazy about him?

Falling in love can create intense physical and emotional feelings. You might feel like you're on a high, have butterflies in your stomach, or even a burning desire to kiss him. These are normal feelings, but at the same time they can be dangerous and complicated. It's important to understand that those intense feelings of being high are often a result of a change in your body chemistry.

Researchers have found that "falling in love" releases various brain chemicals that can mimic the feeling of being high. If your relationship ends and you are still in love, this can be devastating. For many, feelings about a breakup are equivalent to what a drug addict might feel during withdrawal.

Love is complicated. You may have an incredible connection on some levels and yet this person may not be a fit in other ways. It's a hard lesson to learn, but realize that the "falling in love" feeling doesn't last forever. Some researchers estimate that it usually only lasts about two years.

> You can be in love with someone and he (or she) might not be the right person for you.

Finally, it's important to understand when we fall in love, we tend to overlook flaws. Have you ever heard the expression "Love is blind"? Relationship and neuroscience experts are finding that there's some truth to that statement. When we fall in love, some experts believe our brains actually tell us to overlook the flaws that we see in that person.

❝ Around my fifteenth birthday, I met this really cute guy who was two years older. I could tell he liked me, so we started dating. Neither of my parents was happy with the idea that their daughter, barely fifteen, was dating someone who was so close to being a legal adult.

Within about one week of dating, Max uttered the famous three-word phrase 'I love you.' All I could think was, 'Dang, he loves me! I should probably say it now, too.' I told him I loved him, even though I wasn't quite sure I did or what it was supposed to mean. I felt vulnerable and weak and didn't know what else to do but let him love me and to love him in return. My relationship with Max always had a sexual component. It seemed like that was all he wanted from me. It was like he didn't have anything to say to me, but he had loads to do to me.

With everything that was happening in my family and at home, I figured it didn't really matter what I did with Max as long as I wasn't at home. I didn't realize this was emotionally unhealthy for me. Our relationship had an early climax and soon started downhill. I didn't know that the happiness in the relationship was merely sexual and that I wasn't gaining anything but addiction, just as he was. Soon we started having fights, and I didn't see that as a sign of a relationship gone wrong. My family hated my relationship more. They saw what Max was doing to me and tried their best to point it out. But I didn't see his manipulative or controlling ways. After a few months, our parents found out about our sexual relationship, and it was over in a week. We were both devastated, and we tried everything we could think of to stay together, but it just didn't work. That summer I tried to forget Max, but he was the only thing I thought about, and I didn't know what to do. To make things worse, he turned people against me and made them think I was a slut and that it was my fault the relationship ended.

I finally understood that he was a jerk who didn't respect me or care how I felt. I finally felt free of him. I look back now and think about how naive I was. I'm not as angry with him as I was, because I recently learned I can forgive myself for the things that happened. 〞

♥ *Nicole, 17*

How far is too far?

Any type of sexual contact is a big decision on many levels. It's more than just the physical experience. It's thinking about all of your options and choices because they each have consequences. It's important to take your time and really think through what is right for you. *You should never stay in a situation that makes you feel uncomfortable, and if you say no, it means no.*

❝ I started dating Tom when I was a junior in high school. When we first met, we immediately clicked and talked for hours. I decided to go out on a date to the movies with him later that week. He was such a gentleman that when he asked me to be his girlfriend a few days later, I said yes without even knowing him very well. He was a senior in high school, so I thought he would be much more mature and interesting. He was my first official, steady boyfriend, so I was excited to see him every weekend (we went to different schools).

About one week into our relationship, he began calling me after school every day and begging me to sneak out to meet him someplace to make out. I knew my mom would not want me seeing him during the school week, so I constantly told lies about where I was going. Things quickly heated up, and by the end of our second week, I had done more with him sexually than I had ever dreamed of doing with a guy. Valentine's Day was coming up, and instead of the typical roses and dinner, we went to a park and messed around. I knew he cared for me, but I also knew I was in too deep. I just could not let him go.

One night before a basketball game at school, we went to our favorite make-out spot and started kissing. Before long we were undressed, and I remember telling him I wasn't ready, but he would not relent. I should have had more of a backbone, but I was afraid he would break up with me, so I gave in.

I was sad that my first time was in a stupid car, and the worst part was, later that night after the game when he dropped me off, he told me we could no longer be together. I could not believe he had used me this way!

I learned a lot from that experience. I realized I should have been more firm about saying no. I should have taken a stand and waited for a guy who respected me. I'm currently seeing a guy who is amazing. He respects me and likes me for who I am and not what kind of sexual pleasure I can give to him. Being true to yourself and standing up for what is right are always the best way to live. "

♥ *Sydney, 18*

Thinking through your physical relationship

- It's a good idea to talk about sex with your parents, girlfriends, or other adults you trust. There are so many things to consider, and it's good to have a sounding board.
- Specifically, think about how far beyond kissing you want to go. What are your religious or family beliefs about this? What do you believe about this?

- Look at where your information and concept about your physical relationship has come from. Don't believe everything you see on MTV, TV, or movies. Sexual contact is glamorized and made into many things it isn't.
- If you decide to have sex, when is the right time, and how are you going to protect yourself from pregnancy and STDs? How will this change your relationship? Why is this important to you one way or the other? What does love have to do with how far you go?
- Do your research and be sure you understand the risks of being sexually active. Some of the serious consequences of having sex include experiencing emotional harm, getting pregnant, or contracting an STD. (You can read more about these in Chapter 7 on "Dealing with the Tough Stuff.")

These questions and your answers are extremely personal, but fortunately we can learn a great deal from one another's lessons. Hear other girls talk about it at www.youtube.com/girlswithdreams.

When Tracy went to her mom to talk about sex, she was super nervous, but her mom's advice meant so much to her that she wanted other girls to hear it too. Here's a little bit of what her mom wrote.

Dear Tracy,

Before you give your heart to a boy, I hope you will first give it to yourself. I made the mistake of letting others define me and only loving myself if I was being loved by a boy. I put my self-confidence in their words and actions toward me. I didn't realize that I needed to love myself first.

After you've learned to love yourself and you're ready to start dating, I hope you will look for just the right person. Don't just take the first guy who comes along. Look for someone you can trust, who respects you and you respect back. I want you to feel comfortable in

your own skin and love your body so you can stand proud about who
you are every day.

When you get serious with your boyfriend, I hope you'll think
about saving sex for marriage. I know this isn't always the norm these
days, but I have seen some pop stars with purity rings. Really, I want
you to think for yourself, to follow your own intuition, and when
you're ready, I want you to enjoy sex and your relationship with that
special someone to the fullest. I don't want you to get pregnant when
you're 17 or get an STD, or regret giving it away to the wrong boy.

I'll always respect you and your decisions, even if we disagree. I just hope
you will come to me with your questions. It's really important to me that you
get all of the right information so you can make the best decision . . .

How do I know if he's "the one"?

The good news is that you don't have to figure this out right now.
You have the rest of your life ahead of you! You've probably heard
this before, but think about it for a second.

You might genuinely be in love, but you are growing and changing so much that it's important to do things independently, too. *You
need to make important decisions based on what feels right for you,
not what feels right for him.*

Give it time. Maybe he is the one, but there's no reason to rush
into sex or marriage. Both are a huge commitment. While some
people get married before the age of twenty, research has shown
that the older you are when you marry, the more likely it is your
marriage will last. Why not give yourself time?

❝ ❝ I spent all of high school virtually boyfriendless. I had one here or
there, but I always broke up with them very quickly. I was just too happy
single. I was involved in school and very busy.

My senior year of high school started out that way, but about halfway through the year, I realized I wanted somebody to share it with. Bam—I met the perfect guy. He was older, tall, athletic, and sweet, and he never forgot to tell me I was beautiful. Maybe I should have seen the warning signs sooner. He never wanted to do what I wanted. We watched action movies and TV shows I'd rather eat rotten eggs than watch. We agreed on nothing. I liked the arts: music, singing, dancing, writing, history, and design. This was everything he absolutely hated. He said 'opposites attract.'

After only two months of dating, he dropped the L word on me, and at first I said it back. I didn't know what else to do. Three days later, I took it back. I told him I loved my family, I loved my friends, and I loved him in that same way, but I was not in love with him.

He started keeping tabs on me after that, making sure I wasn't hanging out with any other guys, even my best guy friend I'd known years. He'd text my best friends to make sure I was with them when I said I was, and he dropped hints about marriage. That's when I got scared. I knew I'd break his heart, but I didn't want to end up with him. I didn't want to tell my friends my thoughts because I didn't know what I was going to do yet.

Many days he became angry at me for something small I did, and I'd have to smooth it over and apologize. Deep down I didn't want to leave him because he made me feel desirable, beautiful, and attractive. Isn't that what every girl wants?

Finally, I told my best friend all my doubts about the relationship and expressed that I didn't really know how to get out. It was liberating, and I wondered why I hadn't said it out loud before that.

The next day, I didn't answer his phone calls. He came over to my house unannounced, and I knew I had to do it then. I told him I was sorry it had to be this way, but we couldn't be together. He told me he loved me, that I was the one for him. I remember staring at him and wondering how he could have all of these feelings for me when I was so sure he was not the one for me.

I stuck to my decision. We stayed semifriends, and he continued to try to manipulate me for a few months. I realized breaking up wasn't enough. I finally ended it by telling him we couldn't be friends, either. I had to do it to respect myself. I don't regret my decision at all, and I'm a better person because of it. 🙶 🙶

♥ *Abby F., 18*

Breaking up

Breakups are brutal, but there are ways to make them easier.

When he breaks up with you, take a deep breath and put things into perspective. Don't take it personally. This may seem impossible, but just because he doesn't want to be with you doesn't mean there is anything wrong with you; you're just not a fit together. *As much as it hurts, you don't want to be in a relationship with someone who isn't into you.* Try to be thankful for the good times you had and what you learned, and remind yourself that the next relationship you're in is going to be even better.

On the flip side, if you know you aren't with the right guy, don't delay breaking up to save his feelings. The longer it goes on, the harder it will be. Be honest about your feelings. Talk about what worked and what didn't. You might even practice with a friend to figure out what you want to say. If he tries to counteroffer and wants to get back together, give yourself time to think about it.

If he threatens you when you break up with him, this is not okay, and you should take it seriously. Talk to a trusted friend or adult. You'll need to make sure you have the right plan in place to keep you safe.

Regardless of who initiated it, to help you deal with a breakup, do the following:

• Hang with your friends or family.
• Keep busy doing things you enjoy.

- Practice self-care, whether it is sleeping in, going for a walk, or laughing with your friends.
- Let yourself feel the emotions. If you just ignore them or push them away, they will resurface.
- Remind yourself that something better is waiting for you, even if you can't see it now.
- Ice cream and other treats can be soothing, but try not to get in the habit of overindulging.
- Draw or write your thoughts in your journal.

Dealing with older guys

Dealing with older guys can mean a couple of things. It might mean dating a seventeen-year-old when you are only fourteen, or it might mean having a crush on a man who is twenty or thirty. These situations are complicated and even dangerous. Most states have laws about having sex with a minor, and if you are under eighteen, that's what you are. Here are some things to think about:

- Do your parents know about this friendship or relationship?
- Are you being secretive about this relationship? If so, this is probably a clue that you're not in a good situation.
- Where did you meet this person? Online or in person? Make sure to read our section about online dating for more information.
- Be alert to the fact that older guys might be able to pick up on your vulnerabilities or weaknesses easier.
- Check your motives for being with this guy. Do you really like each other, or does he just make you feel special and important?

   I was feeling really alone, and I think he picked up on that. He was the manager of the ice cream shop I was working in over summer break. We started by just talking. We joked around a lot and were friends. Then he started to flirt with me. It was kind of weird, but I was flattered at the same time. One day we were in the cooler, and we just hugged each other. I don't know why. It felt good. I had been so lonely and just needed a hug. The hugging thing happened a few more times.

The problem was that he was married. What was I thinking? What was he thinking? What would his wife say? It wasn't like I saw a long-term future with this guy. I should have quit and found another job, but something kept me there. Maybe it was the extra attention or the curiosity. I'm not sure.

One day, he told me he wanted to talk to me, and before I knew it, he had kissed me. I was so glad summer was almost over. In fact, I had only two days left to work. He tried to convince me that we should meet after work, but I didn't want to do that. In fact, I never went back.

This story is embarrassing, but I wanted to write about it because I think we need to share our stories. I didn't know what to do. I wish I had quit earlier or even made a sexual harassment complaint to upper management. I wish I hadn't felt so lonely, and I wish I had thought of other ways to find companionship besides a forty-five-year-old married man who had no business hitting on girls and playing on their insecurities. 🙋

♥ *Christy, 19*

Meeting guys online

It's very common these days for teens to use the Internet to visit social networking sites such as MySpace, but as great as this technology is, it can be very dangerous. (Read more about this in Chapter 6, "Are You Cyber Savvy?")

Dealing with jealousy

While we all deal with a little jealousy from time to time, how much is too much? Whether he's jealous of you or vice versa, keep it in check. If the jealousy has turned into trying to control each other through whom you hang out with or what you wear, it's not okay. Again, this could be a warning sign of an unhealthy relationship.

Take the following quiz to see how much jealousy you deal with in your relationship.

Quiz

Is the Jealousy in Your Relationship Healthy or Unhealthy?

1. You see him talking to a really cute girl by his locker, and you get jealous and tell him he's not allowed to talk to her anymore. Healthy or unhealthy?
2. He has to study for a biology test with a group of friends. You get a little jealous because you'd like to spend time with him, but you get over it fast. Healthy or unhealthy?
3. He likes your skirt but tells you it's too short and he doesn't want other guys looking at you. He tells you he'd prefer that you wear only jeans to school. Healthy or unhealthy?

Only situation no. 2 is an example of jealousy that hasn't turned destructive. If jealousy is a part of your relationship, make sure you focus on the seven tips at the end of the chapter.

Are you in a violent relationship?

You may not think so, and you may think this will never happen to you, but it's important to recognize that *violence in a relationship can happen to anyone*. Remember Julia from earlier in this chapter? She never thought it would happen to her. It doesn't matter how intelligent you are or how much money you have. It might never happen to you, but it could, and it could also happen to someone you know.

It is very difficult to determine the exact number of teens involved in abusive relationships, because many teens are afraid to report it. At a minimum, at www.cdc.gov/injury, researchers found that one in four adolescents reports verbal, physical, emotional, or sexual abuse from a dating partner each year. This number was reported as one in three at www.acadv.org. Additionally, the CDC reports 10 percent of students nationwide report being physically hurt by a boyfriend or girlfriend in the last twelve months.

It's important to know the signs and what you can do so that if it ever happens to you or a friend, you can get help.

I thought Andre loved me. I thought we had something really special. Every time he called me a bitch, I just blew it off. I didn't want to tell my friends, but then one day we were hanging out with a few of my friends and Andre started making fun of me. Later, they talked to me about this, and I started defending him. I wish I had listened to them that day. My relationship with Andre went from verbal violence to physical violence, and I ended up staying with him for almost a year. It was a long battle to end our relationship, but I finally did it.

Kelly, 18

Dating violence takes different forms. It can be emotional, psychological, physical, or sexual. Violence also occurs in gay or lesbian relationships.

All abusive relationships have good times and bad times. Part of what makes dating violence so confusing and painful is that there is often love mixed with the abuse.

Emotional or mental violence includes things like mind games, constant put-downs, criticisms, insults, name-calling, and intimidation. The abuser may also try to control your activities, destroy your self-confidence or self-esteem, or keep you away from other friends and family.

Physical violence includes things like hitting, slapping, punching, shoving, kicking, biting, and hair-pulling. It can also include the use of a weapon such as a club, knife, or gun.

Sexual violence includes making you do something sexual that you don't want to do, refusing to have safe sex, or making you feel bad about yourself sexually. The term "sexual abuse" refers to forced or unwanted sexual activity or rape. It is also considered sexual abuse to coerce or pressure someone to engage in sexual activity or to try to engage in sexual activity with someone who is under the influence of drugs or alcohol.

Find out more about the warning signs of dating violence and how to help your friends in Chapter 7.

WHAT IF I'M NOT ATTRACTED TO BOYS?

This can be very confusing, but hang in there. Sooner or later you will figure out what's right for you.

❝ For those of you who feel different, who want to be attracted to boys but you're not, life can be pretty confusing. For those of us who struggle with our sexuality in the face of families and a society that thinks we 'should' be a certain way and love certain people, there are so many questions, so many things to consider: 'What will my parents think?' 'How will I tell my parents?' 'My parents are going to kick me out of the house!' 'Where will I go?'

Perhaps you're in a space where you need to experiment to figure out who you are. That experimentation could lead you down many paths: to the realization that you are in fact attracted to boys; to the realization you are attracted to people, not their gender; to the realization that you are indeed attracted to girls. Maybe you will experiment and decide you fall on one side of the fence or the other, and further down the line you will decide you belong someplace else after all.

Coming to terms with your sexuality isn't easy. It takes a ton of courage to be true to who you are in the face of family and friends who may be less than supportive. No matter where you end up down the line, where you are right now—here in the present moment—could be one of the most distressing times of your life.

If I had trusted my instincts so many years ago, my life would be very different. But life is an evolving process. I might not be where I am today if I hadn't gone through this (difficult) process. I still remember the first girl I was attracted to in grade school. She had beautiful brown hair, dark eyebrows, and dark eyes. Her smile is burned into my brain. But I grew up in a family where I was supposed to meet a nice boy, get married, and have children. My next attraction came at lacrosse camp. Surrounded by girls, I thrived. I could relate to them, and I wanted to be with them.

I was too scared to admit my feelings. I suppose it didn't help that I had an uncle who was (shhhh) gay. No one talked about his sexuality. It was a very clear message, at least in my family. It just wasn't who I was 'supposed' to be, so I ignored it. For years I dated men, hoping I could change, but I always felt different. I didn't enjoy men.

When I was twenty-three, I had a relationship with a woman. At the time, I had a fiancé. With his blessing, I pursued the relationship. She was ready, but I was not. Our relationship lasted for nearly a year, and then I cut it off. I was still too scared to pursue what I knew in my heart because I was afraid of what my parents and my friends would think, and how society would treat me.

Finally, when I was twenty-eight, I had the courage to be true to myself. By this point, I had a two-year-old, and I was scared for him. It took me a long time to gather the courage to tell my parents. The most frightening day of my life was the day I told them I was gay. I had run through so many scenarios: them kicking me out of their lives and never looking back, them making my life miserable, them never seeing their grandson grow up, them hating me. What I never considered was that my parents would accept me for who I am. I know this is not the reality for everyone. This is only how it happened for me. Today I am thirty-six years old, and I am with that woman I dated when I was twenty-three, and I have never been happier.

Everyone's experience when they come out to their families is different. I have talked to many people who have lost their families because of who they are. I have also talked to many women who eventually found acceptance, even though they never thought their families would be accepting. No matter what your family's reaction is, you will be okay. Whatever makes us different from other people also makes us stronger. Somehow we have the ability to find the support we need to be okay, especially when times are tough. If you think your family could be supportive, I have some suggestions for talking to them. I make no guarantees that these strategies will work. All I can tell you is that many women have used them with success. 🙶

♥ *Wendy Sheppard, 36*

Wendy's tips for coming out are as follows:

1. Find support outside of your family. I cannot stress how important it is to surround yourself with supportive people during any difficult time in your life. Are there people you know who have struggled with their sexuality? If so, connect with them. Talk with them. How did they deal with their struggle? What things did they find helpful?

Go online and connect with communities of young people who are going through the same things you are. Talk with them about their experiences. (Make sure you follow the cyber-savvy safety tips mentioned later in the book. When you're in an emotionally vulnerable state, it's especially important to have your radar up.) Also, is there anyone at school you think would be supportive? Maybe a teacher, a guidance counselor, a mentor, or a coach?

2. Do your research. Do you have questions about being gay? If so, start there—go online and search for the answers. Save anything you think might help answer questions for your parents if and when you do finally come out to them.

Also search for books that others have found helpful when coming out to their parents. When my partner finally came out to her parents, she gave them three books to read that answered some of their questions and their fears for her future. The more information you can give them, the more understanding they may be when you come out.

3. Consider any support you may have within the family. Are there people in your family you are not afraid to come out to? Some people come out to siblings first. Others come out first to cousins or a close aunt or uncle. Alternatively, some choose to come out to a close family friend who is more like family.

If you do identify someone in your family who you think will be supportive, use the experience of coming out to him or her as a practice run. Ask this person to talk with you about his or her questions or concerns about being gay. Ask about how he or she thinks your parents will react. Ask for help in figuring out the best way to approach your parents. You might even consider asking this person whether he or she would be there to support you when you come out to your parents.

4. Make a plan. First, you need to figure out where you are going to talk to your parents. I strongly suggest you talk to them in an environment where they will be comfortable. Hopefully, this will help them respond in a more relaxed way.

It's important to realize your parents may feel embarrassed to talk about this. While it may be tempting to talk with them in a crowded public place, they may end up feeling resentful that you chose to "drop the bomb" in a place where they couldn't react honestly and openly to the news.

Next, you have to figure out what you're going to say. This is going to be different for everyone. Use words that are comfortable for you, and try to be as direct as possible.

If you feel comfortable, rehearse what you will say with one of your support people. If you do not feel comfortable rehearsing with someone else, then consider writing down your ideas.

Next, rehearse your reaction to their reaction. What if they are silent? What if they ignore what you tell them? What if they get angry? What if they throw you out? What if they start asking questions? What if . . .?

Remember, your parents may need some time to come to terms with the news. When parents ignore or change the subject after a child comes out to them, it's usually because they aren't ready to address the situation. Often, walking away and allowing them to process the information is the best thing you can do.

In addition, even when your parents react negatively, in time they may have a different reaction. For instance, one father had absolutely no reaction when his daughter told him she was a lesbian. It would have been easy for her to assume her father didn't accept her, but she gave him some time. Several months later, out of the blue, he said, "I just want you to be happy." That was it. They never spoke directly about her being a lesbian, but from that moment on she knew he accepted her.

5. Trust your gut. You will know when it's the right time to come out. You just have to trust your gut. If it doesn't feel right, no matter how many people have told you that you "should" do this or you "should" do that, don't do it.

6. Contact a professional. Finally, you can always contact a professional for support before, during, or after the coming-out process. Obviously, depending on your age, you may need your parents' help to contact a professional. Certainly, if you feel like you need professional help, get it!

This can also be a good way to come out to your parents. If you feel like you need more support in figuring out how to tell your parents, go to them and ask whether you can find a counselor to help you with some things. Keep it general if you have to.

Once you find a counselor, you can discuss with him or her how to come out. Most of the time, counselors will agree to have your parents come in for some sessions. The counselor can help facilitate the coming-out conversation with your parents. This can be an effective way of telling your parents, especially for those who are really scared about their parents' reaction.

Seven Tips Every Girl Needs to Deal with Boys

Tip One: You Gotta Use Your Gut

In this chapter, we talked a lot about hormones, those funny chemicals in your body that can make you feel moody, excited, and attracted to others. When you're following your gut, it's important to keep your hormones in check. Get to know what it feels like when you're listening to your gut so you will know the difference.

Your instinct is your best friend, and it's going to help you along the way, from deciding when it's time for you to date, who you're going to date, to how far you're going to go.

> We have all a better guide in ourselves, if we would attend to it, than any other person can be.
> —Jane Austen

❝ It was like love at first sight. Nile and I just connected with each other. We had this amazing bond, and we were falling in love with each other. I couldn't not be with him. The problem was that sometimes he did things that bothered me, like make fun of girls or lose his temper. I just blew it off. It was like my love for him was stronger than these negative traits. I stayed with him for almost two years, and then we had to break it off because he moved away. I was devastated, but eventually I saw how it was actually a good thing. Even though we loved each other, we weren't right for each other. ❞

♥ Paula, 18

This is a great example of how influential those "in love" feelings are and how hard it is to listen to your gut sometimes. It was almost like Paula's instinct was telling her to stay with Nile, but if she dug deeper, it was also giving her clues that he wasn't the right one. She was lucky he moved away, which forced the issue.

Think about it: people in bad relationships often ignore signs and feelings from their guts. What is your gut telling you about dating, about boys, and maybe about one boy in particular?

Take time to figure out whether you want a steady boyfriend or whether you even want to date. *Take time to think about what you want.*

❝ I loved Brian. He was charming, funny, intelligent, and athletic. We had fun together, and I felt really good hanging out with him. As we got more serious, he wanted things to go further. I didn't feel right about it. I really loved him and wanted to keep dating, but I knew in my heart I would have to end things because he wasn't willing to stay around if I didn't have sex. This was one of the hardest things I ever did, and it took a couple of months to get over him, but I was really glad I listened to my gut. ❞

♥ *Tara, 17*

Tip Two: Discover Your Strengths and Use Them

Whether or not you've dated yet, it's important to think through your personal strengths and weaknesses from two standpoints.

First, what are the strengths you generally express? For example, are you independent or dependent? Do you like to talk, or are you shy? Are you smart? Creative? Musically talented? Athletic? Do you like adventure, or do you prefer to be organized? In essence, what do you bring to a relationship? And are you able to express your natural strengths and talents in your relationship?

Make sure he appreciates you for what you're good at. Does he love who you are and what you're about? Can you express your opinions?

Second, what are the strengths you express when it comes to dating? For instance, do you tend to be clingy, or do you give him space? Are you controlling, or do you talk about the opinions you each hold?

If you have dated before, think about what it was like. What did you like about your relationship? What didn't you like?

If you've just started dating, this is the perfect time to start noticing how you act in a relationship.

❝ My first boyfriend wasn't exactly the best choice, but how could I have known? After all, he was the first one. He was cute and funny, but he didn't really express much of an interest in me. And I noticed I was totally attached to him. I think this kind of freaked him out a little bit. 🙌

♥ *Gabby, 15*

Tip Three: Choose the Right Friends and Respect Them

This goes for both the guys you are dating and the guys you are just friends with. Here are a few things to consider. Just because you're friends with a guy doesn't mean you have to date him. It's okay to have guy friends, and it can be really fun, too. A lot of girls like not having the pressure of dating and just enjoy hanging out. Also, just because you're dating doesn't mean you have to ditch your girlfriends. This isn't as straightforward as it sounds, and some girls are better at it than others.

🙌 When I started dating Dylan, I just wanted to be with him all the time, but I remembered what it felt like when one of my best friends had become so obsessed with her guy there was no time for me. So I made sure I had time for my friends. Some weekends I would just have a night out with the girls. Other nights, we'd all do something together. Dylan was cool about this, and actually it was a lot more fun this way because I was able to see all of the people I loved more often. 🙌

♥ *Sarah, 17*

It gives you balance and perspective to hang out with people in addition to your boyfriend. Also, you don't always know how long your boyfriend is going to be around. If you spend time with only him, your friends may not want to take you back if you break up. At the same time, if he is the right guy and the real thing, your guy and your friends are going to be around for a long time.

Tip Four: Be Courageous and Confident

If you know you might be lacking confidence, be careful about getting into a relationship. Why? Many of the girls we talk to who enter relationships just to make themselves feel better are usually disappointed. Typically, they put up with more put-downs and negatives because they're too addicted to getting attention from their guy. If this rings true for you, start working on yourself. Building your courage and confidence won't happen overnight, but if you follow the tips we've outlined in this book, you can make big improvements.

How do you know whether you're lacking confidence? Go back and reread tip four in the Introduction. You might also want to think about the following questions:

• Are you looking for a guy to make you feel good about yourself?
• Do you put yourself down?
• Do you wait to hear compliments from guys and then obsess about them?

Remember, it takes courage to stand alone. This might mean saying no to a hookup or to a guy who keeps pursuing you who isn't right for you. It also takes courage to end a relationship that isn't working. See our tips earlier in this chapter for more on breakups.

Tip Five: Be Fit and Stay Fit

Staying physically fit might be pretty easy to manage, but when it comes to boys, it's easy to get emotionally wrapped up in the relationship and lose yourself.

❝ I fell head over heels for Ryan. Even though we were just friends, he liked hanging out with me. The problem was I became so fanatical about spending time with him that I usually blew off my friends and waited for him to call. I'd wait and wait and no call from Ryan. Just as I'd get tired of this, he'd call, and there we'd go again. It would be just enough of a hook to keep me interested and just enough distance to keep me further and further from my friends. 🙢🙢

> "*Don't back down just to keep the peace. Standing up for your beliefs builds self-confidence and self-esteem.*"
> —Oprah Winfrey

♥ *Kim, 14*

🙢🙢 I wasn't sure what to do the day Alex and I broke up. I remember I was sitting in my room talking to him on the phone when he told me. I was frozen. I felt so much pain I went numb. I had no idea how I was going to handle this. I just hung up the phone and went to bed. My parents came to check on me, and I told them I didn't feel well. This went on for days until finally my mom wouldn't allow it anymore. I finally told her what was going on, and it helped. The pain started to lessen over the next couple of weeks, and slowly things went back to normal. 🙢🙢

♥ *Tish, 16*

What can you do to stay emotionally and mentally healthy? Try these tips.

- Do a reality check. Sometimes it helps to take a step back.
- Keep a journal. Dump your thoughts here and express your feelings with words and pictures.
- Talk to your friends. There's nothing better than a good friend.
- Don't be afraid to ask for help. So many times girls feel they are the only ones dealing with pain. As you can see, you are not alone.
- Sometimes you need professional help. If your feelings are interfering with your grades, schoolwork, or other relationships, talk to

your parents or a professional to figure out the next step.

- Remember, staying physically fit and healthy helps you handle emotional stress. Don't let your exercise and eating habits slip.

Tip Six: Dream Big

What is your picture of an ideal relationship? Look back at the scenes we presented at the beginning of this chapter. Which one feels right for you? Maybe you have another dream.

❝ Tomorrow is my fifteenth birthday, and I'm feeling a little weird because I haven't really had a boyfriend yet. Is that normal? I guess some of my friends haven't dated yet. I know I've been a little picky, and I guess that's okay. I want to date someone who is funny, smart, really into me, and likes to do stuff outside. He won't pressure me to have sex, but he will care about me and give me compliments. I want him to be cute and at least 5 feet, 10 inches tall. Maybe by my next birthday I'll have a new guy to write about. ❞

♥ Gina, 14 going on 15

Does Gina's journal entry sound too dreamy? Maybe it is a little, but it's good that she knows what she wants.

Get clear about what you want and don't lower your expectations. Here are a few more things to think about as you're dreaming:

- What kinds of things will you and your boyfriend do?
- What is your role in this relationship?
- How does he compliment and support you?
- Who do you know who has a great relationship? What do you like about this relationship?
- What do you need in a relationship to feel strong?

Tip Seven: Get Outside of Yourself

For some girls, it seems like boys are all-consuming, but they aren't everything. There is a whole world out there waiting for you. Whatever your situation is with boys, don't forget to get outside of yourself. Whether you are waiting for the right guy to come along or you're in a serious relationship, it's important to get a little outside perspective. Volunteer, get involved, or do something nice for someone else. Just think: if you aren't dating yet, maybe you'll meet him on this project.

Or, you might cheer up a friend who is having guy trouble or help her with her homework. Think about volunteering at a violence shelter or with a hotline. If you already have a guy, think of the great experiences you'll have to share with him. Regardless of the circumstances, it feels really good to take a break from time to time from thinking about boys, to get outside of yourself, and to give back.

Think about it . . .

- Continue to focus on doing things you love to do that bring a smile to your face. Do you love soccer? Dance? Hiking? Playing drums? Gymnastics? Making jewelry? Hanging out with friends? Whatever it is, do it. You will feel happier, and when it's the right time, you will find companionship with someone who also likes those things or who has respect for the things that make you, you.

- Be yourself. This is the best way to find the right guy. We've been asked many times, "How do I get that guy to like me?" The answer is simple: be yourself. Do what you love to do. If you're faking it, it's going to cause terrible stress, and sooner or later, it's all going to come crashing down. If you have a boyfriend, does he like who you are and what you're about? Can you express yourself and your opinions?

- What's your version of a good boyfriend? What do you want him to like you for? Get clear on this in your mind. Know when you're willing to accept a different image and when you're not. For example, maybe you want him to love dance because you're a dancer, but for your part it's okay that he's into baseball.
- Don't let boys stress you out! Dating and the events leading up to it might be very stressful, whether you are in pursuit of someone, being pursued, or just feel lonely for not having a guy. Wherever you are in this process, focus on the positive things in your life. Think about all of the things you have going for you. Try to do the things you love doing!
- Can you tell the difference between your intuition and your hormones?
- Make sure you are in a relationship that is safe emotionally and physically. This means your guy doesn't put you down, call you names, or push, hit, or hurt you in any way. He also doesn't coerce you to have any kind of intimate contact that you are not comfortable with. Dating can be an incredible high. Sometimes you will have intense feelings of attraction. Be smart. Don't let a physical attraction and your own hormones trick you into a relationship that is dangerous.
- Playing it safe is cool! Your safety is the most important thing.

Try it!

- Try all of our quizzes in this chapter and on www.girlswithdreams. com to test your relationship IQ.
- Know your strengths, weaknesses, and moods and how these affect you and your relationships.
- Work on being happy on your own. Get a journal and write down your thoughts, feelings, and ideas.
- Make a point to hang out with friends a couple of times a week.

- Try telling the guy you're dating how you really feel about things, from your opinions on politics to your thoughts on your relationship. Can you be open with him?
- Remember that just being friends with a guy can be a lot of fun, too.
- Try going on a group date or hanging out with a big group of friends.
- Try talking to your parents about stuff you're dealing with. They might be cooler than you think.
- Give yourself a confidence boost! Put on your favorite outfit, stand up tall, tell yourself you're beautiful, and surround yourself with friends who love you!

3

Best of Friends or Worst of Enemies?

How do you define a "friend"? Is it someone who brings out the best in you? Is it supportive? Is it loyal? Is it funny? Is someone you can turn to in your time of need?

Life for most teenage girls swirls around friends. Whether you have a lot of friends or just a few, the girls I've talked to care deeply about their friendships.

> A blessed thing it is for any man or woman to have a friend, one human soul whom we can trust utterly, who knows the best and worst of us, and who loves us in spite of all our faults.
>
> —Charles Kingsley

❝ I remember laughing so hard with Courtney, we both practically peed in our pants. There's nothing like a good belly laugh with your friends. ❞

♥ *Savannah, 15*

❝ It just feels good to know you've got someone who knows you better than anyone else and who you can call anytime you need anything. ❞

♥ *Jane, 13*

Friends come into our lives for all sorts of reasons. They provide a shoulder to cry on, the sister we never had, or the sister we always wanted. We love them; we hate them. They are the girl to borrow cool clothes from or the one to laugh with about our mistakes. They come in all shapes, sizes, and interests. Best of all: *you* get to decide what a friend is. Friends have the ability to lift us up but also to bring us down. Friends help us make good decisions but may also help us make bad ones. Friends may keep our secrets and/or spill our secrets, and we might keep some of our biggest secrets from our friends.

SECRETS GIRLS KEEP FROM THEIR FRIENDS

Secret diaries and quiet whispers about secrets—these are the memories you might have of some of your first friendships in grade school. For girls, it always seems like friends and secrets go together, whether it's about keeping secret the boy you like, some embarrassing moment, or a bad grade you got on a test. Yes, secrets bring girls together. Some secrets might even be the glue of a friendship, but secrets can also tear friends apart. And some secrets seem too embarrassing to share, even with our best friends. Here are some of the secrets girls told me they keep from their friends.

I do drugs.

I was abused.

My boyfriend hit me.

I am failing some of my classes.

I think about hurting myself.

No one understands me.

I make myself throw up.

My parents fight too much.

Do any of these sound familiar? Or maybe it's not your secret, but one your friend told you not to tell anyone. Think about why girls are holding their secrets so tight and how we can help each other find the courage to open up to our friends or someone we trust to get help and get better.

Ideas on opening up

If you're having doubts about opening up, consider a few things. Are you hanging out with the right people? If you worry they are not trustworthy and might tell your secrets, maybe they are the wrong friends. Or consider, maybe this is a secret you need bigger help with. Remember how I told you I thought about suicide at times? I needed professional help but I was too embarrassed and scared. If I hadn't held so tight to this secret and others, I think my path might have been a little easier.

GOOD FRIENDS BRING OUT THE BEST IN YOU

When I was in high school, I was grateful for the friends who saw the real me. I was quite a perfectionist. I overstudied, over-worried, and under ate. I loved having fun, but I didn't let myself do this very often. That's why Jeff and Kathryn were so good for me. They teased me (lightly) about my habits and made me laugh, and it worked! I began to lighten up and really changed for the better in many ways.

Real friends allow you to be you. They love who you are and

what you're about. Real friends allow you to express yourself and your opinions, but they also express their own opinions. When you're doing something stupid or harmful to yourself, a real friend will tell you the truth and try to help. She won't look the other way, because she cares what happens to you!

Friends help you laugh at your mistakes

If we didn't have friends to help us laugh at our mistakes, we'd be in terrible danger of taking ourselves too seriously.

❝ I was horrified. I was at my dance recital, and somehow my outfit got switched around backstage. When I danced onto the floor, I was wearing the wrong thing. I was so embarrassed! I saw Kelsey right after that, and I wanted to cry, but I looked at her, and we started laughing. I guess it was pretty funny, even though I was completely devastated at the moment. ❞

♥ *Raegan, 16*

Friends know just what we need and are there for us

Sometimes when we are caught up in our problems, we lose our perspective and our ability to respond appropriately to the challenges we face. Friends can really help us in these trying times.

❝ I was dealing with depression, and Deanna, my best friend, knew it. Actually, neither of us realized it was depression—we both just knew I was sad at times and having a really tough time. I was at camp for the summer, and I still remember the day I got a letter from her with the song "Don't Give Up" by Peter Gabriel written out. It brought me to tears, and it was exactly what I needed to help me make it through this tough time. ❞

♥ *Kim, 14*

PROBLEMS WITH FRIENDS

As much as we love and appreciate our friends, some of our toughest issues and most trying times come along with our friendships. As most of us know, with friends come issues. Do any of these sound familiar?

- You get invited to do something but already have plans with another friend, and you are torn.
- You both like the same guy.
- You aced your history test while your friend got a D.
- Your best friend began drinking and hanging out with a crowd you aren't comfortable with.
- You don't have nice clothes or "toys"—a cell phone, iPod, and so on—like your friends do.
- You don't really feel like you fit in. When you get to school, no one is particularly glad to see you. At lunchtime, you don't really have a group to sit with. You are more or less alone.
- Your so-called friend has been spreading rumors about you.
- Your friends talk openly about parties you're not invited to.
- Your friend puts you down in front of other people, but she always says it's just a joke or she's just kidding.
- Your friend is jealous of everything.
- There's an odd number in the group of girls you hang out with.

A few things might help in many of these situations. As hard as it might be, be honest about your feelings. If a friend is doing something hurtful or something that you don't agree with, tell her.

Also remember that friends can change. Sometimes friends grow apart or just can't relate to each other anymore. If it's time to go your separate ways, be okay with that. Sooner or later, it happens to everyone.

Help! I don't have any friends!

It may be true. Perhaps you don't have any friends—at least not any real friends. Or maybe you sometimes just feel like you don't fit anywhere. This happens to lots of girls. Possibly you do have friends and don't realize it. I have talked to many girls who think no one likes them, but when we talk about their lives further, they see other kids do care about them.

Other times, you might be in transition and need to make new friends, but it doesn't have to be as hard as you think. There are thousands of people out there who have similar interests and ideas and who want to be your friend.

❝ Making friends was always very difficult for me, especially girlfriends. I never got the 'secret signals' they gave each other and was excluded a lot. Now I've learned a little about how to do it successfully. First, I think the best strategy to get people to like you is to make them laugh and to help them out in little ways instead of just telling them about your endless problems. In turn, you'll be pleasantly surprised at how much people will come to care about you and support you in your time of need. ❞

♥ *Katie, 17*

If you need to bring friends into your life, take stock of a few things:

- First, notice where you are hanging out. Do you spend most of your time at your locker? In the cafeteria? At an after-school club? All of these are possible spots to find friends and strike up a conversation.
- Give a compliment. Everyone loves getting compliments. Just make sure you are sincere and see where the conversation goes from there.
- You can also offer to help a potential friend with something. Maybe you see someone who needs help carrying something or maybe

you're really good at math. Your offer of help might be the start of a great friendship.

- You can also look for friends at after-school activities or outside of school. Are you a part of any youth groups? Any organizations?
- Invite a potential friend to do something, whether it's having your nails painted, going on a school trip, or studying together.
- Also, think about making friends on the Internet versus in person. Ask yourself: are more of your friends online or in person? Make sure you have a healthy balance.
- Finally, be open to becoming friends with boys, too.

❝ One thing that stops me from making girlfriends is DRAMA. There is so much drama with girls these days, and I can't and don't tolerate it. That's why I hang out with boys, and that is what I tell people. ❞

♥ Kylie, 17

My friends and I are jealous of each other

❝ The competition between us almost destroyed our friendship. It was like we were always trying to 'one-up' each other. Marquita would get an A on her Spanish test, and I would try to get an A+. I would finish running the mile in eight minutes, and she would try to do it in seven. Everything was a race and a competition. ❞

♥ Shawnda, 15

Girls can be downright mean to each other. You know what I mean. For example, you're wearing a new outfit you just adore, and some girl you barely know walks by your locker at school and starts laughing at you. Competition between girls happens all the time, but it happens between friends, too.

Is competition ever good? In some cases, maybe. Some people

might argue that competition pushes them to be their best or that they thrive on being competitive.

But in many cases, competition and jealousy hurts friendships. Competition also comes in other forms, such as competing for the same guy or trying to look good at a school dance. It can be painful and can spark an inner battle if your best friend's success in getting dressed up and looking beautiful makes you start to second-guess every part of yourself.

❝ I loved Libby, but it was like she was perfect. She was pretty, smart, and athletic. She had even done some modeling. I was flattered she had chosen me to be her friend. Some days our friendship was normal, but other days I got really jealous. I couldn't help it. I just wanted to be pretty, smart, and athletic just like Libby. ❞

♥ *Dawn, 14*

Sometimes our friends genuinely hurt us, even though they are our friends, for reasons having to do with competition.

❝ I walked in smiling, and Tammy asked why I was so happy. I told her I had just made the varsity swimming team. 'Great,' she said. I could tell by the tone in her voice and the fake smile she was jealous. My heart sank. This was supposed to be a happy day. I tried not to let it bug me, but it did. I had two choices to make. I could ignore it and try to make Tammy feel better by complimenting her successes, or I could talk to her about it directly. Either way could have worked, but I decided to talk to her about it. At first she denied feeling jealous, but eventually she admitted it. I was really glad I brought it up because we became closer friends. ❞

♥ *Tiffany, 15*

If you feel jealous or competitive, try this:

• Consider how often you get this feeling.
• Answer truthfully: has your jealousy or competitiveness ruined friendships before?
• Ask yourself what you can appreciate in yourself as a success.
• Do you have a genuine compliment you can give?

If your friend is jealous or competitive with you, try this:

• Put things in perspective. If you had to guess, why is she feeling this way?
• How often does this happen?
• What can you do to make her feel better?
• Would it be helpful to acknowledge how she's feeling? For example, could you say, "I can see you're really upset about my [whatever it is she's jealous about]. How could I make you feel better?"

Popularity and cliques

If you're popular or part of a clique, you might not think much about the terrible pain other girls feel who just can't and don't fit in. Where do you stand on this issue? Are all of your friends in the same group? Do you consider yourself to be part of the "in" crowd or the "out" crowd? What are the benefits to being popular or not being popular? Can you be happy and fulfilled if you're not part of a clique?

 I've just never fit in. I'm a little shy, and some of the humor the popular girls use seems so cutting to me. I'm not really into boys or drinking, either. I like being in track, and I like spending time with my family, but I'm a little lonely sometimes. I'd like to have a close girlfriend. No one is really mean to me at school, but no one is particularly glad to see me, either.

I'm going to join the band. I want to learn to play the clarinet. I hope I meet some new friends in that class. 🙖

♥ Charlotte, 13

Lily's attitude is a little different.

🙖 I decided early on I wasn't going to let being popular run my life. Nor was I going to get caught up in a clique and ignore the rest of the world. I watched my older sister work herself into a frenzy just to belong, and I watched some of her classmates get ignored as though they'd never been born.

I'm lucky. I have a good sense of humor, I'm a good student, and I'm friendly to everyone. I have friends all over school, from all different groups. I don't let the way someone looks or dresses influence me. I get to know people in class, and then they're my friends. I think I have more fun this way. I don't like to see peoples' feelings hurt. This is working for me. I feel like I can pretty much join in anywhere I feel like it and have a good time. 🙖

♥ Lily, 17

So, what do you think? Can you be happy and fulfilled if you're not part of a clique? We'd love to hear your thoughts at www.girls withdreams.com.

We like the same guy!

This problem has destroyed some friendships but not all of them. If you both like the same guy, you have a decision to make. Who are you going to put first—the guy or your girlfriend? Will it be your best friend or a boyfriend?

Beth and Carly both liked the same guy. He was fifteen, one year older than they were, and had the nicest smile. They both nearly swooned over him every day in the cafeteria, and they both tried to flirt with him whenever they could.

One day Beth wore a low-cut top to school. Carly was shocked. This wasn't really their style. Beth must really want to impress this guy, she thought. Sure enough, she could see him checking Beth out when she sauntered past him at noon.

Carly decided to take a backseat and see what happened. Later that day, Beth told her that Sam had asked her out. Beth was so excited that Carly couldn't help but be happy for her, and she shrugged off her own mild jealousy.

The very next day after their date, Beth called to cry on Carly's shoulder. Sam wanted to have sex on their date, and Beth was shocked. She was also sorry she'd worn such a low-cut top to school.

For her part, Carly was glad she hadn't succeeded in going out with this guy after all.

Usually, real friends can work it out. There are tons of options. For example, both of you can pursue different guys. Or, like Carly did, one of you can back off. Maybe the guy himself will settle the whole thing. Perhaps he's not interested in either one of you, or possibly he's clearly interested in one of you and not the other. Then you have jealousy to deal with, but at least you know where you stand.

All in all, don't take it too seriously. Let nature take its course, and stay cool and it will all work out.

My friend is doing something I don't agree with

❝ I remember it like it was yesterday. The day I found out my best friend snorted cocaine was the day I died inside. I yelled at her. I pleaded with her. I begged her to tell me it wasn't true. The girl I always considered my best friend was then nothing more to me than a repulsive traitor. I couldn't look at her. I ran from her sight and went home to cry for hours. I immediately wrote about it in my journal. If I wasn't the one who did the drugs, why did I feel so guilty?

I ignored her at school for days. I didn't want to associate myself with a druggy. 'It was only once,' she'd tell me. 'Bridget, please hear me out.' In my book, once was one time too many. 'Okay, so maybe it was twice. But Bridget . . . Bridget . . . please listen.'

I superglued my ears shut. No excuses.

And then the guilt rolled in again. I cried and cried and cried. I felt like it was somehow my fault. I could have—no, should have—prevented her from doing it. At this point my problem had grown twofold. I was mad at her, but even worse, I was mad at myself.

Eventually, she forced me to talk to her. She asked for my forgiveness. And I gave it to her. I had this overwhelming feeling of sorrow and pity. I began to realize it wasn't my fault; it was hers and hers alone. It was at that point that I made a promise to myself to stop being so critical. She was my best friend and she always will be. While I would have preferred something a little less extreme, I discovered this 'test' only brought us closer together. It showed we could get through the worst and taught me to put away the superglue and be there for my best friend.

And might I add . . . she hasn't done any drugs since. 🍃🍃

♥ Bridget, 17

Peer pressure

Temptations are all around teenage girls, and our friends are frequently a huge part of the decisions we make. Peer pressure, or the influence of our friends and peers on our decisions, is a natural part of adolescence, and it's fairly typical for teens to listen more to their friends than to their parents.

🍃🍃 She didn't even have to say anything. I just looked up to her in every way. When she studied, I wanted to study. If she got a new outfit, I wanted to get one, too. And those times I really wanted to give up? Camille wouldn't let me. She was there with a good nudge. 〞

♥ *Sarah, 14*

Peer pressure comes in many forms

Think about when you've been pressured by your friends or pressured them. Are any of these on your list?

- Pressure to try new things
- Pressure to dress a certain way
- Pressure to lie, steal, or cheat
- Pressure to get better or worse grades
- Pressure to be mean to someone
- Pressure to do drugs or alcohol
- Pressure to have sex

Friends shape our lives for better and worse. The key is to think for yourself but still be friends—if you want to be. Listen to your friends and their opinions, but ultimately remember: *you* are the one who has to live with the decisions you make. Sometimes this feels impossible if you are the only one in the group making a different choice.

❝ It was my freshman year in high school. I had transferred last minute from my small Christian school to the public school. I was playing on the freshman volleyball team and had my small group of friends, but I wanted the perfect movie-style high school popularity. One of those girls, Madison, was in my first-hour class. She sat in front of me. We had casual conversations, which slowly turned into an out-of-class friendship. I was in with one of the girls!!!

A couple of months went by and it was time for homecoming. I went and bought my dress. It was fabulous! One day Madison and I were talking about homecoming, and she invited me to ride in the limo with everyone to homecoming. Seriously, how much better could it get? I'm in with the 'it' crowd, riding in a limo with senior boys, and I'm only a freshman!!! We made our plans for getting together to take pictures and eat dinner before the dance. Then, a few days before homecoming, Madison double-checked to make sure we were still on. But one little thing had changed. She asked me if I knew that everyone would be getting high in the limo. Everything fell apart. Perfect crowd, perfect night, but I knew I couldn't compromise my standards. So even though the choice was rough, I knew what I had to do. I told my mom I no longer wanted to go to homecoming, and she didn't understand why. I just told her I was no longer interested, and the subject was dropped.

What I wasn't planning on was one of my other friends calling on my home phone. My mom asked my friend if she knew why I didn't go to homecoming, and my friend told her. My mom called me into the room so I could take the call and when I got off the phone my mom gave me a huge hug and told me how proud she was of me. Come to find out, I ended up earning a lot of respect from the popular girls because of my decision. It really does pay to stand your ground and hold tight to your beliefs. Sometimes you will have to compromise, but doing the right thing will always be worth it. 🙠

♥ *Darya, 18*

Did you know brain studies show that the part of the brain that is responsible for controlling risky behavior doesn't develop until close to the age of twenty-five? This is why teens tend to feel invincible, and it's also what makes peer pressure so potentially dangerous.

This means that if you know you're going to be in a situation where you might have to make a tough decision, you need to think about it ahead of time. Make a plan with an exit strategy. For instance, if you are going someplace and relying on others to drive you, make sure you have a cell phone or another way to call for a ride if you feel unsafe.

If you're sorting through where you stand on a tough issue, do your research. Know the risks and talk to someone who might be able to provide some insight.

❝ When I was fifteen, some new friends invited me over to their house. I didn't realize there was going to be a party. I was a little uncomfortable and probably should have left, but I stayed. I think I was flattered that they had invited me, and I was curious. As the night wore on, they started playing spin the bottle. I wasn't going to play at first, but they made a good argument for it. By the end of the night, I completely regretted my decision. I was drunk, and I had done stuff with boys I was embarrassed about. ❞

♥ *Mikala, 16*

MEAN GIRLS AND BULLIES

Cutting comments, snide remarks, and losing friends are just the tip of the iceberg when it comes to mean girls and bullies. Whether it's a small remark or a physical push, this must stop! All of us need to see how powerful we could be by coming together, instead of trying to pull each other down.

Andrea was very uncomfortable. She'd just sat down in the cafeteria with her friends, and they were laughing at a girl a few tables down. The girl had worn an ugly green dress to school, and it looked terrible. Her hair was frizzy, and she was wearing ugly glasses.

Andrea's heart went out to her. She had no one to sit with, and Andrea's friends were loud and rude. She knew this girl could hear what they were saying. "Hey, you guys. Give her a break. Let's talk about something else." Andrea had to be pretty insistent to get them to quit, and she could tell they didn't exactly appreciate what she had to say, but when she thought about it later that night, she was glad she had asked her friends to stop making fun of that girl.

Andrea clearly did her part to stop bullying. What role are you playing? If we all are going to put a stop to mean girls, first you need to figure out if you are a bully, victim, bystander, or friend. Take the quiz to find out which fits you best.

Quiz

Are You a Bully, Victim, Bystander, or Friend?

Look at each statement below and put a check mark in the box if your answer is true.

Bully
❑ I've said mean things to other girls or called them names.
❑ I've written negative comments, gossip, or rumors about another girl.
❑ I've set out to exclude someone from our group of friends.
❑ I've said something mean online, in an e-mail, or in a text message that I wouldn't say in person.

Victim
❑ Other girls have threatened to hurt you, called you names, or hurt you.
❑ Girls isolate you by moving away from you at lunch or by your locker.
❑ Girls have taken things from you.
❑ You've felt picked on or teased, but didn't tell anyone.

Bystander

❏ You've watched girls tease other girls.

❏ You've listened as girls chatted about why they hated so and so.

❏ You've laughed as girls said or did something mean to another girl.

❏ You've seen your friend push another girl but didn't tell anyone.

Friend

❏ You've refused to participate in teasing or hurting someone and walked away.

❏ You've stuck up for your friend.

❏ You've changed the subject when girls start making fun of others.

❏ You've invited someone new to your group.

Give yourself one point for every checked box. Now, look at each category. Which one did you score the highest in? That is your friend profile. Wherever your score lands you, remember, we can all work to be a better friend. Use the tips in the next section for more ideas on dealing with mean girls.

If you are a Bully, how long has this been going on? Ask yourself why you need to put other people down to feel better. Do you want to make a change? Are you ready? It's not going to be easy to change by yourself. Find an adult you trust to talk this through. Yes, this will take a ton of courage, but you can do it! Here are a few more questions to think about:

• What are you gaining by being mean?

• Who bullies you in your life?

• What are you going to do when you grow up?

• Who can you talk to for help with your anger?

If you are the Victim, I'm very sorry. You are not alone, and things can change. It's really important that you get the right kind of support around you. A good place to start is by finding someone you really trust, like a teacher, school counselor, or social worker who can help you brainstorm more ideas and come up with a plan to change your situation. (Find more help in the resource list at the back of the book.)

If you are a Bystander, you aren't usually the one to start it, but you don't stop it either. This can be just as harmful and encouraging to the bully. See what you can do to help other girls the next time you see them being bullied. Can you get other friends to help you stand up together? If you're scared to do this yourself, maybe another friend will help you. Look at the girls you are hanging out with—are these really the people you want to be friends with? Will you stand up with all of us and help stop mean girls? Social pressure goes a long way with bullies.

If you are a Friend, congratulations. You're helping all of us come together and move forward in a positive direction. Your actions likely helped other girls who were being bullied.

Why are girls so mean?

❝ From a young age I was the one who picked on other kids. I had gotten in trouble several times for it. This changed when I transferred schools in second grade. I didn't know anyone in school, and it was tough. I remember watching everyone greeting their friends after summer, feeling left out. From the first day on, I was picked on. Everyone in that class just didn't like me. To this day, I still can't figure out why. ❞

♥ *Elizabeth, 14*

The bottom line is that girls are hurting. When a girl has been picked on or put down in her life, one of the ways to deal with it is to put someone else down. Another one of the main roots of girls being mean comes from insecurity. Whether you are the girl who is picking on someone else or the one who can't stand up for yourself, the basic problem goes back to feeling insecure. Some of the best ways to put a stop to mean girls are to stand up for others when you see them being picked on and also to look for more ways to build up confidence. Confidence is built from little things, like giving compliments, playing sports, and making sure we're using our strengths.

❝ In grade school, I never hung out with people in our class, although it was hard to ignore my classmates, because we were in a small Catholic school. Our fifth-grade class had eleven boys and three girls. I didn't get along with the other two girls, and I wasn't even going to try to get along with the boys.

After we merged schools in sixth grade, it got a bit worse. People would spread rumors about me. I had at least two good friends who were always there for me, telling me not to worry about what others said. But I knew that most of the people in our class just hated me. In sixth grade, this girl started calling me names and said I couldn't wear the jacket I was wearing because I wasn't cool enough to wear a brand name. We ended up yelling at each other, and I think if the teacher hadn't stopped us, we would have gotten into an actual fight.

These experiences have made me stronger, and I now know how to deal with situations like these. I am able to control my feelings and treat others with respect, even if they don't return it. I'm a better person, and I think this will really help me in the real world. I learned that not everyone is going to be nice to you, and you have to learn to deal with it.

The one person I really want to thank is my mom. No matter what, she was there for me. She was there, even if my friends weren't. I don't know where I would be without her today. I know for sure, I wouldn't be the same person.

I don't think anyone should have to go through this. If you ever face something like it, just remember who your real friends are, be strong, and never give up. That's what I kept telling myself over and over. And talk to your parents, too. They are there to help through tough times.

♥ Elizabeth, 14

Bullying can happen in person and online. Whether it's the girl who talks behind your back, the friend who gets everyone to gang up on you, or the nasty e-mail that is blasted to 100 people, bullying hurts.

We can all put a stop to mean girls and bullies

I love the advice Barbara Colorose shares in this quote, "The beauty of empowering others is that your own power is not diminished in the process" because it reminds all of us to work on building our own as well as our friends' confidence, self-esteem, and security. Too often girls think they have to be the best, or by complimenting or lifting someone else up they will be less of a person. The best way to combat this is to look at the tips in this book. Where do you have security? With your looks? Academic talents? Sports? What if you have nothing you feel good about?

The beauty of empowering others is that your own power is not diminished in the process.
—Barbara Coloroso

I always knew I was a great basketball player, but I got teased for being so tall. I think the other girls were just jealous. Sometimes I cried at home, but I just kept believing in myself. I laughed off their comments and eventually they stopped.

♥ Roxanne, 16

❝ Before I moved, I was always the one to be picked on, but somehow I made it into the 'in' crowd. Because of my past, I guess that's why I was a little more sensitive when Fern wanted to pick on other girls. I couldn't stand it. I talked to Kelly and we decided to take a stand against Fern. It worked! Fern decided to back down. ❞

♥ *Missy, 14*

Simple ways to talk to your friends or to handle conflicts

Understand your role and be open to change. Practice conflict resolution skills. Some of the sentences you might use are:

I feel ... when you ...

I don't like it when you ... I'd like you to stop and ...

When you X ... I feel ... I want you to ... Or, I really like ...

But I want you to stop ...

I want to be your friend, so how can we work this out?

If someone is bothering you, you might try:

• Ignoring her. This might seem hard or ineffective, but bullies usually want a reaction. If you can ignore them, many bullies give up eventually because they're bored.
• Making a joke or laughing it off.
• Getting help. Tell a friend or an adult you trust.
• Walk with your head high. Or you might try a self-defense class or tae kwon do.

KEEPING FRIENDS

❝ When I think of friendship, I think of love, laughing until your stomach hurts, ice cream, hugs, tears, and people who stick with you through it all. I consider myself blessed to be able to say I have more than one best friend. They all are different, and they keep me going, no matter what kind of lemonade life gives me. With friends, lemonade will always be made, even when the sourest lemons come my way, which is why I love my friends and would not trade them for the world. 🙶🙶

❤ *Mo, 18*

What keeps friendships together? Sometimes it is location, ease, genuine concern, or even parents. Some of us have friends for a long time, but some of us don't. People change, and sometimes friendships do, too.

By staying open to new friendships, you stay open to a world of more experiences. Take the Friendship Quiz on the next page to see how good you are at being a friend and choosing friends.

Build yourself up with your own Girls with Dreams Friend Circle

One of the best ways to get real support is to surround yourself with a group of four to eight friends who really bring out the best in you. When we build each other up and help each other succeed, we all win. If you've ever seen the movie or read the *Sisterhood of the Traveling Pants* books, it's a lot like the group there. As I told you earlier, I had a group kind of like this in high school, and I've continued to see the power of bringing girls and women together in my adult life. To start your own Friendship Circle, here are a few things to think about:

- Set an intention for what you want. Get clear about what type of qualities or attributes are important to you in your life and with your friends and mentors.
- Figure out how you want to check in with each other and how often. Where will you meet? Will it be in person, over the phone, or via webcam?
- What's the overall purpose? What kind of goals do each of you have?

Friendship Survey Quiz

Making friends

1. You are there for your friends in most of their emergencies.
2. You listen to your friends.
3. If your friends are doing something dangerous, you talk about it with them respectfully.
4. You are honest with your friends.
5. You build your friends up and make them feel good about themselves.
6. Your friends say they can trust you.

SCORING: Give yourself one point for every yes. If you scored six points, you are a stellar friend. If you scored five points or fewer, pick one thing you can do today to be a better friend.

Choosing friends

1. When meeting people for the first time, you keep an open mind and try to get to know them.
2. Your friends make you feel good about yourself.
3. Your friends respect your decisions even if they are different from theirs.
4. You can count on your friends in a time of crisis.
5. There is a healthy balance of give-and-take with your friendships.
6. Your friends challenge you in a good way and help you to be a better person.
7. You have fun with your friends. They make you smile.

SCORING: Give yourself one point for every yes. If you scored six or seven points, you are great at choosing friends. If you scored five or fewer, you may want to take a look at how you are meeting and choosing friends.

If you're serious about starting your own Girls with Dreams Friend Circle, you can find out more by visiting us at www.girls withdreams.com. Then you will be able to start your own group and swap stories with other girls like you.

Seven Tips Every Girl Needs to Deal with Friends

Tip One: You Gotta Use Your Gut

Deep inside, we all know whether we're hanging out with nice people or people who aren't nice. We all know whether we're nice or not nice. Let your intuition guide you toward the people you really ought to be hanging out with and the behavior you really ought to be engaging in.

What's more, if you rely on your gut, you won't let a friendship overrule your best judgment and get you into a situation where your safety is compromised, such as going to a party with drugs and alcohol, driving with someone who's been drinking, and so on.

> ❝ Know who you are. Often people aren't in touch with who they are spiritually and mentally. That leaves them stuck in a hole and able to fall for anything. Know your likes and dislikes. Know who you are as a person and what makes you unique. Don't rely on your friends' opinions to decide who you are as a person or what you like and don't like. ❞
>
> ♥ *Rukiya, 16*

Tip Two: Discover Your Strengths and Use Them

We can learn a lot from our friends, and we can also share our strengths. Our friends don't have to be just like us. In fact, sometimes we're really different from each other.

" Take me and my best friend growing up. I enjoyed talking to people but felt like I lacked social skills. Denise was a social butterfly. She loved talking to people and was very friendly. This is one thing I really appreciated about our friendship. I learned so much from Denise just by watching how she interacted with others. On the flip side, I was more organized than she was, and that is something I shared with her. "

♥ *Melita, 19*

Tip Three: Choose the Right Friends and Respect Them

Be your own best friend first. Get clear on who you are and what you like to do. Know what's important to you and make sure you treat yourself well. Then, when it comes to your friends, you'll be ready to give 100 percent.

> The most basic and powerful way to connect to another person is to listen. Just listen. Perhaps the most important thing we ever give each other is our attention. . . . A loving silence often has far more power to heal and to connect than the most well-intentioned words.
> —Rachel Naomi Remen

" Make time for just being alone. Although it may sound odd, some of the best times of my life have been spent alone doing something I love, like writing. This is definitely important for girls who get overstimulated at school easily; we need to recharge our batteries for the next day. It's also kind of therapeutic in a way. "

♥ *Bella, 14*

" One of my best friends for a couple of years shared so many good times, but she also completely deflated my confidence in my singing abilities. It was subtle and under the surface in our friendship. I couldn't see it at the time, but I recognize it now. I was a good singer, but I felt like a midget in her shadow. It wasn't all her fault. A big portion of it was my own low self-confidence. I just wish that we could have supported each other in our singing instead of feeling like we were in competition with each other. "

♥ Steph, 19

When you are choosing your friends, remember that friends can pick you up or pull you down. Do your friends make you feel talented and beautiful? Do you make them feel talented and beautiful? If you value honesty and people who are nice, are you choosing friends who are honest and nice? Do your friends make you feel marvelous? Or do they make your insecurities come out?

> Treat people as if they were what they ought to be and you help them to become what they are capable of being.
> —Goethe

Tip Four: Be Courageous and Confident

Why do we let people take advantage of us? Why are we afraid to speak up when a friend is bossing us around, or a boyfriend is going too far, or when we see our friend being bullied?

Because we lack the confidence and courage to stop them. Maybe we don't want to be embarrassed, are more comfortable going along with the crowd, or we want to avoid a disagreement with our friend.

" Think for yourself. Most girls rely on friends, family, or other outside sources to make decisions for them. It's okay to get advice or a different outlook from other people, but don't solely rely on their beliefs to make decisions. Don't let others speak for you. Speak up and fight for what you believe in. "

♥ Rukiya, 16

It takes courage to give your opinion and stand up for yourself or to friends when they're making bad choices. Don't let people walk all over

> Whatever you do, you need courage. Whatever course you decide upon, there is always someone to tell you that you are wrong.
> —Ralph Waldo Emerson

you, even your friends. Be a courageous friend! You will feel better in the long run when you've stood your ground and held on to what you value. If your friends don't respect you for that, it's probably time to find new friends who do. *Always remember—it is within your power to say no, and it is your right to say no.*

Sometimes this can be hard to learn, especially for girls, because most of us are people pleasers. We don't want others to be mad at us. We don't want to hurt people's feelings. This is partly why we don't always stand up for what we want.

Tip Five: Be Fit and Stay Fit

Friends are a great way to help us stay fit physically, emotionally, and mentally. By the same token, arguing with or having problems with friends takes its toll on us physically and emotionally.

Because you need to stay fit, why not consider doing it with a friend? For instance, if you're going for a run, why not call a friend to go with you?

Friends contribute to our mental health as well. They cheer us up, make us laugh, and help us deal with our day-to-day dramas, but sometimes they stress us out if we're arguing with them or dealing with an issue.

The bottom line is that being physically fit will help you stay mentally fit!

Tip Six: Dream Big

Ask yourself, "What is my picture of an ideal friend? If I had to pick a best friend or a couple of best friends, what would I want to do with them? How would I want them to treat me?"

Get clear on this and hold your ground. If a friend can't understand why it's important to you to get good grades so you can get into a particular college, try to explain it to him or her. If your friend still doesn't get it and tries to make fun of you or undermine you, well, this friendship may be on its way out.

Tip Seven: Get Outside of Yourself

Make sure you're not always saying, "What can you do for me?" Instead, try "What can I do for my friends?"

For example, maybe one of your friends is running in a big cross-country meet. Why not make a poster and stick it on her locker to surprise her and cheer her on? What about surprising your best friend on her birthday with a picture collage and her favorite lunch? How about creating a survival kit filled with her favorite magazines and treats when your friend has to go to hang out with her stepsiblings over the weekend?

If you're thinking about a community service project, invite a friend to participate with you. This will benefit the agency you're serving, and it can be a lot of fun to work with a friend.

> *"It's amazing what can happen if you just put your arm around somebody. It's the truest thing and the simplest thing that does the most good a lot of times, and I hope that we can all just reach out to each other."*
> —Julia Roberts

Think about it . . .

- Who are you hanging out with, and how's it going?
- Are you true to yourself? Do you think for yourself?
- Do you make a difference in the lives of your friends?
- Are you a good friend? How can you be a better friend?
- Are you overly competitive with or jealous of a friend?
- Do you influence your friends for better or for worse?
- Do your friends support you 100 percent?

Try it!

- Make a new friend. Step outside of your comfort zone.
- Tell your friends how much you appreciate them.
- Give a compliment.
- Keep an open mind.
- Do something nice for your friend without expecting anything back.
- Send your friend a care package or a card.
- Put this quote up, "The beauty of empowering others is that your own power is not diminished in the process." —Barbara Coloroso
- Start a Girls with Dreams Friend Circle. What's that? Visit us at www.girlswithdreams.com to find out.
- Plan a slumber party.

READER/CUSTOMER CARE SURVEY

HEFT

We care about your opinions! Please take a moment to fill out our online Reader Survey at **http://survey.hcibooks.com.**
As a **"THANK YOU"** you will receive a **VALUABLE INSTANT COUPON** towards future book purchases
as well as a **SPECIAL GIFT** available only online! Or, you may mail this card back to us.

(PLEASE PRINT IN ALL CAPS)

First Name		MI.		Last Name

Address			City

State		Zip	Email

1. Gender
❏ Female   ❏ Male

2. Age
❏ 8 or younger
❏ 9-12   ❏ 13-16
❏ 17-20   ❏ 21-30
❏ 31+

3. Did you receive this book as a gift?
❏ Yes   ❏ No

4. How did you find out about the book?
❏ Online
❏ Store Display
❏ Teen Magazine
❏ Interview/Review

❏ Book Club/Mail Order
❏ Price Club (Sam's Club, Costco's, etc.)
❏ Retail Store (Target, Wal-Mart, etc.)

5. Where do you usually buy books?
(please choose one)
❏ Bookstore
❏ Online
❏ Book Club/Mail Order
❏ Price Club (Sam's Club,
❏ Retail Store (Target,

6. What magazines do you like to read? *(please choose one)*
❏ Teen Vogue
❏ Seventeen
❏ CosmoGirl
❏ Rolling Stone
❏ Teen Ink
❏ Christian Magazines
❏ Other

7. What books do you like to read? *(please choose one)*
❏ Fiction
❏ Self-help
❏ Reality Stories/Memoirs
❏ Sports

8. What attracts you most to a book?
(please choose one)
❏ Title
❏ Cover Design
❏ Author
❏ Content

How did you find out about the book?
❏ Friend
❏ School
❏ Parent

FOLD HERE

Books for Life

Comments

4

Funky Family Stuff

We don't choose our families. Some of us are very fortunate and have a loving home, supportive parents, and siblings we usually get along with, but it doesn't always work that way.

The truth is that families are all different. Some of us are adopted, some live with one parent, some live in foster care, some live with stepfamilies or relatives, some live with gay parents, and some live with both parents.

> The family. We were a strange little band of characters trudging through life sharing diseases and toothpaste, coveting one another's desserts, hiding shampoo, borrowing money, locking each other out of our rooms, inflicting pain and kissing to heal it in the same instant, loving, laughing, defending, and trying to figure out the common thread that bound us all together.
>
> —Erma Bombeck

Our families may be stable, argumentative, loving, awkward, supportive, unbearable, and even humorous. Sometimes our blood relatives make up our family, but sometimes we aren't related to those we consider family. However we define "family," most of us have one, and we all need one.

❝ I was always very close to my grandparents. My parents divorced when I was five, and I lived with my mom and saw my dad a few weeks during the summer. My mom worked hard to support me and my sister, but that meant a lot of time with Grandma and Grandpa. That was okay with me. My grandpa made me laugh with his magic tricks, and my grandma loved helping us with our homework. ❞

♥ *Meredith, 13*

❝ I live with my mom and her partner. They're lesbians. This is normal to me. I don't remember anything else. My dad's been out of the picture since I was conceived. Sometimes I wish I had a sister. I'm a little lonely once in a while, but I have a few close friends. My best friend's parents are a married couple, but they're really cool. I think they have some gay or lesbian people in their family. They don't care that my mom is a lesbian. ❞

♥ *Leslee, 15*

SECRETS GIRLS KEEP ABOUT FAMILY

If only girls would open up about some of the secrets they keep about their families, most would see they are not alone. Here are a few of the secrets girls shared with me. Do you think they are really as alone as they feel, or do you think we all have secrets we keep?

I worry about my alcoholic brother.

My mom has a new boyfriend (and he's kinda weird).

My parents aren't cool enough.

I have nightmares at night about my mom (she's in the Navy).

My dad just got out of jail.

My sister is depressed.

I hear my mom crying at night.

My family argues all the time.

My dad used to hit me.

What's normal, anyway?

Hopefully, I've gotten my point across that nothing is "normal." Yes, the traditional two-parent family exists, but more and more children are residing in single-parent homes or other combinations of family members. In spite of the problems, "family" for most of us serves as a place where we are unconditionally accepted. It is a safe harbor, a place to go home to. Even so, we all deal with stuff that is a little funky at times. There is no way to cover the thousands of issues that come up in families in one book, but we've tried to cover the big ones.

Sometimes one of the toughest family problems is just dealing with our siblings. How can it be that people in the same biological family can be so utterly different? Well, it's just a fact of life.

COMMON SIBLING PROBLEMS

Our siblings are supposed to be our friends. After all, they are the ones who will be with us for life. As much as we may love them, sometimes it's very hard to get along.

❝ My sister is my best friend. Well, at least I feel like that on most days. Sometimes I get mad when she borrows my favorite pair of jeans and won't give them back, but I know she's just trying to be like me. ❞

♥ Vicky, 14

Jealousy

This goes both ways. You might be jealous of a sibling, or he or she might be jealous of you. In either case, it's normal to feel jealous once in a while. The key is figuring out how to deal with these feelings.

If you are feeling jealous, stop and think about the situation. Are you being rational? Try to stop focusing on your brother or sister and switch your attention to something else. For instance, what can you celebrate about yourself? What else can you do instead of letting this eat away at you?

If your sibling is jealous of you, try to put yourself in his or her position. Can you understand why your sibling might feel this way? Can you show your sibling any type of appreciation for something he or she does?

We argue with each other

Arguing, putting each other down, and fighting are fairly typical between siblings, but only to a degree. If you think you and your sibling are over the top, ask yourself how often you fight; once a week versus a couple of times a day makes a big difference. If you argue on a regular basis, you need to figure out what is going wrong and what you're doing right when you're not arguing.

You might want to ask yourself what triggers your conflicts. Is it the same every day? Maybe your brother is tired when he comes home, and that is when you argue, or maybe it's always about something you borrowed and didn't return. Once you know the trigger, you can start to deal with the real issue.

Think about what you want your relationship with your sibling to be like. Do you want to hang out a lot together or not very much at all? Are little arguments okay? Now think about the next time you get mad at your sibling, how are you going to handle it? Some brothers and sisters wait to calm down. Others write down what is bugging them and talk about it later.

Also, ask yourself what you've done in the past to get along and what you can do now to help the two of you get along better. If you have ideas on how to get along better with siblings, we'd love to hear your tips at www.girlswithdreams.com so you can help other teen girls.

My brother/sister gets into trouble

❝ Here we go again, I said to myself. I woke up at 2:30 AM to hear Seth yelling back and forth with my mom and dad. I just wanted to go back to sleep, but they were yelling so loud I couldn't. And, truthfully, I was worried about my brother. Where had he been for the last three days? We all knew he was probably getting high with his friends, but he had never been gone this long before. ❞

♥ Kira, 14

Does your brother or sister get into trouble often? Is he or she the one you all worry about and the one who gets all the attention? When a sibling is having problems, whether they are academic or potentially more serious, such as a drug habit, it may take a huge toll on the family. It's easy for this person to become the "squeaky wheel" that consumes the bulk of the family's time, energy, and attention.

What can you do? For starters, make sure that you take care of yourself. It's hard to help someone else if you're not in good shape. Then notice what is happening and talk to your parents about it. Try not to take out your anger on people who don't deserve it. If you're angry, don't keep it bottled up. Instead, release it through journaling, exercising, talking about it, or all of these.

My parents play favorites

It can be pretty tough to have a big brother or sister who couldn't be more perfect. It may feel impossible to live up to this sibling. On the flip side, if you're the big sister in this situation, think about how this makes your younger brother or sister feel.

❝ This is unbelievable. Makena is untouchable. She has perfect grades, perfect friends, and perfect awards. My parents are always talking about how Makena did this and Makena did that. It gets annoying after a while. I mean, don't they see that I'm a pretty cool kid too? I may not have straight As, but I sure work hard to try to. And what about the Future Movie Makers Club I started at school? It's like I'm invisible. ❞

♥ *Maria, 13*

When a sibling seems perfect, it might feel hard to get any attention or appreciation in your family. You can begin to deal with this by pointing out to your parents how you're feeling and giving them specific examples of what you've experienced.

If that doesn't work, remember that family patterns are hard to change. One way you can help yourself is to think about your strengths. If you get stuck here, ask your friends or parents what they think. You might be overlooking things that come easily to you, like being social or having artistic skills or thinking creatively.

While recognition feels good and is important, it isn't the end of the world if you aren't recognized. The truth is, sometimes a lot of good things we do don't get noticed. Do good things because they feel right and good, not simply to be praised.

COMMON PARENT PROBLEMS

As common as problems with siblings are, problems with parents are even more prevalent.

We don't agree on anything

How often do teens and their parents disagree? Every day? Once a week? What do you think the norm is? Parents and teens don't always see eye to eye, but is it normal to be yelled at and humiliated? No. Is it normal to have disagreements? Yes. Is it normal to think your parents aren't fair? Yes.

Whether you are arguing a little or a lot, here are a few ideas to try.

- **Look for common ground.** Is there anything you might be able to agree on? Now put yourself in your parents' shoes. Are their requests reasonable? What are their motives? What are yours?
- **Think about both sides.** What are your views on this particular issue? Let's say you want to get a job, but your parents don't want you to work. What are some reasons that will support your wishes? Perhaps you might like to make extra money to help buy your own clothes. On the flip side, your parents might be concerned with the amount of time it would take you to work. You might want to ask them how you could meet in the middle on this issue.
- **Prepare for a standstill.** What if your parents won't budge? Ask them what it would take to change their minds or when you could discuss this again.
- **Find a good time to talk for both of you.** Don't just expect to talk to them when they walk in the door. Ask them when it's a good time to talk or wait until you know they're relaxed.

- **Practice.** Rehearse what you'd like to say in advance and then start with something you agree on. Finding common ground can go a long way toward patching up bad feelings. If you need to, consider writing out your thoughts.

We argue too much

I haven't talked to too many teens who haven't had some type of argument with their parents, whether it's fighting about a messy room, bringing up their grades, or disagreeing about dating rules, curfews, friends, or something else.

The battles can be little, or they can be huge. It's not fun to be in frequent arguments, so here are a few suggestions:

- Give each other space.
- Take a break and talk about it later.
- Try not to yell. Keep your tone positive and volume down.
- Think about why you're upset. Are there other factors at work, such as a bad day, or other things on your mind? Or theirs?
- Think about what you want your relationship with your parents to look like.
- Consider what it would take for you to get along.
- Think about what you can talk about with your parents. Start somewhere, even if it's something little. If talking is hard, there's always texting or e-mail. It's not as personal, but it's a great start.
- Make time to do fun things. This is important too!

My parents don't understand me

In your teen years, it's common for teen girls to feel misunderstood or like they can't talk to their moms or dads, but this doesn't mean you shouldn't try.

Even if your parents don't seem interested, perhaps it's because they feel you don't want to talk to them. They may think your friends are more important to you than they are, or they may not be sure how to talk to you now that you're maturing.

❝ ❝ I was having this problem at school. I was kind of embarrassed because kids were teasing me for what I was wearing. I knew my dad was working as much as he could and that we didn't have money to get new clothes. I didn't want to make my parents feel bad, and I thought they'd never really get what the problem was, so I just kept it to myself. ❞ ❞

♥ Tara, 13

Like Tara, you might think your parents would never understand your problems, whether it's about the girl who keeps teasing you, problems with guys, or something to do with drinking.

What can you do? One of the most important things is to open up the lines of communication. Use the tips on talking to your parents to get more ideas.

❝ ❝ You will be surprised by how receptive your parents will be to a discussion like this. Despite what you might think, your parents really do want to know what you think, because they want to understand how you feel. Every time I needed to discuss a difficult topic with my mom, I was always uncomfortable at first. However, once I approached her and we started talking, I felt better instantly, and I was glad I had opened up. ❞ ❞

♥ Kate, 23

If you really can't talk to your parents, find an adult you can talk to, perhaps someone at school or another relative.

❝ ❝ My parents just don't get me. They don't know how hard it is to be a teenager, let alone deal with boys. There was no way I was going to talk to my mom about Nick. I just knew she'd start lecturing me. Then Nick's mom called her about the 'date' we had this weekend. It forced me to talk to her about Nick, and it didn't go as bad as I thought. She still let me go with Nick and my friends to the movies, and she actually had some good advice and didn't lecture me. " "

♥ *Denny, 15*

I don't know how to talk to my parents

This is common for so many teens! As girls grow up, for many it takes a little while to get used to a new way of communicating with Mom and Dad, or whoever their guardian is. Why? As you're growing up, it's common to feel like your parents won't understand, it's awkward between you, you're both really busy, or you feel like you don't know where to start. The truth is that you don't have to make this complicated. Check out these ideas.

Simple tips to help you talk to your parents

- Start with e-mail or text messages (this isn't as ideal as face-to-face contact, but it's a great way to start).
- Share a journal between the two of you. Take turns writing notes or messages to each other.
- Start with simple stuff and build on it, even if it's only for ten minutes a day. You can work your way up to more serious stuff.
- Calmly and respectfully, tell your parents how you feel.
- Ask open-ended questions (typically the sentences start with "what" or "how." Don't use "yes" or "no" questions because they will shorten your conversations).
- Schedule some fun hang-out time together. Just keep it fun.
- Show appreciation (get creative, make a card).
- Are you experiencing any roadblocks? (i.e., one of you lectures, talks over each other, doesn't listen, etc.). Tell your parent how you

feel. You could say, "I don't like it when you [fill in the blank]

_____ or "I

want you to _____."

My parents don't trust me

❝❝ I hate asking my parents if I can go to the mall. I get the third degree, and they have to call every single parent of the friends I'm going with. I just feel like they don't trust me. I feel like I'm constantly under police surveillance. ❞❞

♥ Sophie, 16

Does this sound familiar? Even though Sophie felt like her parents didn't trust her, there is a lot of information missing from her story. Have her parents always been like this? What was the intention behind their actions? Did Sophie ever do anything to lose their trust? Have any recent events like thefts at the mall or kidnappings in the news affected her parents' decision?

Think about the times when your parents don't seem to trust you, and consider the situation from their perspective. Maybe there's a reason they're acting this way. However, if your parents have always had a hard time trusting you, think of a way you can talk to them about it. If they haven't always had a hard time trusting you, ask yourself what's changed. Talk to them about how you appreciate their concern, but you want to be able to figure out a way you can be more independent and trustworthy. Consider that lying to your parents never works. Not only is it wrong, but your parents will find out eventually—they always do!

❝❝ I was homeschooled until the seventh grade, and as a result, I was mature, yet sheltered when I entered the world of public school. I managed to stick to my roots pretty well, stayed close to my parents, and got involved at school. Things changed the summer after my sophomore year. I started rebelling. Every kid goes through it at a certain age. I thought my mom was a strict, judgmental dictator and my dad a blind puppet who did whatever my mother said.

I met some new friends and started hanging out with a new crowd. They got me to drink with them, saying only prude losers didn't drink. I withdrew from my family and talked less and less at home. I knew they wouldn't understand because they didn't know what it was like to be part of the 'in' crowd. I knew they wouldn't want me staying out late, so I'd spend the night at a friend's house whose parents would let me stay out. If that didn't work, I'd wait until my parents were asleep and sneak out the window.

One night I lied about where I was and went to my friend Tyler's party. We played drinking games, and I had way more than my small frame could handle. I don't remember much after that. What I do remember is my friends waking me up and telling me my car was wrecked by a sophomore who had attended the party.

I was very confused. My friends drove me to the wreck. Red and blue lights flashed from the police cars and the tow truck. I found out my best friend had been in the passenger seat and had helped find my keys to take my car. My dad showed up and silently took me home.

Later, none of my friends at the party would agree to testify in court that my friend had taken the car without permission. They 'didn't want to take sides.' Not one of my friends backed me up!

I was grounded for three months, but worse than that, I completely lost my parents' trust. They caught me sneaking out twice during my grounding. Eventually I went into a depression. I'd lost my friends, and my parents didn't trust me.

I realized I needed to change because the people around me weren't going to. I started being more honest with my mom, spending time at home, and helping around the house. I didn't party on the weekends anymore and hung out with my family instead.

Soon, I realized how great my family was. It took me more than a year to get their full trust back, but now they completely trust me and even take advice from me. I learned that trust is important, and it's better not to break it in the first place. But if the damage is already done, the ball is in your hands to make the right changes and move toward a better future. Family will always be there for you, even more than your friends, and their trust is more valuable than the trust of anyone else you'll ever know. 🎔🎔

♥ *Abby F., 18*

You might even ask them what it's going to take for them to be able to trust you again. Talk to your parents about your mistake. Take responsibility for what happened and don't make excuses. Talk about how you are going to make amends or fix the problem. Remember, trust takes time. If you're willing and committed, you can prove to your parents you are trustworthy.

> If you've done something to violate your parents' trust, remember—it takes time to heal.

Rhys knew she messed up by taking the car without asking. This really changed things with her parents. She decided to talk to them about it. She talked about why she'd done it and how it was a big mistake. She talked about what she had learned and asked her parents how they could work things out.

My parents have impossible or different expectations

Do such statements sound familiar? Do they sound a little extreme? They are. Most parents have expectations. They want you to do well. They may be your biggest cheerleaders, and they can have big dreams for you. Such expectations are good for us when they hold our best interests at heart and when they are a guide for us to follow, but sometimes parents who love us and want what is best for us have impossible expectations.

> "You will get into Yale. And you are going to get a scholarship."
> "I don't care if you have to study all night; you are going to ace your calculus exam."
> "I want you to get the best grades in your class. No excuses."

There are countless examples of this. For example, Tina loved dancing ever since she was a little girl, but by the time she got to high school, her interests had changed. She didn't want to be a ballerina anymore, but her parents insisted she continue to dance. Or think of poor Sabrina. She tried with all her might to get an A in physics, but even with regular after-school tutoring from the teacher, it was impossible.

> "My parents wanted me to be a lawyer. But I don't think I would have been very happy. I'd be in front of the jury singing."
> —Jennifer Lopez

With verbal or even subtle demands, sometimes parents let us know they expect us to get the best grades, be the best dancer, get into the top college, and the list goes on and on. The second we don't live up to those expectations, it starts chipping away at our confidence.

If this happens to you, take some time to figure out what you really want and why. Try having a conversation with your parents. Make sure you are ready to listen to their point of view, but also be ready to share what it is you want and why. If you can't agree, be respectful, but don't ever give up on your dream!

" My parents wanted me to be this awesome athlete. They had this dream I would play in college and be a star. They pushed me hard, always criticizing my game, never encouraging it. Don't get me wrong, I really loved the game, but it wasn't my game anymore. It wasn't my dream. They didn't know their actions were affecting me; they wouldn't understand. I couldn't work up the courage to tell them how I felt, and I didn't want to cause a fight. But most of all, I couldn't handle disappointing them. I played so I wouldn't let them down. I didn't want to be a failure in my parents' eyes. Ignoring worked for me; I didn't push myself for a college position and there was only so much they could do. I think eventually they understood my silence. Eventually, I found my new passion and made my own dreams. Don't let anyone stand in your way. I have seen it happen to too many girls, and I've had enough. Stand up. Speak out. Dream your own dreams! Trust me, it's worth it. "

♥ *Courtney, 18*

My parents put me down

If you are in this situation, I'm sorry. It's very painful when those closest to us put us down. Oftentimes these emotional wounds are more painful than physical ones. Here are a few things that might help.

- **Focus on your strengths.** Even if you feel like your parents constantly put you down, stop and think about what you are good at or about praise you have received from teachers or friends.
- **Look at their motives.** Are they angry about something else? Are they trying to make themselves feel better? Is this a motivational tactic? Trying to understand why this is happening might give you some relief.

- **Try to talk to them.** Wait until a good time and let them know how this is making you feel. If they aren't open to talking, don't sweat it. You can only be responsible for yourself.
- **Get others to support you.** Look to them for encouragement. It might not feel the same because it didn't come from your mom or dad, but it might be the only way to have support right now.

My parents argue a lot

❝ I don't think there was always yelling in our home, but it really got bad this last year, right after Dad lost his job and Mom started working extra shifts. There was this unbearable tension between them and in the entire house. It made me not want to be there anymore. I coped by staying busy at school and going to my friend's house as much as possible. I felt bad for my little brother because he couldn't leave. ❞

♥ *Sierra, 16*

If your parents argue a lot, don't take it personally and don't let it cause negative behaviors on your part. At a good time, let them know how you feel about how they interact with each other. If possible, try to talk to them in a neutral place.

If talking to them doesn't work, maybe you can spend time at a friend's house or occasionally at a relative's house. Or maybe you can go to your room and play music or go for a walk. *In spite of your best efforts, remember—the only person you can truly control is yourself.* Make it a goal not to grow up to mirror those behaviors you don't like and that make you uncomfortable.

Also remember that physical violence is not okay. If you or anyone in your family is being hurt, call the National Domestic Violence Hotline at 1-800-799-SAFE (7233) and come up with a safety plan.

My parent is an alcoholic

If your parent is an alcoholic, you are not alone. Read Mackenzie's story to see how she deals with this.

❝ My family has its up and downs. It is not just a hilly road but a rocky one that causes some bumps and scrapes along the way. Ever since I can remember, my dad has been an alcoholic, my mom has smoked, and both of my brothers picked up on both. When people get drunk, they might be mellow and laid-back, angry and argumentative, funny and joking around, or emotional and depressed. At first we never know what kind of person dad is going to be, but he always ends up being angry and argumentative.

My older brothers and sister moved out, while I'm stuck at home. When my dad drinks he might start by arguing with my mom or me and then calls us names. Usually we get yelled at for no reason. I've been called every name you can think of. Worse, I never get to go out and be with my friends or have a date. I went through a period where I was a wreck and didn't talk to anyone. I skipped out on a lot of my childhood that I can't get back. Sometimes I am sad for no reason, and the little smile I used to have without even trying disappeared.

With it being my senior year, I told myself that I deserved to have the best last year with my friends. I went on my first real date and now have someone I can call my boyfriend around my family. It's still a roller coaster in my house. I get yelled at almost every single day, while other days I'm the absolute favorite child. I just think to myself that maybe I won't get yelled at until I cry like all the other times.

Now I am trying to find little good things each day and spend time with my friends every chance I get. My dad still drinks and yells at me, but from where I stand, there isn't much I can do. After I get yelled at, I just go to my room and calm down or call and talk to someone. It's times like that when I am thankful to have those friends and family members. There is always hope when you have people that care about you. 🙶 🙶

Mackenzie used some really great coping tips, like taking a stand for herself, realizing this wasn't her fault, focusing on good things, making her own space, and talking to and hanging out with loved ones. If your parent is an alcoholic, here are few other things you might be feeling and ways to handle it.

- **Guilty feelings.** It's typical to feel that this is all your fault. Just as Mackenzie learned she couldn't control her parents and it wasn't her fault, you need to tell yourself the same.
- **Frustration with ups and downs.** It might feel like you're riding an emotional roller coaster. Look for ways to calm yourself down, from going to your room, listening to music, or getting involved with dance or sports.
- **Anxious feelings.** You might worry about yourself and family members. Talk to someone you trust about your feelings.
- **Difficulty trusting others.** Because your parent may not have always been there for you, it might feel hard to trust people. Don't let yourself become emotionally isolated. Reach out to friends and other adults who are positive.
- **Embarrassment.** Many teens keep this as one of their biggest secrets. It is embarrassing when you don't know how your parent is going to react, but you are not your parent.
- **Anger.** You might feel very angry at your parents, the world, or just anyone in general. Learn positive ways to get your feelings out.
- **Depression.** Just like Mackenzie felt at times, it is so easy to feel hopeless about your situation. Don't get stuck here, though. Reach out to others and put positive supports and activities around you.
- **Overachieving or underachieving.** Many teens will go to either of these two extremes. They will either act too responsibly

(almost acting like a parent) or begin to have major problems of their own (academic problems, fighting with others, etc.)

- **Join a group.** Get support from others who understand, such as an Al-Anon group (they offer Alateen for younger members and offer help to families and friends of alcoholics).

My parents do things that make me uncomfortable

When parents engage in behaviors we don't like or aren't comfortable with, such as smoking cigarettes or even doing something illegal, it is natural to have mixed feelings. You probably love your parents but are also angry and even hurt by what they are doing.

This is never easy to deal with because you may feel loyal to them and frustrated by their actions, but eventually you have choices to make, just like the girls in the following paragraphs.

Katie had been living with her dad and his girlfriend. Her father's drug habit was getting really bad. He was yelling a lot and drove when he was high or drunk, and Katie was terrified. She decided to talk to the school counselor and resource officer. It was a really hard decision to make, but she decided to turn her father into the police for doing drugs. His drug habit was out of control, and she feared for her life.

Alison spent most of her time at her friend's house. Her parents' fighting was too much to cope with. When she turned eighteen, she planned on moving out.

Maddie felt really stuck. Her dad drank a lot and got very violent with her mom. She didn't feel like she could be gone a lot because she was worried about what would happen to her mom. She had tried to convince her mom they should all leave. She was thinking about talking to a school counselor to get more help, but she worried this would put her dad over the edge if he ever found out.

Hang in there. You aren't going to be underage and living with your parents forever. You will find your life, and you will have the opportunity to make choices different from those your parents make. You can start making those different choices now.

❝ I've been angry with my dad for a long time. After my parents got divorced, it seemed like he did everything wrong. Your dad is supposed to take care of you, but my dad couldn't even take care of himself. Over the years, we remained distant, and I remained angry. I'm only now starting to realize it's much easier to forgive people than to stay mad at them. I realize my anger toward him is one of the reasons we have remained distant for so long. He has made a lot of mistakes, but I'm trying to remember good things about him instead of focusing on his flaws. ❞

♥ *Kate, 23*

My family is violent with me

We've talked about arguing, yelling, and even things parents do that we disagree with, but what happens when the violence is against you? Unfortunately, this happens, but you need to know that it isn't your fault—and you can get help.

Violence comes in many forms. Verbal violence includes mean comments, put-downs, humiliations, or cussing. Physical violence includes punching, kicking, slapping, biting, and hitting. Sexual violence includes touching, kissing, and sexual intercourse. Neglect means you don't have adequate food, clothing, or shelter, and/or that your parents leave you in dangerous situations or without appropriate supervision.

If you are in one of these situations, it's normal to feel terrified, alone, embarrassed, or ashamed. This is a time when you need to muster up every ounce of courage you have and to remember this is not your fault. As lonely as you may feel, remember you aren't alone. Thousands of other girls have been in a similar situation. You are resilient and strong! As hard as it might be, you need to talk to an adult you trust who can help you get in touch with the right people who can make sure you are safe. The resources section at the end of this book lists more places that can help.

I lost a parent

I'm sorry if you are reading this and you are in this situation. It's hard to even put into words how painful this is to deal with. Read Stevie's story on how she handled it.

❝ There are many things in life moms are good for, whether it's going shopping with us, letting us vent, talking to us about boys, helping us with girl things, or even getting on our nerves. It doesn't matter, because we love everything about them. They are our moms and no one can replace them. But what if you don't have a mom? There are so many girls out there without one, and I'm one of them. We don't realize how good we have it until it's gone. My mom passed away when I was four. It was hard, especially since she didn't get to be there with me as I grew up. I would wake up in the morning and not know if what I had on matched, or if I did my makeup the right way. She was never there to answer all those embarrassing questions moms and daughters talk about.

Thanks to my dad and best friends, I got through it all. I have a father I can talk to about everything, and if there was something I couldn't talk to him about, I know I have my best friends. It's really hard dealing with a loss, especially if it's your mother, but no matter what you have to deal with, lean on people. It will help you so much. Find a group of friends you can trust and grow with. I've been best friends with mine for four years, and they have been the best years of my life. ❞

♥ Stevie, 17

More tips on handling grief can be found in Chapter 7 on "Dealing with the Tough Stuff."

My parents are divorcing or divorced

With around 50 percent of all marriages ending in divorce, millions of young people are affected by it. Every divorce and its aftermath are different. In many cases, it makes things better, but usually there are some tough feelings and situations to deal with before you feel the calm after the storm.

I guess I was okay with my parents getting divorced because they fought all the time, and I figured maybe it would stop if they just ended their marriage. Boy, was I wrong. Things slowly and progressively got worse. When I was fourteen years old, my mom, brother, and I moved to a different state, and that is when all hell broke loose. No one seemed happy with anything that was taking place in our lives. I was very unhappy about being at a new school, my brother was unhappy that he was in a different state than my dad, my dad was furious that we had moved away, and my mom was in tears every night because no one was happy.

Months went by where every night there was yelling, screaming, tantrums, or fits taking place in my house. I considered where I lived a house, because it definitely did not feel like a home.

♥ *Nora, 17*

If your family is experiencing a divorce, here are some common emotions you might be feeling:

- **Stuck in the middle.** When parents split, it is easy to feel this way, and sometimes parents accidentally put you in the middle of their issues. They may ask you questions about the other person or make you feel like you have to choose one or the other.

- **Like a referee in a bad game.** This is the worst position to be in. Sometimes parents have you serve as a mediator or referee between them and the issues they are trying to deal with. If this happens, try to point this out to them at a good time.
- **Like a "little adult."** When divorce happens, kids often have to assume more responsibility and independence than before.
- **Confused.** It's rough adjusting to different parenting styles and going back and forth between two homes and two sets of rules.
- **Frustrated** by constant on-the-go packing for two different houses.
- **Relieved** because the fighting has stopped.
- **Shocked** even when you might have thought this was going to happen or your parents warned you it was coming.
- **Sadness** because you moved away from the other parent or don't see him or her as often.

My parents got divorced when I was young, and I still remember how they broke the news. We all gathered together on the couch, and they started reading a children's book about divorce to us.

While the book was supposed to help us understand what was happening, I still didn't grasp what 'divorce' meant for our family. Once the divorce actually started happening, I learned it meant my mom was taking my sister and me to live somewhere else and my dad could visit us on the weekends. Eventually, we moved a couple of states away from my dad, and we hardly ever saw him anymore.

♥ *Kate, 23*

As difficult as divorce is, it's important to remember a few things that can help you get through it in better shape. First, remember—it's not your fault.

❝ ❝ The only point I remember from the divorce book was that the decision for your parents to get divorced is not your fault. It might be hard for you to understand why your parents made the decision to split up, but you can start by accepting that there's nothing you could have done to stop it from happening. ❞ ❞

♥ *Kate, 23*

Communicate how you are feeling. We've talked a lot about this in this chapter. As simple as it sounds, it isn't always easy to share your feelings, but it's common to act them out. Instead of telling your parents what you're angry about, you may become irritable or get into arguments that are unrelated to the real problem. Even if you have to start by writing your parents a note, it's important to tell them how you're feeling. They can't guess.

> It is never the fault of children when parents divorce.

Look for the positives, regardless of how bad the situation is.

❝ ❝ My parents' divorce taught me to set high standards for myself and to always look on the bright side. Although divorce is never a pleasant experience, it helps to know things could always be worse and they'll definitely get better. Both of your parents still love you, and they want what's best for you. Things will be bumpy in the beginning, but try to stay positive and turn to your friends and family for support.

Although I grew up without the presence of a father figure, I was happy to have one strong parent instead of two unhappy ones. Plus, having a strong woman as a mom taught me how to be a strong woman. ❞ ❞

♥ *Kate, 23*

If you start going downhill, get help. If your grades are dropping or you start having problems with friends, get help. Talk to an adult

at school, look into counseling, or find a support group. Don't let
divorce ruin your life.

Remember, it takes time to heal. Reactions to divorce are different for everyone. Some may get over it in a few months, while for
others the process may take years. Just be patient with yourself and
the healing process and try to get counseling and support from other
friends who are going through the same thing.

If your parents are divorcing, read the tips in Chapter 7, "Dealing
with the Tough Stuff," about dealing with death to help you cope. Even
though your parents haven't died, your dream of a two-parent family
has. *It's common to grieve as though you've experienced a death.*

❝ It's okay to feel weird about what's going on. You might feel angry
and even left out. I had to learn to be patient. My parents couldn't always
give me the attention I wanted right away. I just tried to make the most
of the situation. My mom and dad were really cool about things and didn't
mind me spending the weekend at my best friend's house once in a while.
This helped me feel stress free for a day or so. ❞

♥ *Daisy, 16*

My parent is remarrying

When parents remarry and stepparents and stepsiblings enter the
scene, this adds yet another complication to divorce. If you find
yourself in this situation, consider finding a counselor or support
group to talk to.

You might feel your stepparent is trying to take the place of your
other parent. He or she probably isn't, but talk to your own parent
about what you are feeling. Also figure out what name you are
going to call your stepparent. You don't have to automatically use
"Mom" or "Dad."

You might not think you like your stepsiblings or stepparent, but give it time. Try to have some one-on-one time with your parent. Also try to find time for all of you to do something together.

Remember, adjusting to this new family reality is going to take time. Be patient with yourself and with your stepparent and potential stepsiblings.

❝ I was so angry when my dad told me he was getting remarried, but I should have known it was coming. They had been dating for two years, but somehow I just didn't think it would happen. *I'm not going to call her 'Mom,'* I thought to myself.

Then I thought, *Oh, no, where are her kids going to stay when they visit? Has Dad thought this through?* I had so many questions for him.

It's been more than a year now since my stepmom and Dad got married. I just call her Nancy, and that works. It took a little while, but we're all getting along pretty well. Sometimes there are rough spots, but I just try to take a deep breath and give myself time to think things through. ❞

♥ *Ashlee, 16*

Seven Tips Every Girl Needs to Deal with Funky Family Stuff

Tip One: You Gotta Use Your Gut

Be honest with yourself about your family situation. For starters, as bad as things may be, perhaps there are some good aspects to your family. Try to hone in on what is good. For instance, maybe you're upset because your parents got divorced, but you really like the way you can talk to your mom about school issues.

One of the things I wish I realized when I was a teen is that love is expressed in different ways. Some people show love by spending time with the ones they love, some by their verbal expressions, and others by giving gifts. What does this have to do with family? Everything. If you and your parents and/or family members are not speaking the same love language, think about the problems that might result. You can find out more about these love languages in the books written by Gary Chapman. Maybe your gut is telling you your parents really do love you, but you're frustrated by the arguing or your day-to-day relationship.

Try to take a step back from the situation you are dealing with. If you can put yourself in the shoes of your parent, sibling, and/or stepparent or stepsibling, ask yourself what was this person's real motive for grounding you, arguing with you, or missing your game.

Next, get quiet and listen to what your gut is telling you. This can be really hard when painful and hurt feelings are in the mix, but take your time, be patient, and keep listening to your instincts.

❝ I was really angry at my stepsister for lying to me. Why would she have done that? We always told each other everything. It took me a few days to cool down, but then I started thinking about this more. I think Casey lied because she didn't want to disappoint me and she didn't want to put me in an awkward position. I decided to talk to her about it. She came clean, and my instincts were right. She had actually been trying to protect me. We worked it out, and I'm glad we didn't stay mad. ❞

♥ *Ragan, 14*

Tip Two: Discover Your Strengths and Use Them

Families are a great place for us to try out our strengths and also a place where some of our strengths can inadvertently be buried.

For example, you might usually be a shy person, but when you're around your family, you love telling stories.

On the other hand, maybe you're a great artist but that skill isn't valued in your family. Instead, your parents want you to focus on academics because they think art is frivolous.

Pay attention to what is happening in your family. What traits or strengths do you strongly express around your family? Does your family value softball, science, or talking to people? Is there a skill or talent you have that isn't appreciated by your family?

If it is hard to express your real strengths in your family, try to identify where you can get support. We are inevitably cast into roles, and it's hard for family members to see us differently. If you've tried talking to your family about this and it's still a problem, consider finding other role models and cheerleaders.

With siblings, it might feel impossible not to compete at times. Look honestly at your individual strengths. Even if your big sister is an honors student and you are left in her shadow, maybe you can take pride in the way you lead the student government or handle a tennis racket.

By the same token, if you are the one always recognized for good grades and you have a younger sibling who is seldom recognized, don't forget to celebrate both of your accomplishments. By honoring and celebrating what each of you do, you may find that the two of you can accomplish much together.

Tip Three: Choose the Right Friends and Respect Them

We don't pick our families, but we do pick our friends, so choose them well. Most teenagers feel like friends are family. At times friends may even take over as the top priority. Perhaps your friends can provide an opportunity for you to get new role models if you need them. For example, maybe your parents are very kind people but they are shy and not very outgoing, so you find friends who are outgoing and social. Another way of looking at this strategy is to ask yourself if your friends respect your family and how your friends affect your view of your family.

Most important, as you start spending more time with friends, don't forget about your biological family members. You need them, and they need you, too!

Tip Four: Be Courageous and Confident

Parents usually have the best intentions, but sometimes they can inadvertently or purposely be our biggest deflators. Whether or not you have a great family, you might need to use your courage and confidence to be more independent.

❝ Being the youngest has its perks but also its problems. A lot of times, I'm treated like the baby in the family. Like when I wanted to go to the movies by myself at the age of fourteen, my parents first said no. I had to remind them that that was the age when they let my older brother, Peter, go, and they changed their minds.

Also, I had my heart set on being a Rotary exchange student. Was I nervous about it? Yes. Scared? Yes. Excited? Yes! It took a while, but I convinced my parents to allow me the chance to try this. And guess what? I'll be going to Japan next year. ❞

♥ Meg, 16

If your family isn't getting along, use your courage and confidence to deal with the issue or get the help or role models you need. Or if you've had a crisis in your family, draw on a shot of courage and confidence to get through it.

❝ I was scared, but I didn't really have a choice to not move forward. My parents had lost their parental rights, meaning they had treated me and my little brother so poorly that the court wasn't going to let them parent us. I didn't know what our future was going to look like, and I was worried about my brother.

We were sent to live with my aunt and uncle. It was a new town, new school, new friends. It was a big adjustment and really scary at times, but I just kept holding on to this idea that things would get better, and they eventually did. ❞

♥ *Justice, 14*

Tip Five: Be Fit and Stay Fit

Girls report that much of their stress comes from their families, whether it is arguing with parents, going through a divorce, or dealing with siblings. One of the best ways to stay on top of stress is to stay fit physically, emotionally, and mentally. This can help you deal with the typical everyday challenges within your family.

As you're working on your physical fitness, invite a family member to help you keep your commitment. Go for a walk with your dad or go mountain climbing with your brother or mom.

To help your emotional fitness, stay connected with and get support from your friends and family. Researchers have found that having friends or social support can greatly help our emotional fitness.

❝ When my parents were divorcing, I really relied on my friend Trina. She had a great family. You could just see the love her parents had for each other and their kids. I know my parents both love me, but they sure didn't feel that way about each other.

It was really soothing to be at Trina's. Watching her parents and interacting with them gave me a sense of what a good marriage is like. I'm going to set my sights on a marriage like theirs. ❞

♥ *Marlene, 15*

Tip Six: Dream Big

What is your picture of an ideal, yet realistic family? Is this something you can create for yourself down the road? What will it take—and whom will it take—to create this family? How can you start to take small steps toward this goal?

Maybe you have a vision in which you feel comfortable talking to your mom about problems you're having. One way of taking small steps toward this goal would be to let your mom know what you want. Then, pick one thing you are going to talk to her about this week. It doesn't have to be serious. Maybe you're going to ask her about a movie you just saw.

What if it isn't possible to create the ideal family now? Your ideal may be to have your parents get back together after a divorce. Focus on the things you do have control over. Think about the qualities you want in your family and what you have to be grateful for right now.

If your parents put you down, maybe you have loving grand-parents, or a favorite cousin, or an amazing teacher at school who really understands you and makes you feel good about your work.

Does your family inflate or deflate your dreams? If they are deflators and you've tried to deal with it and there are no changes, don't keep banging your head against the wall. Talk to people who will support your dream and listen to your big plans.

Tip Seven: Get Outside of Yourself

As bad as you may have it at home, trust me—there are many girls (and boys, for that matter) who have it worse. A little dose of perspective can sometimes be really helpful. What about the girls who have never had parents and have been in foster care all of their lives? Or the girls who have been abused? Or the girls who have lost their parents in tragic accidents?

Maybe you can think of a friend who is in a tough spot with her family. How can you help her? Can you listen to her? On the flip side, as you're dealing with your own family,

Make an effort to be grateful to the people who care for you.

can you try to add a dose of humor? Sometimes laughing at your family's quirks is one of the best ways to get by. Can you look at things from your family's perspective? Try thinking about it from this angle. You might be surprised at what you realize.

Think about it . . .

- What are the good things about your family?
- Whom do you appreciate in your family and why?
- What can you do to improve things?
- Where can you get what you need?
- Have you ever thought about going for counseling?
- If you could change one thing about yourself and your family, what would it be?
- What are you grateful for?

Try it!

- Surprise your mom, dad, or brother or sister with a favor or their favorite thing.
- Appreciate your family members. Thank them for the big and little things they do.
- Do something with your parent or parents. Go to a park, see a movie, or find something you both like to do.
- Compliment people in your family. A little compliment goes a long way.
- Find a good time to talk.
- Laugh at yourself.
- Put your thoughts and ideas down in a journal.
- Ask your mom or dad to go to lunch.

5

Dealing with School, Now and Beyond

Most of us will spend thousands of hours and days going to school. Whether you're in a public, private, or home school, this time of your life holds some of your best and worst experiences.

School is where we make some of our greatest friends, try new things, push ourselves, and try to figure out our place in the

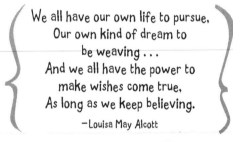

We all have our own life to pursue,
Our own kind of dream to
be weaving . . .
And we all have the power to
make wishes come true,
As long as we keep believing.
—Louisa May Alcott

world. In this chapter we'll talk about some of the biggest school-related issues teen girls face. Girls keep secrets about school too! Here are some of the most common.

SECRETS GIRLS KEEP ABOUT SCHOOL

I cheated on a test.

I have a crush on my teacher.

No one likes me.

I didn't make the team.

I'm smarter than people realize.

I'm getting bad grades.

I've been harassed, and boys make sexual comments to me.

I have a learning disability.

My parents can't afford college.

I have really good grades.

I'm way too stressed.

I'm living my parents' dream, but not mine.

However you look at it, girls keep many secrets about school. We're going to cover all of these and more! Let's start at the very beginning, and that's with teachers, of course.

TEACHERS

Teachers can be wonderful. They know how to build us up, dream the best for us, challenge us, and encourage us to do well, but sometimes things don't go so well. What if you don't click with your teacher? Then what?

Put yourself in his or her shoes

Take a minute to think about your involvement in your teacher's class. Is there a reason why your teacher might be upset with you? If the answer is yes, try to address the root problem. For example, maybe you're late to class several times a week. Is there any way you can make sure you're on time? Is there a reason you're late so often? If so, you may want to schedule a time to talk about it with your teacher. If your answer is no, keep reading to help with your situation.

Be patient

Handling disagreements takes time. Whether you are mad at your teacher or he or she is mad at you, hurt feelings take time to heal.

Vanessa was an excellent and conscientious student. She always worked hard and gave her best in every class. She was very excited about the paper she'd just turned in to her English teacher. She knew it was the best work she'd ever done.

When she got the paper back, she was shocked to see a B on it and no explanation, no comments, nothing that would indicate why it had received a lower grade than her usual A.

She didn't know what to do, and her mom suggested she talk to the teacher about it. When she did, the teacher brushed her off and said she didn't have time to talk about it today, but she said to leave the paper and she'd take another look at it.

When Vanessa got to class the next day, the teacher handed her the paper. The B had been changed to an A, but there was still no explanation of what had happened in the first place. Vanessa was very confused, but the teacher said she had a meeting after school and couldn't talk that day, either. Vanessa let it drop, but she never felt the same about the teacher again.

Look for common ground

While you're trying to get along with this person, can you find any common ground? Maybe you love the way your teacher dresses or appreciate the way he gives tests, or perhaps you enjoy looking at the picture of the beach she keeps on her desk. If you really want to go out on a limb, tell your teacher what you appreciate or strike up a conversation about something you have in common. Make sure you're genuine and not just trying to be a teacher's pet.

Schedule a meeting

In many cases, it's a good idea to find a time that is good for both of you to sit down and discuss what is troubling you. After you make an appointment, plan out what you want to say. It could help you feel more comfortable if you write your points down. Be honest and real. Adults appreciate honesty, and even if you don't get the result you want, you will gain your teacher's respect by being honest.

When nothing seems to work, it's never a bad idea to run your situation by a friend, an adult, or a parent. If you're in a situation that is getting worse, you may need to get your parents involved.

GRADES

Grades are huge. There's just no way to overstate it. If you're serious about going to college, you already know this. If you don't know whether you're going to go to college, don't make it more difficult to get in by messing up your grades. If you're having trouble keeping your grades up, make it a personal goal to overcome whatever is challenging you so you, too, can "make the grade."

Oddly enough, sometimes girls keep their mouths shut too much in class, even when they know the answers. I can't help but wonder why girls wouldn't want their brilliance to shine.

❝ I knew the answer, but I didn't want to raise my hand. I don't know why not. I guess I was afraid of looking like a know-it-all. ❞

♥ *Kay, 14*

Whether you don't want to look too smart, you're trying to impress that hunk who sits next to you, or you think it's cute, think twice before playing dumb. Whether you go to college or not, your high school grades will follow you. If you apply to college, the classes you've taken and the grades you've earned will make a big difference in whether you're accepted.

If you decide not to go to college, your employer may still want to see your high school transcript. The fact is, if you're a slacker in high school, there's a real possibility you'll be a slacker in the workforce, too. I'm biased here, but I think most people would agree with me that going to college is vitally important if you want to get a good job. Even if you want to be more of an entrepreneur and create your own job, there are still classes, skills, and experiences you will want to get from college and internships. Kids from all around the world are competing for the same jobs and are seeking a quality education, too. If you have a desire to go to college, you can make it happen with the right support and plan in place.

If you're just not good at school, talk to your parents and teachers and get help. You might benefit from an extra study hall or a tutor. You might need to be tested to rule out a learning disability.

Also, remember—this is the time to discover your strengths. Some kids don't do well in school because most schools are very language- and math-based. What if your talents are artistic or athletic? This doesn't mean you can blow off school. Talk to your parents and teachers try to come up with a plan that works for you.

In the meantime, these study tips can make a big difference in your grades:

• If you need help, don't be embarrassed to ask for it.
• Decide what grade you want and figure out what you need to do to make it happen.

- Use a calendar to write down assignments, activities, and study times.
- Consider when you study best. Are you a morning or night person?
- Be smart about it. Can you study on the bus? Do you like it quiet? Or do you like music in the background?
- Start with your hardest subject first. This might seem counterintuitive, but by getting your hardest subject done first, the night becomes easier and easier.
- Ask your friends what works for them.
- Don't wait until the last minute. If you get a big project, break it down into smaller pieces.
- Keep your priorities straight by identifying what is important to you. Pick three things. For example, maybe your priorities are to pass physiology, spend time with your friends, and start on the volleyball team. Make sure your choices reflect these priorities.

School is primarily about learning, but it would be impossible not to talk about the social scene. For many girls, when things go awry socially, every other area of their lives is affected.

THE SOCIAL SCENE

❝ I had just moved to Chicago, and things were a lot different than in California. The way kids dressed, what they did after school—it was all unusual to me. I found the best way to deal with my move was to get involved. I made a lot of different friends right away because I was a drifter. What I mean is I didn't stick to any one group. ❞

♥ *Alexa, 15*

Gossip, teasing, and rumors

It's one of those things that girls don't want to make a big deal about when talking to me, but it is a huge deal. Nobody enjoys being made fun of for not making the basket in gym class, for getting a D on an exam, or for something they're wearing—and most girls say girls are meaner than guys! This topic is handled more in depth in Chapter 3 (on friends) and in Chapter 6 (on being cyber savvy), but here's a quick overview:

If you're being teased:

- Try your best to ignore the teasers. They want you to react.
- Try to have a sense of humor about it. Sometimes laughing it off works too.
- Count your blessings. Be glad you're not mean enough to tease anyone else.
- Stay close to your friends. They're your source of strength when you let bullies get to you.
- If the teasing continues, get help from your parents or a person you trust. You don't have to face this alone.

If you're the teaser:

- Identify what you are gaining from teasing.
- What typically sets you off? What do you get angry about?
- Ask yourself if teasing others makes you feel better about yourself.
- Think about how the other person must feel.
- Ask yourself what you can do instead.

That doesn't mean we need to be best friends with everyone, but it does mean we don't backstab or put each other down. Think of how much more we could all accomplish if we lifted each other up instead of tore each other down!

> I'm a big believer in us girls sticking together, no matter what.

Unfortunately, I've never heard of a high school that doesn't have cliques. They seem almost like a part of growing up, but that doesn't mean you have to be in one. I've talked to many girls who have managed to navigate their way around this.

WHAT IF YOU'RE TOO INVOLVED?

Erica is president of student government and the captain of the softball team. She is a member of the National Honor Society, plays the violin, works, volunteers regularly at a nursing home, and is also an honors student. She wants to get into a good school to be a doctor and feels like she needs to be doing all of these things, but how is she supposed to get everything done?

More and more students today feel more and more pressure. With college expectations rising, it almost seems like a race to see who can outdo whom or sign up for more activities. How do you fit everything in and handle the pressure? Follow these tips:

- Prioritize. Figure out what is important to you. Is it college? Is it a certain career path? Is it your friends or family? Is it sports?
- Now ask yourself how well you are managing your top three priorities. Map out each week in your calendar and make sure you have made time for your priorities.
- Be open to letting some things go. It's better to do a few things well rather than spread yourself so thin you do a poor job in many areas.
- Brain dump. This works great when you're feeling overwhelmed. You might think it will take hours to do the exercise I'm proposing, but I promise it will take under fifteen minutes:
  a. Take out a sheet of paper and write down everything you can

think of that is bugging you or that you need to get done. Then try to clump things into specific and manageable categories. This is one form of mind-mapping.

b. Next, make a list of things you want to accomplish based on your priorities. Don't overwhelm yourself. Put only three to five things on your list to accomplish every day.

- Are you feeling extremely anxious or worried about tests, friends, or school stuff? If you constantly worry, have problems sleeping, are irritable, or can't focus, this could mean you need professional help for your anxiety.
- Dance!

    My favorite way to destress is to dance. By 'dance,' I mean jumping up and down while listening to my latest favorite song. You can even throw in a few jumping jacks or kicks to work up a bit of a sweat. Not only is this a great way to gain an energy boost during a study session, but it also reminds you that sometimes all you need to do to feel better is have fun.

♥ *Mandy, 14*

- Reassess what you're committed to. Is there anything you're spending time doing that isn't in line with your future goals? If you need to, talk to someone who has experience dealing with stress and organization. Sometimes talking with another person helps us look at things from a new perspective. Be open to making changes if necessary.
- Ask friends who seem really organized how they get it all done and swap ideas with each other.
- Get support from the girls in your Girls with Dreams Friend Circle. There's nothing more powerful than a group of motivated and supportive friends helping each other.

This is a great time to try new things, new clubs, and new experiences. Find a balance between doing too much and doing nothing at all. From sports to school clubs and national organizations, there is so much to choose from. To decide what to join, ask yourself, "What am I passionate about? What have I always wanted to try? What would stretch me a little out of my comfort zone?"

MONEY... NEVER ENOUGH!

School can be expensive, between parking permits, prom, and paying for extra activities. Some parents give their kids money for all of this, including unlimited lunch money, but other parents just can't afford it, and kids work to pay for their own things.

❝❝ My mom and I had a great deal in high school. She gave me a certain dollar amount each week for lunch, and I had the choice to spend that money or make my own lunch and save the money for other stuff. Which one did I choose? I usually made my lunch. Buying new clothes and CDs and having gas money was more important to me than eating out. ❞❞

♥ *Dallas, 16*

It's critical for girls and women to establish financial independence

I never realized this until after I was in college, but if you can start good financial habits early, you will be well on your way to financial success. Don't wait until you graduate high school. Take these ideas to heart and learn your money smarts as soon as possible!

One of the great tips many financial experts talk about is breaking your money into three categories: saving, spending, and giving. Budget an amount of money you are going to allocate into each of these areas. For example, if you bring in $100, you might allocate

10 percent, or $10, to your giving fund, 30 percent, or $30, to your savings fund, and the remaining 60 percent, or $60, to your spending fund. Figure out a system that makes it easy to keep your commitment. For example, you might put your savings in your savings account, your giving in a special place, and the spending in your checking account.

Just by saving a small amount every month, you can be on your way to millions. Did you know that if you save just $75 a month at a 7 percent interest rate starting at age sixteen, you'll be a millionaire by age seventy-nine? If you can save $125 a month, you'll be a millionaire by age seventy-two, and if you can save $200 a month, you'll have your million by age sixty-five. Once you get a job after college, you'll be able to put away even more money each month. The point is to start saving as soon as possible!

Finally, think about your own beliefs about money. Do you think money comes easily, or is it hard to get? Think about how your beliefs have been shaped by your parents. Do they operate out of abundance or scarcity? Do they believe in sharing? For more ideas, look at the resources at the end of this book.

Job or no job?

Getting a job is a great idea for a number of reasons. You will be able to meet a lot of new people, make a little money to spend or save, and have something to list on your résumé if the job is in the field you plan to study. If you're looking for ways to bring in more money, there are many possibilities, from getting a job during the school year versus in the summer or both. Ask yourself why you need a job and what the benefits and consequences will be. For example, will you be able to keep up with your schoolwork if you take on a job? Talk to your friends about their experiences.

How did they like their jobs? How did they find them?

Also, if you decide to work, try to find a job that is in line with your passions. If you love photography, can you find a studio that needs extra help? If you like children, can you babysit? If you love the outdoors, can you work for the city parks department? Not only are jobs great because they provide you with opportunities, they also give you money, teach you new skills, and help you identify what it is you truly do and do not enjoy.

> I was really shy before I got my first job as a bus girl at a restaurant. People I worked with even playfully teased me about how quiet I was. It didn't take long to bust out of my shell. Cleaning tables was a great first job for me because it allowed me to be in an atmosphere other than home or school, but I didn't have to interact with many customers. This allowed me to overcome my shyness in my own time. Since then, I've always recommended getting a job as a way to combat being quiet.
>
> ♥ *Sabrina, 18*

Interviewing for your job

When you decide to interview for a job, visit www.girlswith dreams.com to find out more about the process and how to apply, interview, and follow-up.

Follow Kate's tips below to ensure yourself a good experience.

Before applying

- Brainstorm a list of possible places to apply. If you love working with pets, apply at a pet shop. If you're studying art, apply at a gallery or studio.
- Don't limit yourself to one type of work. Applying to a variety of places will increase your chances of finding a job that suits you.

- Apply a month or so ahead of the time you want your job. You will avoid the seasonal rush and have the chance to pick from a wider variety of opportunities instead of scrambling to find a job out of what opportunities are left after everything has been picked through. You might even be able to apply online in some cases.

The process

- Keep track of the places you've applied to. About a week after turning in the applications, call each company to see if they've had a chance to review your application.

The interview

- Before the interview, do your homework. Be familiar with the company's history and products. Come up with a few questions about how things work or what responsibilities you will have as an employee.
- When the person interviewing you asks why you want to work here or why you would be a good addition to the team, have a great answer.
- Dress nicely for the interview, make sure your clothes are clean and pressed, and arrive about ten minutes early and let someone know why you're there. Be polite, friendly, and enthusiastic.
- During the interview, just be yourself. Waiting for the interview is the hardest part of the process, and since you did your homework, it should be more fun than scary. Once the interview is over, thank the interviewer for his or her time.

The follow-up

- You're almost done! The last step is the follow-up. Take the time to let the person who interviewed you know how much you appreciate his or her time. You can send an e-mail or a card in the mail. This extra step is the icing on the cake. Good luck!

BIG BLOWS

Everyone deals with big blows at some point in his or her school career. Some of us don't make the basketball team or the dance team. Others change friends or don't get into the college they want. Here are a few of the biggest blows you've told us about with some ideas for how to handle them.

I failed a test after studying really hard

❝ I felt like all I did all week was study. I studied with my friends, by myself, and with my mom. I reviewed the material over and over. I actually thought I'd done okay, so I was shocked to see a D– on my exam when I got it back. My heart sank, and I was on the verge of tears. ❞

♥ *Rhonda, 16*

If this hasn't ever happened to you, it might someday, and I'm sure you can imagine how devastating it feels. If you're ever in this situation, you need to take the results in stride. We all stumble sometimes. Instead of getting wrapped up in the failure, try to see past it and do the following:

- What's the lesson you can take away from this? Was there a certain area on the test that was especially hard for you?
- Talk to your teacher about what happened. Maybe he or she will have some suggestions for future tests.
- Try not to beat yourself up.
- Ask your teacher to review the areas you had the most trouble with.

I didn't make the team

Sooner or later, we all have this experience or its equivalent.

" 'Coach wants to see you out in the hallway.' As the assistant coach said this, my heart started racing. We were only three days into basketball tryouts; why did he need to see me out in the hallway?

Questions raced through my mind as I jogged out the door to show my effort. There he was, waiting for me, and by the look on his face, I knew it was over. My heart leaped into my throat as I listened to the normal formulated speech of 'You're a great kid but not what we're looking for.'

I walked back into the gym where everyone else was still practicing, got my stuff, and headed out the door. As I walked to the parking lot, I could not feel the floor. Everything around me was swirling, and I felt as if my life were over.

I did not understand where I'd gone wrong. Everyone said I was a great player, better than most of the girls who had been on the team in previous years. I could not believe I hadn't made the girls' basketball team.

For a week, I was distant and kept to myself. There were so many emotions to deal with. I felt I had let everyone down, even though my friends and family said they loved me just the same and were proud of my efforts.

I did not know what to do with myself. I started doubting not only my ability to play basketball but my ability to do other things as well. I questioned myself. Was I smart enough? Was I pretty enough? I just kept struggling with why I hadn't made the team. This was my dream, and now it was shattered.

It took a lot of time to get over not making the team, but I was lucky to have some great friends who saw I was down and picked me back up.

Luckily, my days of playing basketball were not over. In playing with my friends, I discovered I enjoyed playing for fun, and it was nice not stressing out over winning the state championship.

When you do not make the team, whether it's for a sport, a spot in the marching band, a social clique, or a part in the school musical, do not give up. If you give up, you let the world win, and you miss out on life.

There will always be other opportunities. Take the other opportunities you are given and live them to the fullest. These will soon turn into great memories, and soon enough you will forget about your failure.

Life is not about counting all the times you have failed; it's about counting all the times you tried again and never gave up. 🙴 🙴

🍀 Mo, 18

I think I have a learning disability

In most cases, learning disabilities are diagnosed before middle school, but that doesn't always happen. Some kids fall through the cracks. If you have a learning disability or think you have one, this doesn't mean you are stupid. It means you learn differently from the average person. It also means you need to know how you learn best and to include and share those strategies with your teachers.

> Life is not about counting all the times you have failed; it's about counting all the times you tried again and never gave up.

The most important thing to remember is not to be embarrassed by your learning disability. You can't help it, and it's not your fault. It's important to get support, and there are numerous resources online and in books that can help you understand and deal with your learning disability. See our resource section at the end of this book for more.

LIFE BEYOND HIGH SCHOOL

Nothing can truly prepare you for life after high school. Half of you is excited to be on a new adventure and making decisions independently, while the other half is terrified, not sure what life will hold or what it will be like to be at a new school and possibly away from most of your friends and your home.

Whether you are going far away or staying close to home, whether you are going to a large school, a community college, or not going to college at all, the unknown can be scary and exciting all at the same time.

> Thinking is easy, acting is difficult, and to put one's thoughts into action is the most difficult thing in the world.
>
> —Goethe

Before you start college or your next adventure, get clear on what you want to happen.

Preparing for college

In today's world, most employers are looking for people with college degrees. It has also been shown in many research studies that the more education you have, the higher your salary will be.

Many girls already know they want to go to college, while others know they're going but have no idea how to pay for it, and still others doubt they can ever get in.

> This is a time of big decisions, and it is a critical time to rely on your gut.

Don't give up on your dream or idea of college. It will open up countless opportunities for you. If you think you can't do it, keep reading, and we'll help you figure out how to get there.

You might think you have lots of time to think about your future and college, but you need to start looking at your options now. As I said earlier, grades make a huge difference, whether you know what you want to be when you graduate or not.

Junior high and high school are the time to prepare, so whether you're on the fence or you've decided to go to college, you might as well make the most of your time and act as if you want to go.

Here are a few ideas to help you plan each year:

Seventh and eighth grades:

- While you're still in middle school, develop a general understanding of what college is.
- In eighth grade, many students outline their high school schedule. Ask for help in making sure your schedule will prepare you for college. Pay attention to things like foreign language and requirements in the areas of math, science, and English.

Freshman year:

- Talk to your guidance counselor about what you will need to do, from taking the SAT and ACT to making sure you have the right classes.
- Start thinking about college, but don't obsess about the details.
- Find an activity you like to participate in. Also consider finding a volunteer experience you can continue during high school.
- Start a list or résumé of all of your activities and accomplishments. Make sure you add new experiences. This list will be very helpful when applying to colleges.

Sophomore year:

- Pay attention to your grades and the skills you are developing.
- Check in with your guidance counselor.
- Some students take the Preliminary SAT this year.
- Keep in mind that while the ACT and SAT are important, college requirements can vary. However, these tests are usually very important in deciding scholarships.
- If you find a job, try to find one that compliments your interests.

Junior year:

- Find a self-assessment tool so you can start deciding what is important to you in a school. Your guidance counselor should have some good suggestions.
- Determine when you will be taking the ACT and SAT. If your score is really important to you, consider taking a class to prepare.
- Think about the characteristics you want in a college. There are many factors to consider, including size, location, faculty, social life, dorm setup, and more.
- Keep in mind that the admissions office will look at everything you have to offer, including how you did in high school, what classes you took, your activities and leadership roles, recommendations from teachers, and your application essays.
- Visit some of the colleges you're interested in. There is nothing like seeing a campus in person and talking to current students to help you decide whether you can picture yourself there. It's also important to have an interview with an admissions counselor if you like the school. This can help put a face on your application.
- Start looking into financial resources for college. Talk to your guidance counselor about scholarships and other options you can research.

Senior year:

- Research application deadlines. Map out a time line for yourself.
- Visit any schools you still need to see in the fall.
- Apply to a couple of schools that are a stretch for you, meaning you're not sure whether you will be accepted. Also apply to a few you will definitely be accepted to and a few others you are fairly certain you will be accepted to.
- Make sure you give yourself the right amount of time to apply for financial aid, complete your essays, and put all the pieces together.

- Consider most of your applications will need to be submitted by January of your senior year if not before.
- Once you've been accepted, you might think about visiting or revisiting the campus.
- Remember to keep your options open. The college acceptance process can feel very random. Some of the more competitive schools may accept only 7 to 10 percent of those who apply.

Seven Tips Every Girl Needs to Deal with School, Now and Beyond

Tip One: You Gotta Use Your Gut

You may feel like a lot of things happening at school are out of your control, but don't forget the things you do have control over: yourself, the way you think, and the way you handle tough situations and talk to people. This comes from your intuition.

You also have control over your future. What do you want to reach for? Where do you want to go to school? As you enter the world after high school, remember that your gut is your best friend. *Keep listening to yourself with every decision you make and you'll always make the right one!*

Tip Two: Discover Your Strengths and Use Them

Don't be afraid to try new things. I limited myself in high school because I didn't want to mess up my GPA, but it inhibited me from trying new things, which would have helped me get a better sense of what I liked and what I was good at. Take a class outside of school if you're really that scared of ruining your GPA.

Too many girls are walking through life without ever tapping into their strengths. They are under pressure from parents or maybe have never even thought to ask the question. It's never too late to get in tune with your own strengths.

> *Once you make a decision, the universe conspires to make it happen.*
> —Ralph Waldo Emerson

Chloe loved to dance. For as long as she could remember, she had loved dancing. She went on to dance in college and later became a professional dancer.

Follow Chloe's example. She knew what she loved, and she made it happen.

Madison had no idea what she was good at. She felt like she didn't excel at anything. This scared her, and she wondered whether she shouldn't avoid college until she had a better sense of what she wanted to do with her life. After all, college costs a lot of money.

Many girls feel like Madison, but this situation doesn't have to be complicated. Here are some tips for Madison and girls like her:

• Know thyself. Identify your natural talents and abilities. Do you love numbers, drawing, reading, talking? When are you most happy? Is there any way to turn what makes you happy into a career?
• Ask other people what they love about you and what they see as your strengths. Visit www.girlswithdreams.com for more fun quizzes and tools.

Ultimately, the key to success is combining your strengths with your passions. When you start thinking about going to college and what your future is going to be like, remember this equation to determine whether you are thinking about both sides. If you're not, ask yourself whether you can live with that. Don't forget to be easy on yourself. Your interests and passions may change, and it's important to remember that as well.

Tip Three: Choose the Right Friends and Respect Them

As always, the right friends support your best efforts to make the most of yourself and keep yourself safe. The right friends will support you in making the grades you want, in dealing with tough situations with teachers, and moving your life forward in the best direction.

Whether you're in middle school, high school, or getting ready to go to college, take care of your friends. Be open to new friends and experiences. I made some of my best friends in college, but that doesn't mean I forgot about my other friends.

Tip Four: Be Courageous and Confident

Odd as it is, we sometimes get teased in grade school and high school for getting good grades. It takes courage and hard work to get good grades, to stand up for ourselves when we're being inappropriately teased, or to stand up for someone else.

Also remember that our stress goes up when we feel less confident! What do I mean by this? If you don't feel like you're a strong writer and you have a big paper to write, you will feel more stress than someone who enjoys writing and considers it a personal strength.

It also takes courage just to go to college, from making the first decision to leave home to finally being on your own. In reality, all change requires courage and confidence.

❝ Life should be exciting, but many times when we fear, it is because we are facing something we don't know or are unfamiliar with. When I entered high school, I was terrified! Two thousand students? Are you joking? I was sure I was going to die.

Instead of worrying about what was going to happen, I should have been excited and eager to see what was going to happen next. This was a new opportunity. I was done with close teacher supervision and monitored lunch sessions. In high school, I would be free, treated more like an adult, yet I was running the other way, scared silly!

If you want to know the true secret of how to be more confident, it's this: be yourself. Do not think of new experiences as doomsday but as a day of adventure. Where are you going to go, and what are you going to do? Who knows what might be lurking around the next corner? You'll never know until you turn the corner!

Find confidence in being yourself and knowing you can do great things. The more you practice this, the more confidence you will gain, and the more you will learn and grow to be yourself. ""

♥ *Mo, 18*

Tip Five: Be Fit and Stay Fit

If there's anything that causes stress, it's school. There's always so much to do and so many people to please! Now more than ever, you need to keep stress under control by keeping fit physically, mentally, and emotionally. By taking care of yourself, you are essentially creating a stress shield to help deal with stress. Eat a healthy, balanced diet. Get plenty of sleep. Work exercise into your schedule. In short, keep your life balanced.

Tip Six: Dream Big

Okay, this isn't a new concept, but think about it. Do you still have big dreams? *Always dream big for yourself and know what you want, not what others want for you.* Can you relate to the following girls?

- Allison loved to sing, but instead of trying out for one of the leads in the school musical, she talked herself into doing makeup instead.
- Julie loved to play basketball, but instead of playing year-round for a select team and going for varsity, she settled for the school JV team because she didn't think she'd ever make it big.
- Katie loved photography and took pictures every chance she got. She dreamed of studying photography in college and then opening her own business.

Which dreams need to be rewritten? Allison's certainly does. Julie's dream needs to be rewritten, too, but Katie is doing just fine on her own. Don't touch that girl's dream!

Tip Seven: Get Outside of Yourself

Don't make the mistake of losing perspective. Don't make the mistake of thinking you're the only person in the world dealing with your particular challenge. It just isn't true.

What would you dream if you weren't afraid?

A great way to get started is to get involved with a student organization or start your own group. Figure out what your passion is and follow it. Check out groups like Amnesty International, the National Honor Society, the school yearbook, the green club, and others.

If money and resources weren't an issue, what would your dream be?

❝ I just didn't get it. Why was our school throwing away thousands of plastic soda bottles and cans every week? Why weren't we recycling? I wanted to change this and asked my favorite teacher what I could do. She suggested I talk to the principal about my concerns. I got a few friends together, researched how others schools were recycling, and made

an appointment. It wasn't easy, but six months later, we were
recycling! 99

♥ *Isabella, 15*

Who helps you dream big?

Get outside of yourself and volunteer to do your part
in the community. Many girls tell me that they have organized toy drives during the holidays, blood drives to benefit the community, or recycling campaigns in their schools. You can also read
the newspaper or lose yourself in a good book. Whatever you do,
don't wallow in yourself!

Think about it . . .

Who are some of the people you look up to who dream big?

• How do you get help if you need it, whether it's with
grades or with the pressures of choosing a college or
a career you're genuinely interested in? Start by asking.
Most people are glad to help. If you need help, ask, and
watch the doors open for you.

• Begin recognizing the things you're good at or the things
you've succeeded at. Start a journal of successes both big
and small. For example, make a list of things you're good at,
like this:

I'm good at math.
I'm good at cheering people up.
I'm good at computers.
I'm good at puzzles.
I'm good at listening.
I'm good at problem-solving.
I'm good at running.
I'm good at expressing my opinion.

Make a list of anything you can think of. Try to add one thing to it every day and keep the list where you can see it.

- Start noticing when your self-talk pulls your confidence down. Replace such thoughts with a confidence builder. Instead of saying, "I'm never going to make the team," say, "I don't know whether I'm going to make it, but I'm going to give it my best shot."
- Instead of saying, "I have no friends," say, "I feel pretty lonely, but I do have friends, and maybe I need to think about meeting new ones."
- Instead of saying, "No guy is ever going to like me," say, "I am likable. I'm a good friend. I will find the right guy who likes me for me."
- Instead of thinking, "Who am I to think I can make the honor roll?" say, "If I work hard, I know I can make the honor roll."

[Unless you try to do something beyond what you have already mastered, you will never grow.
—Ralph Waldo Emerson]

- What's the best way you've handled a high-stress situation in the past? Have you used exercise? Talked to a friend? Shared your ideas with someone you know or at www.girlswithdreams.com?

Try it!

- Try something new you've been curious about each month.
- Make a list of all the things you love to do and/or are good at.
- Notice when you get really excited or when you are really happy. Is there any way this passion can help guide you when choosing a college and/or a career path?
- Ask yourself, "What would I love to stay up late doing? Doing my biology assignment? Playing the guitar? Reading? Making a movie?"
- Talk to your friends about your dreams and help each other.

- Dedicate a notebook or journal to your dreams. Write down where you see yourself and what you are doing in one month, one year, five years, and in ten years!
- Get outside of yourself. Start a new club at school.
- Visit the colleges you are thinking about attending.

6

Are You Cyber Savvy?

Can you imagine a **day** without your cell phone, computer, texting, or the Internet? For most girls, it's impossible to imagine. Advances in technology have made all of these a part of our everyday lives. They connect us with people, ideas, information, and knowledge, but also expose us to dangers such as cyber bullying and on-line predators. Every girl needs to be cyber savvy, so she can use technology to make the most of herself while warding off risks.

> This is perhaps the most beautiful time in human history; it is really pregnant with all kinds of creative possibilities made possible by science and technology which now constitute the slave of man—if man is not enslaved by it.
>
> —Jonas Salk

SECRETS GIRLS KEEP ABOUT CYBERSPACE

Girls keep secrets about their cyber business for many reasons. They may have strict rules set by their parents, or they let fun override their own intuition, or maybe they are just embarrassed or afraid. It's much better to be knowledgeable. Most girls think nothing can happen to them, and even more don't realize some of the threats lurking. Here are a few of the secrets we heard girls keep.

I joined Facebook and didn't tell my parents.

I am being picked on in an online group.

My friend shared photos of me I didn't want people to see.

I sent mean text messages about my old best friend.

I downloaded a movie illegally.

I've been chatting and flirting with older guys online.

I saw sexually explicit material I probably shouldn't have.

IS THE INTERNET GOOD FOR YOU?

❝ I'm actually worried about the Internet. It's become everyone's everything. We use it for shopping, communicating, meeting new friends, and more … what's next? As much as I love it, the Internet isn't as great as we'd like to think it is. ❞

♥ Betsy, 17

Betsy has a point here. How do we balance these great advances with practicality and humanity? The Internet isn't all bad, and it is going to be around forever. Without it, our lives would be more difficult in many ways. We must figure out how to use it in a way that brings our best self forward. There are millions of people using the Internet to make a positive impact, such as these young people:

Ashley Qualls created www.whateverlife.com when she was a teen. This popular and unique site for girls lets them create their own web layouts and graphic designs but also talk to each other about what they care about most.

Started by **Craig Kielburger**, www.metowe.com helps everyone
answer the question, "What have you done to change the world
today?"

Lindsay Giambattista founded www.taylorscloset.org for girls
in foster care to "shop" for clothes they like—completely free of
charge. The idea was just to put a smile on their face for a
moment and let them know they weren't alone.

These are just a few of the thousands who are using the Internet
for positive motives. What will you do?

So, who's at risk online?

Unfortunately, everyone is. It's very common for teens to visit
social networking sites such as Facebook and MySpace, but this
technology can be very dangerous. I'm not saying we shouldn't be
online. It's our way of life now, but we all need to be more savvy
and safe!

Researchers don't know exactly how many teens are using the
Internet to set up meetings with strangers, or how many have tried
cybersex or have received solicitations from others. Predators can
be anywhere online, from social networking groups to chat rooms.
Clearly, the risks increase when teens meet strangers online.

It won't happen to me

Clearly, the Internet and advances in technology have changed us
for good. It's important to stay current with trends and know how
to stay safe. So many girls have a false sense of security when it
comes to interacting online.

❝ People are always saying, 'It'll never happen to me.' So they don't watch what they do. I can't explain how frustrated I get when I see my friends adding total strangers online, nevertheless actually TALKING to them! We've all heard stories—the Internet is dangerous! People are dangerous! I don't understand why girls overlook that so often. When I get a friend request from someone I don't recognize, I add them, but check out their profile immediately, and then I delete them right away if I still don't know who they are ... Seriously, it's common sense! ❞

♥ Betsy, 17

When you're online, it's very easy to forget that things are not always what they seem to be. You may think you are talking to a new guy who really is an older man, or maybe it looks like a cute guy, but it's really girls who are trying to tease you. Read the scenarios below to see how some girls, just like you, faced major problems when online.

CYBER BULLYING

❝ I was so mad at her I didn't know what to do. I decided to seek my revenge by posting pictures of her that I knew she didn't want to be seen. ❞

♥ Tyler, 13

❝ I couldn't believe it. My friends started the 'Meggan is the biggest geek' group. Was this even allowed? ❞

♥ Elsie, 15

❝ I didn't mean for it to get so out of control. I just wanted Lizzy and Drake to see the pictures of Lauren. I didn't think they would send them to the entire school! ❞

♥ Veronica, 14

Many kids admit that someone has said mean or hurtful things to them online and many kids admit having said something mean or hurtful to another person. Maybe it's because we don't talk to people face-to-face; when people go online, it seems so much easier to be hurtful or mean. Some polls and researchers found as many as 33–75 percent of teens have been bullied while online, and experts believe this number is increasing.

❝ My sophomore year was the worst year of my life. I was having a really hard time getting along with my friends. They changed and wouldn't be friends with me anymore. To make things worse, they made fun of me by sending nasty text messages. I felt like the whole school was against me. I tried to keep my mind off things. I ran track and thought that would distract me, but I soon lost interest. I just didn't care anymore. I didn't want to go to school, either. ❞

♥ *Carmen, 18*

While bullying at school is a genuine problem, the issue of cyber bullying is on the rise, and at times it is more dangerous than physical bullying. Actually, girls are more likely to engage in this behavior than boys. In Chapter 3 (on friends) you can read more about bullies, victims, and bystanders and take a quiz to see which one you are. Because cyber bullies tend to feel anonymous, the threats and tactics may be more severe. In fact, as a result of cyber bullying, a shocking number of teens have committed suicide after incidents.

After losing their son, the parents of Ryan Patrick Halligan started a website to talk about the risks of cyber bullying (see www.ryanpatrickhalligan.org). Similarly, Megan Meier took her life after being cyber bullied, and a foundation has been started in her honor (www.meganmeierfoundation.org). In addition, Megan's pledge was created to remind us all what is at stake. Her pledge reminds us to take a stand against cyber bullying and not to use technology as a weapon to hurt others. It reminds us to think before we click and to think about the person on the other side of the screen. Most important, if you help put a stop to cyber bullying, you can save lives!

What is cyber bullying? Cyber bullying occurs through electronic media like cell phones, the Internet, blogs, and discussion groups when a young person is tormented, threatened, harassed, humiliated, embarrassed, or otherwise targeted by another teen or teens who do things like send rude messages, spread rumors, trick others, impersonate people, or exclude someone from an online group. Interestingly, researchers have found that kids usually change roles and go back and forth between being a victim and being the bully.

What is cyber stalking? Otherwise known as cyber harassment, this is what it is called if an adult commits an act like this. What is sexual exploitation? This is when an adult or sexual predator tries to lure children into offline meetings.

Has anything like the following scenario ever happened to you?

❝ Liz was spending the night, and we were having a blast instant messaging our friends and hanging out on MySpace. I don't even remember giving her my password, but I guess I did. It was no big deal. After all, we had been good friends for a long time.

About a month later, we got into a huge fight. I forgot that she had my password, and Liz went into my account and changed my profile and sent messages to people pretending to be me. I was devastated and embarrassed. ❞

♥ *Cora, 17*

What Liz did is against the law, but most of the time cyber bullying does not go that far. Parents often try to pursue criminal charges, but this typically results in a child losing an ISP or IM account as a terms-of-service violation. However, laws are beginning to change as our justice system gets caught up with technology. In some cases, if hacking or password and identity theft is involved, it can be a serious criminal matter under state and federal law. One place you can report incidents is at www.cybertipline.com.

Even if you sincerely think you'll be BFF (best friends forever), follow these simple tips when online.

- Never give out your password.
- Follow the advice of the recent campaign called Think Before You Post, which reminds teens that once they post an image anywhere online (including e-mail and text messages), everyone can see it.
- Remember, if you are being bullied, don't stay silent. You are not alone. Thousands of teens are bullied every day, and it is important that you get help by checking out the resources we've shared and by talking to an adult whom you trust.
- More important, if you witness a friend or another teen being bullied, don't be a quiet bystander—speak up! This will make a huge difference. If you see someone posting cruel messages online, post a positive message instead. Don't support hateful or mean gossip or teasing. And make sure you tell someone who can help.

Peer pressure and cyber world

Peer pressure is everywhere, especially online. It's easier to buy into because you can't see the immediate impact you're having on the other side. Whether someone is asking you to go along with teasing or a practical joke, it's easier to go along with because you can't see facial expressions. To deal with peer pressure online or off, read more tips in Chapter 3.

MEETING GUYS AND FRIENDS ONLINE

❝ I absolutely hate it when my friends add guys on Facebook just because they're good-looking ... not only do I preach to them that good looks aren't all that matter, but adding a total stranger and allowing them to see all of your pictures and information is NEVER a good idea! Surprisingly enough, after chatting for a week online, a couple of my friends have actually ending up dating these guys they hardly know. Not only is it stupid, it's dangerous. Meeting someone at the movies that could secretly be a different person entirely? I just don't get it ... ❞

♥ Betsy, 17

Facebook, MySpace, and Bebo are just a few of the many social network sites popping up. Because they are a meeting place for friends, it's easy to forget about some of the basic safety tips, like not accepting friends who you don't really know. When you're using social media sites, it's just as important to follow safety tips as when you are online in any other capacity.

❝ I went to a seminar over summer and they preached the importance of Internet safety. When they asked how many people had their addresses on their Facebook pages, I couldn't believe how many hands went up in the air! ❞

♥ Wimberly, 16

Some girls are even more at risk for forming online relationships. These include:

- Teens who feel like they have no friends
- Teens who are sad/depressed
- Teens who are not getting along with their parents

Before you join a site

Here are a few more quick tips from Kate based on information from www.ftc.gov.

" • Learn about how a site works before you decide to join. Some allow only a defined community of users to access posted content.
- When on social media sites, consider restricting access to your page to a select group of people.
- Make sure your screen name doesn't say too much about you. Don't use your name, age, or hometown.
- Flirting with strangers online could have serious consequences. Some people lie about who they are, so you never really know who you're dealing with.
- Trust your gut. If you feel threatened by someone or you're uncomfortable, tell an adult you trust and report it to the police and the social networking site. You could end up preventing someone else from becoming a victim. "

♥ *Kate , 23*

Too good to be true

In addition to Kate and Betsy's tips, watch out for friends who seem too good to be true. That cute guy you never met who wants to be your friend could be anyone. Or the lonely girl who just moved to your hometown and is looking for friends may not be who she says she is. It's important to know what you're doing and how to be safe.

Sophie learned her lesson well. She had been on several networking sites like MySpace. She thought she was being careful and had started talking to this guy named Dave who told her he was eighteen. Well, a few months later, Dave showed up at her house. He wasn't eighteen; he was twenty-five. Fortunately, her parents were able to call the police, and he never got to her. This really shook Sophie up because she thought she knew him so well and never thought something like this would happen to her.

How Cyber Savvy Are You?

Quiz

Answer True or False to each question below.

1. It's okay to give my best friend my password if I totally trust her.   ○ T   ○ F

2. It's okay to share some personal information as long as I'm careful.   ○ T   ○ F

3. I never talk about where I'm going when I'm online.   ○ T   ○ F

4. I always believe everything I read online.   ○ T   ○ F

5. If someone asked to meet me, I would consider it after I got to know them for a few months.   ○ T   ○ F

6. If someone swears or uses inappropriate language online, I report it.   ○ T   ○ F

The best answers for each statement:

1. **False.** You probably love and adore your best friend, but it's not safe or cool to give anyone your password. Things change between friends, and by giving someone your password, you open up your personal life to great harm.

2. False. Giving out any kind of personal information from your full name to anything that can identify you, like the name of your dog or mentioning that your parents aren't home, is not a good idea.

3. True. You might think it's innocent to mention that you are going to a school football game on Friday night, but these types of clues can give away your location and identity.

4. False. Don't assume what the other person is telling you is true. For example, someone might tell you she's just another lonely girl who needs a friend when really you're communicating with a thirty-year-old man. *Remember—you never really know the identity of the person you're chatting with online.*

5. False. Never agree to meet someone. You have no way of confirming who this person is or how old he or she really is.

6. True. If someone is swearing, using inappropriate language, or making sexual advances, go offline and tell your parents and possibly law enforcement. You can report incidents at www.cybertipline.com and find out more at www.perverted-justice.com.

How well did you do? If you answered all of them correctly, great! You are well on your way to staying cyber savvy. If you were off on any of them, take it to heart. These are all based on key safety tips. Do everything you can to get on track.

Sophie learned several lessons from this situation. Take the Cyber Savvy quiz to see how much you know.

Pornography online

It's unfortunate we have to talk about this in this book, but if you're going to be online, there's a good chance you will be exposed to some form of pornography, so it's important to keep your radar up and be informed. Experts suggest that as many as one in five youths have been approached by online predators, and often they go unreported. Additionally, teens have started sending their own porn in the form of text messaging or "sexting." This happens when a teen sends a nude or partially nude text message of himself or herself. More about this later in this chapter.

Predators use e-mail, instant messages, bulletin boards, and chat areas to gain a person's confidence and then arrange a face-to-face meeting. Child predators are excellent at "grooming" their victims. This means they build the trust with their victim from the beginning. Some predators may not even mention any type of sexual content in the beginning. It's important to know that there is no "typical identity of a predator." They can be any age, sex, background, or even someone who is married with children. Once a predator gains your trust, he or she might try to meet you in some way.

Be alert to anyone asking you to send pictures or who wants to take pictures of you. The Internet has become a highway for exchanging explicit photos and has increased the communication lines for predators.

Whether or not you use the Internet frequently or you're saying to yourself, *This would never happen to me,* it can happen to you. Take these tips to heart, and pass along the info to your friends!

Chat rooms

It was a Christian chat room and he seemed so nice, but Carissa told me to be careful. She warned me that he might not be as nice in person as he was online. It started off with just one message, but we were talking every day before I knew it. We talked for about two months before my parents found out. At first they let me keep talking to him even though they were skeptical. They started doing research and found out how dangerous chatting with strangers was. They showed me some stories they found at www.perverted-justice.com, and I stopped dead in my tracks. I never went back to that chat room again. And I'm not starting conversations like that anymore. It's just too dangerous. 🙶🙶

♥ *Rachel, 16*

Rachel shared great tips in her story. Chat rooms are a very easy place for predators to find victims. Since chat rooms are often anonymous, they tend to draw more predators. If you are in a chat room, it's important to let your parents know what you're up to. You should never lie about your age or share personal information. Just like anywhere else, people in chat rooms can lie about their age, gender, or anything else.

Online gaming

Games are fun, so it is very easy to forget these parts of the cyber world have dangers too! Gaming sites are all over the Internet and have expanded with many of the gaming systems like PlayStation, Nintendo, and Xbox. If you play games online, use the same precautions you'd use anywhere else on the Internet. You might start talking to someone about the game, and before you know it, they are asking you for personal information or a password.

DOWNLOADS AND FILE SHARING

If you've spent some time online, then you've probably noticed many places that offer software that makes it easy to share music, movies, and other personal information. Some of the sites like this include LimeWire, Napster, YouTube, SwapNut, and iMesh, to name a few. This may sound great at first, but there are risks involved you may not have thought about. For example:

• Your computer could be exposed to unwanted spyware or viruses.

- You might be given access to sexually explicit material.
- Your personal information could be given to anyone who has the same file-sharing software.
- Depending on what you're downloading and sharing, you might be infringing on copyrights.

These types of violations have strict fines and penalties.

Be careful when you're on these sites. Make sure your downloads are safe, secure, and legal.

COMMUNICATION MISHAPS

Without body language, facial expressions, and general face-to-face communication, it's easy for communication to get mixed up, whether you're talking to someone in an e-mail, text message, or social media site. Communication mix-ups and mishaps are very common. Some teens are even starting to send explicit text messages. Read more about Charlotte's story.

Sexting

❝ I wish I could take back that day. I wish I had never hit send. I was in love with Travis, or so I thought. He went to a different school so we didn't get to see each other every day, and it was really hard over spring break because our schedules didn't match up. He was in Florida with his friends, and he kept begging me to send pictures of myself to him. Sure, head shots were easy and I loved doing it, but his begging became more persistent and he wanted me to send a picture of my breasts. He even started to say things like, 'If you really love me, you'll do it.' I don't know what got into me, but I decided to send him a picture. That was one of the biggest mistakes I ever made. He didn't just keep the picture to himself. It spread like wildfire. I actually think his friends spread it to be funny, but whatever happened, this was one of the worst days of my life. I was mortified and embarrassed. I did this for love? The results of this have been devastating. I couldn't handle going to school for weeks because I was so embarrassed. I also was suspended for a few days because of the incident, and I had to talk to the school resource officer (the police, basically). This was a huge mistake that I'm still getting over and learning from. I know I'll never do anything like that again, and I hope other girls will learn from my story. 🙶🙶

♥ *Charlotte, 17*

Unfortunately, stories like Charlotte's are more and more common today. Recent surveys done at www.thenationalcampaign.org found more than one in five teen girls (ages 13–19) reports sending/posting nude or seminude pictures of themselves. And, 37 percent of teen girls are sending/posting sexually suggestive messages. Here are a few important tips to consider:

- **You never have complete privacy online.** Anytime you click send, it's easy to be fooled into thinking your message will only be viewed by the person you're sending it to. But it's critical to remember anyone can see the picture or message you send.
- **Your decisions in cyberspace are permanent.** It's natural for teens to be impulsive, but this is one area you want to really think carefully about. Even if you regret sending that text, IM, or picture, you can't take it back. You have no idea how many people have already copied or forwarded it on to others. This could include not just friends, but your coaches, teachers, employers, or potential college admissions office.
- **Think before you forward.** If you get a "sext" message, think carefully before you continue sending it. Did that person really want thousands to see this picture or e-mail from them? This is

one place where we really need to stick together as girls!

• **Don't fall into the guy trap.** In the www.thenational campaign.org survey, 51 percent of girls said they sent an explicit message because of pressure from a guy. You don't need to fall for this one like Charlotte did. If someone truly cares about you, they wouldn't want you to do something that makes you feel uncomfortable or that could get you in trouble, or be embarrassing.

• **You are never fully protected online.** Even if you're using very little personal information to identify yourself online and in social networking groups, it can still be fairly easy for someone to find you if they really want to. Some girls have sent messages to strangers or people they might want to meet. This is very dangerous.

• **Consider legal risks.** Recent news headlines have talked about people being charged with pornographic crimes for sending nude images. The legal systems are starting to catch up with technology. Think about all of the risks before you send.

Easy Mix-ups

Because messages we send electronically don't include our facial expressions or body language, it is very easy to have misunderstandings. Sometimes, these are a little more serious, as Savannah found out.

❝ One day I was sitting at home, using AIM on the computer. All of a sudden, an AIM box popped up. It was some girl who was saying all these mean things about how I was racist, and kept referring back to my Xanga site.

One of my friend's sites had my name in the comment box and some racist jokes were next to it, so people thought I said them. I was completely appalled at what I read and couldn't believe someone would put me in that kind of position. I tried telling the girl that it wasn't me, and she still doesn't believe me to this day. She still gives me dirty looks at school, all because someone thought it would be fun to say those things.

If you ever read something someone has 'said' and don't believe it's something they would say, they probably didn't say it. I think things could have gone completely different if that girl let me explain. We could have been friends, but she chose to express herself in a different way. ❞

❤ *Savannah, 17*

Jeslyn decided the Internet might help her talk to her friends when an argument got in their way.

❝ One year, my two best friends and I planned to go trick-or-treating. We had our costumes and sleepover plans all set up one year in advance. Over the summer, they told me the costumes changed to fairies, and that another girl was tagging along. I didn't know her that well. They even uninvited me to the sleepover later that year. I got really mad and tried sticking up for myself, but they got mad back.

After a long fight, I wrote a note on Facebook to the three of them saying that the fight was dumb and we should just forget about it. The girls didn't react well, so I figured the best way to handle the situation from that point on was to ignore them. I acted like nothing happened the next day at school, but the girls were never nice to me again. My attitude paid off, though. Three other girls invited me to trick-or-treat with them. We had a blast and realized we just needed true friends to have fun. ❞

❤ *Jeslyn, 13*

Clearly, our cyber world offers many opportunities for communication to get mixed up. Use these tips to help you!

• Before you click send, think about what you've just written. Can it be misinterpreted without having your voice or body language to accompany your message?

- When is it better to communicate in person versus online?
- What was your biggest communication frustration online? How can you learn from this and not do the same thing to others?
- If you have a misunderstanding like Savannah did, try not to over-react. Stay calm and try to talk it out. If that doesn't work, know when it's time to move on.

Seven Tips Every Girl Needs to Be Cyber Savvy

Tip One: You Gotta Use Your Gut

When you go online, it's equally important to keep your radar on. If you get a weird feeling about someone who is contacting you or something that is happening, listen to it.

❝ Jake asked me to be his friend on Facebook. He didn't look familiar, and when I asked him how we knew each other, he said we had met at my friend Sarah's party. I didn't remember this at all. My gut was telling me, 'Wow, he's cute,' but it was also telling me not to accept him as my friend because I didn't know him. I decided not to and felt like I made the right choice. ❞

♥ *Annabelle, 15*

If a friend approaches you to join in on the mean messages they're posting about someone, stop and listen to your gut. Is this really what you want to do? On the flip side, if you are being bullied online, don't be afraid to get help. This happens to most kids who are bullied. One of the voices inside your head might be saying you are no good, but that isn't your gut talking to you.

Tip Two: Discover Your Strengths and Use Them

Figure out how you can use your strengths online. Take note at what you're good at.

Are you good with computers? Do you enjoy writing? Researching? Design? You may find you can improve your strengths by using them more online, or you may discover you have other talents that have nothing to do with the Internet.

❝ I was really nervous, but I decided to take this graphic design class my sophomore year. This was always something I was curious about, but hadn't explored. I loved it! I found I really was good at this stuff. I can't wait to take more classes. Maybe this is something that will turn into a career! ❞

♥ *Jada, 16*

Tip Three: Choose the Right Friends and Respect Them

Choosing the right friends when you're online is almost more important than when you are in person. One big reason is because you never really know who you're talking to online. If you're going through a tough time, please don't look for help from new friends or strangers online. Predators are really good at empathizing and getting kids to trust them. If you need help, it's better to talk to your friends in person or only those friends you know for sure are your friends.

❝ When I'm on Facebook or MySpace, I only add people I know. I don't want someone I add to not be who they are and steal my life. ❞

♥ *Katie S., 18*

Katie's right. You should never become friends with strangers online. Watch out for strangers who are extra nice—they might be predators, or they could be posing as someone they aren't.

When you are hanging out with friends online, make sure you surround yourself with people who build you up. Are your friends into picking on others or pressuring you to do things you don't want to do? Or do you have fun? Do they make you a better person? If you're involved in a crowd that is putting you down, it might be time to find some new friends. Finally, make sure all of your hangout time isn't happening online. Make sure you have a life outside of the cyber world, and get outdoors once in a while!

Tip Four: Be Courageous and Confident

You'll always need courage and confidence, whether you are online or in person. One way courage might show up is by helping someone out.

       I couldn't believe how mean they were being to Jennifer. I didn't like Jennifer all that much either, but I didn't believe in putting people down. For weeks, they had been sending her mean text messages and saying things about her on MySpace. I had had enough. I talked to Maria first. I knew she didn't like what they were doing very much either. We decided to stand up to the rest of them. I was so scared, but I knew it was the right thing to do, and I could tell this was really starting to hurt Jennifer. After we talked, they did decide to stop, but it kind of ruined our friendship. That's okay with me, though. I figure I don't want to hang out with people who spend so much time making fun of others.

♥ Catherine, 17

On another note, keep in mind that the Internet isn't the place you want to announce something you'll be embarrassed about later. What you put online stays online. Whatever you are writing online, would you be willing to say that in person? It's okay to talk to people about things online, but don't hide behind it if you really need to talk to someone in person. This is what takes real courage and confidence.

Tip Five: Be Fit and Stay Fit

Can you be stressed out by technology? Yes! How long could you live without text or e-mail messages? A few minutes? Hours? Days? For some, it's easy to be so obsessed with their computer that they forget to get out, exercise, and get away from the screen. Take a break from technology once in a while and turn off your computer and phone.

❝ I got to the point where I couldn't let go of my cell phone. I would even sneak it into class with me. I had to get my e-mails and be ready to text message on a blink. It really became an obsession. I started to realize that this was just too much! ❞

♥ *Regina, 17*

Tip Six: Dream Big

Can you just imagine where technology and computers will take us in five or ten years? What cool things will cell phones do then? How can you use the Internet to help others? What's your big dream? Will our cars be driven by computers? Will video conferencing over the web be an everyday thing?

Maybe you have a big idea that will impact millions or billions. Read Maria's vision below.

❝ I started Your Allure to empower, encourage, and express the importance of good self-esteem and body image in women. Our long-term goal is to create a whole movement using media in a positive way to communicate messages of self-confidence and alluring beauty with an upbeat, cool, and funky approach. **" "**

♥ *Maria, 21*

Maria is taking the best of both worlds. She's starting a college organization that meets face-to-face, but she is also tapping into the power of Internet media through www.yourallure.org to help her reach millions of young women. You could say she's dreaming big and getting outside of herself!

Tip Seven: Get Outside of Yourself

When it comes to being cyber savvy, there are numerous ways to get outside of yourself, from buying ecofriendly devices, to being nice online, to helping others via the web. Take note of these tips:

- Keep the environment in mind. We produce an enormous amount of waste from our computers and electronic devices. Try to recycle as much as possible and look for ecofriendly devices. You can find more products and resources at www.gengreenlife.com.
- Before you post, put pictures up, or say something about someone else, think about how that might impact them; do they want you saying or posting that?
- Take a walk out of cyberspace every once in a while.
- Tell your school about http://www.bullyingawarenessweek.org and plan some activities.
- Take Megan's pledge (www.facebook.com/meganpledge) and help spread the word to end bullying.
- Help spread the word about online safety by using info at www.teenangels.com.

7

Dealing with the Tough Stuff

We all deal with tough stuff. Some of us have more on our plates than others, but I would guess that most of us have experienced that "How am I going to get through this?" feeling—or worse yet, an "I don't care" attitude.

Whether it's the divorce of our parents, depression, drugs, alcohol, the loss of a loved one, flunking out of school, an eating disorder, or something else, these painful experiences connect all of us. Many of the toughest problems talked about in this chapter are often kept secret. I'd like to thank all of the girls who broke their secrecy to come forward to share their stories with you.

> Courage, it would seem, is nothing less than the power to overcome danger, misfortune, fear, injustice, while continuing to affirm inwardly that life with all its sorrows is good; that everything is meaningful even if in a sense beyond our understanding; and that there is always tomorrow.
>
> —Dorothy Thompson

SECRETS GIRLS KEEP ABOUT TOUGH STUFF

Unfortunately, the secrets about our passions, addictions, pain, and fears are often the biggest, most private secrets we keep. Whether it's cheating on a test or drinking alcohol, here are more of the secrets girls shared with me.

I was raped and now I'm pregnant.

I'm failing most of my classes.

I think my boyfriend is harassing me.

I stole something and got caught.

My uncle committed suicide.

My mom gets high.

I hate myself.

No matter what your secret, it is very common to feel alone. It is common to believe you are the only one dealing with a problem. It is easy to feel scared and that no one would ever understand. The problem with believing this is that none of it is true!

All girls deal with stuff. We all have problems and challenges we face. We aren't the only ones, and there are people who understand. Girls deal with their secrets in a variety of ways. Being aware of what type of secret-keeper you are is critical, because many of the tough stuff situations described in this chapter can have horrible consequences, including death. Make sure you take the quiz in the introduction that gives you your secret-keeper profile.

As you read about the tough problems, keep in mind the following questions: What can girls learn from one another? How can we all learn to deal with the pain in our lives in a way that doesn't hurt us or those around us? How can we learn to stop hiding and begin to share our secrets safely?

Girls deal with all kinds of problems, sometimes more than one at a time, as Lee explains.

❝ What's going on in me was something I couldn't describe. I was more tired. I started crying often, and I couldn't sleep at night. When I started having thoughts of suicide, I was worried. A very important woman in my life saw what I was battling. She saw it before my own mother did. When I did tell my mother, she said, 'It's a phase; you'll grow out of it,' and I never did. My suicidal thoughts were getting more frequent. I really thought something was wrong. I think what hurt the most was that I kept telling people something was up, and no one would listen. I was in a dark hole, scared out of my mind, screaming like my life depended on it, yet no one could hear me. ❞

♥ Lee, 18

When you've tried like Lee to get people to listen and they don't, it's important to keep trying!

❝ After months, I discovered a disgusting habit. Cutting. It's something I regret and I wish I could stop. But the pain helped me think, and it calmed my spirits to a new level. This stopped my crying, until I realized what I had done. Every time I hid my arm and lied to my friends, saying I'd stopped, but this just dug me in deeper. No one saw my true pain, the one I'd been screaming about. I was ashamed of what I'd done, and I wanted to change.

It's now two years later, the beginning of my senior year, and I've talked to a counselor and shared my problems. I'm finally taking a step out of the dark. I can see my life now. I can see where I want to go. I don't know why, but I'm finally smiling and meaning it. It's like I have some invisible force telling me I'm going to be okay, and I'm going to live. I want to thank those who have helped me the most, especially my mother. Once she realized I was having a REAL problem, she helped all she could. And my friends are the ones who listened to me cry and vent. 🙲

♥ *Lee, 18*

DEPRESSION

Miranda was a freshman in high school. She was having a really good year. She played on the volleyball team and had many friends. As the year went on, she started feeling sad. It didn't help that her best friend was moving, and Miranda's sadness worsened. Eventually she realized she was depressed. She felt off. She was sleeping a lot, lost her appetite, and lost interest in the things she used to love. She eventually told her mom how she felt, and they decided to get her help.

Miranda started by talking to her doctor and then a therapist. She didn't realize there were so many girls with depression and so many ways to get help. She decided to take medication, though this isn't always necessary. Before long she was back on her normal schedule and talking to her friends again. Yes, her best friend moved, but she called a lot, and Miranda didn't feel so down anymore.

The causes of depression are very complex. Family history, severe stress, or trauma are some of the big contributors, but sometimes depression happens to girls who are just trying to deal with all the challenges of growing up.

Medication and counseling aren't always necessary, but they might be part of the formula that professionals recommend. Since many teens with depression don't get help, the important thing is to tell someone and seek help, like Miranda did.

How do you know whether you're depressed?

Depression shows up differently for everyone. In a nutshell, it is a constant mood of feeling down, sad, blue, or even irritable. For a complete list of the characteristics of depression, visit www.girls withdreams.com.

What should you do if you're depressed?

If you're depressed, instead of feeling ashamed:

- Talk to someone you trust and tell them how you're feeling.
- See a physician. They can rule out physical illnesses that may be contributing to the depression and they can refer you to a counselor.
- Think seriously about seeing a counselor. Be picky and find one you feel comfortable with. See www.girlswithdreams.com for information about the differences between therapists, psychiatrists, and psychologists.
- Depression is very treatable. You don't have to feel this way forever, but you need to be willing to get help. Untreated depression can lead to suicide.

By the same token, if you think a friend is depressed, do the following:

- Talk to your friend about how she's feeling.
- Let her know she's not alone.
- Be a good listener. Don't just blow off her feelings and tell her to get over it or cheer up. This doesn't help.
- Make sure to read the section on warning signs for suicide. Many teens who are depressed are at risk for suicide.

Depression is common and treatable. Don't let it derail you or keep you from living the life you were meant to live.

SUICIDE

❝ I had a secret, and I'm glad I'm here to tell you about it. I tried to kill myself, and I'm glad I wasn't successful. My life is so different than it was my freshman year. I had started dating this guy named David. I thought I loved him. He made me feel incredible.

One day I saw him talking to Kathy in biology, and the next thing I knew, I heard David had cheated on me with her. I was devastated. How could he do this to me after he said he loved me? I felt like no one would ever love me again the way he did. I stopped eating, and my grades dropped. David stopped talking to me, and I felt completely lost. My friends were still kind of mad at me because I hadn't spent much time with them when David and I were together, and I wondered how I was going to get through this. Would anyone even notice if I were gone?

One day I tried to kill myself, but my parents came home and found me. Deep down, I was relieved. Somehow my parents hadn't known how bad I felt. They called the school the next day, and we met with the social worker. I also started therapy sessions. I didn't think I could ever feel better, but Ms. Maxwell and my therapist made a huge difference.

I'm a junior now and have great friends. I haven't found the perfect guy yet, but I know I will someday. I wrote this because I don't want anyone to think suicide is an answer. I was really lucky I had a second chance. ❞

♥ Liz, 17

According to the CDC (www.cdc.gov) in 2007, 14.5 percent of United States high school students reported they had seriously considered attempting suicide. More than 6.9 percent actually attempted.

Think about it: in a school of 1,000 students, that means around 145 kids have thought about suicide and 69 have attempted it. Statistics show there is one suicide for every 100–200 attempts for fifteen- to twenty-year-olds. Just one student thinking about it or trying it is too many, and yet many teens deal with it every day.

Earlier in the book, I told you my story about suicide. I hid my pain really well, but I struggled off and on for several years with thoughts about dying. I wish I had known more about depression when I was a teen, because I think I would have made different choices about how I dealt with all of this. I was depressed and didn't realize it.

What I know now is that I wasn't alone and should have got help, but I was fortunate my coping strategies of relying on friends, staying involved in school, and turning to my faith worked.

❝ As a freshman in high school I wanted nothing more than to be accepted and make as many new friends as I could. I was so excited to start a new chapter of my life and make new memories. Soon after my first few weeks I met a guy. He was older, mature, and really charming, so it was easy to find myself starting to like him. I was really surprised when I found out from one of his friends that he liked me too. We started dating and it seemed to be like the perfect relationship.

Things quickly started to go sour after about the first six months of our relationship. He always seemed to be upset. If I couldn't come and see him, he would call me names and just try and make me feel the worst I possibly could. To make him happy I started to rebel and argue with my mom more than ever before. I felt like no matter what I did, I was always disappointing someone. Things progressively got worse, and my family started to dislike him more and more because of the way he would treat me, but I always make excuses for him. I was always depressed over the things he would call me, but I feared what his next move would be and I didn't want to make him mad so I stayed with him. Two years of the cheating and name-calling ended when he broke up with me unannounced and told me he never wanted to talk to me again because he wanted to have multiple girlfriends who didn't care what he did. I was devastated. I told him I would do anything for him and I didn't understand why he was doing this. He told me to leave him alone and if it meant taking my own life, then that's what I should do. That same day I attempted suicide, so I ended up in the hospital for a week, and even though I was upset at the time, I'm extremely thankful I spent time there and got better. I don't talk to my ex-boyfriend anymore and I'm proud of myself for letting the situation go. I don't look at it as if I wasted two years on him, but as a learning experience that helped me mature and changed my whole life in a positive way. ❯❯

♥ *Darya, 18*

If you're thinking about suicide, do the following:

- Talk to or call someone you trust. If you don't know anyone, call the suicide hotline at 1-800-273-TALK (8255) or call 911.
- Remember that as much as your life hurts, this pain is temporary and suicide is permanent.
- Come up with a plan for what you can do when you start thinking of hurting yourself.

If a friend is thinking about suicide, do the following:

If a friend tells you she is thinking about suicide, either you are probably going to think she's exaggerating and would never really do it or you are going to panic. Neither extreme is helpful. Instead, do the following:

- Remain calm.
- Listen to her.

- Ask her directly whether she is thinking about suicide.
- Don't make a deal with her that you won't tell anyone that she is thinking about suicide.
- Tell an adult.
- Don't leave her alone.
- Assure her she won't feel like this forever.

Know the warning signs that a person might be contemplating suicide. These include:

- Feelings or expressions of hopelessness or depression (belief that things won't change or get better)
- Wrapping up personal matters
- Giving away possessions
- Talking about dying (including writing notes about, talking about, or threatening death or suicide)
- Low self-esteem (feelings of extreme worthlessness, shame, or guilt, a belief that the world would be better without them)
- Previous suicide attempts
- Changes in sleeping or eating habits
- Change in personality or behavior

“ It was the scariest moment of my life when I found out the truth. A long time of keeping secrets poured out during a deep heart-to-heart. She was my best friend, my not-related sister, my advisor, my world. I knew she was depressed, but I had no idea what had been going through her mind. I listened to her cry, gave her advice, and encouraged her every step of the way. She thought she was fat and ugly; she was far from it. She is the most beautiful person I have ever met, with the kindest heart. But her thoughts were too much, and her depression became so intense, she was hospitalized.

I had no idea a friendly invitation from me saved her life. I learned about that a few years later. It was devastating, but I was so thankful for our friendship, that she accepted my invitation. With help, she has improved greatly. I am so glad I stuck with her all the way, encouraging her and supporting her. Most important, I am so glad I chose to listen to her. I was always afraid: afraid I would lose her, afraid I would make a mistake. I didn't know if I was helping, but I learned that being a good friend was help enough.

Don't run away when a friend needs you—stick with her and be on her side. Don't make someone fight alone. Would you want to? 🙴

♥ *Grace, 18*

If you've lost a friend to suicide

If you've lost a friend to suicide, you might be feeling very angry and have a lot of unanswered questions. You might also be blaming yourself for not preventing it. There are specific support groups for survivors of suicide that can help you. Also, read our section on dealing with grief later in this chapter for more ideas.

🙴 I'll never forget the morning of April 6. My mom woke me up and told me she had something terrible to tell me. My friend Adam had killed himself. At first I thought this was some awful joke. I had just talked to Adam yesterday.

At his funeral, I couldn't believe he was gone. Then the guilt set in. I should have noticed his mood. I should have stopped him or called him or something. How was I going to deal with this? It helped to talk about it. My mom told me there were support groups for survivors of suicide, and I thought that was kind of dorky, but I decided to try it.

The first couple of times at group were awkward and painful. I didn't want to talk about it, but then it got better. As I heard other people's stories and how they were coping, I started coping with Adam's death. I decided to write him a letter with all my questions, feelings, and anger. I read it to him and left it at his grave. There were lots of ways the support group helped. I was glad I went because it helped me heal faster than trying to do it on my own. 🤍🤍

🤍 *Bree, 16*

Final thoughts on suicide

Teens who are thinking about suicide are often afraid to get help. They don't want to be teased, they are often ashamed or embarrassed, they don't want to be labeled as mentally ill, they are afraid of counseling, and the list goes on. There are a lot of reasons why they're afraid to get help, but if you are feeling suicidal, *you are not alone*. Please, hold on one more day, reach out, don't keep this a secret, and let other people help you through this. You can always call the Suicide Hotline at 1-800-273-TALK (8255).

DRUGS AND ALCOHOL

🤍🤍 My first experience with drinking was at my cousin's house when I was fourteen. At first, I didn't try any, but I was curious about what it would taste like. My parents always looked like they were having so much fun when they drank. I didn't think it would hurt to have a couple of beers, and at first it was kind of fun. I felt relaxed and talked more, but then I felt really sick. Yuck, I didn't think it would be this way. 🤍🤍

🤍 *Lydia, 15*

Most girls I talk to say drinking and drugs are everywhere. For many, it starts to show up in middle school but definitely by high school. Some find that it's really hard to find a group where their peers aren't drinking on the weekends. Knowing the facts, learning how to stand up to peer pressure, and finding other ways to have fun are helpful in dealing with drugs and alcohol in your life. Watch other girls talking about this at http://www.youtube.com/girlswithdreams.

❝ My drinking started my freshman year in high school. I knew where my parents kept their alcohol. They didn't pay attention to how much they had, so it was pretty easy to sneak it. At first it was just with my friends, but then I started drinking whenever I was upset.

Pretty soon I started hanging out with other kids who drank. They also did drugs, and before you knew it, I was doing them, too. I almost didn't graduate from high school. At the time, I didn't think it was a big deal, but now that I'm trying to get my life on track and finish college, I can see how the drinking and drugs just created problems. They were masking the real issues. Looking back, I wish my parents had found out. Maybe I could have gotten some help. ❞

♥ Annie, 21

Mixed messages

It's confusing to sort out all of the mixed messages. On the one hand, you hear "Don't do it," and on the other hand, ads make it look like fun, parents enjoy it, and some adults even allow underage drinking in their homes.

Teens and adults use alcohol and drugs for many reasons, but here are the most popular. If you've ever tried drinking and drugs, ask yourself, "What was my reason?"

- You might have been curious or wanted to experiment.
- You were trying to fit in.
- You wanted to hurt yourself.

- You were trying to escape pain or feel good.
- You wanted the excitement of it.
- You thought it would be fun.

❝ I was the designated driver for this party. I didn't really like to drink, but then someone offered me a pill. I thought, *This won't hurt if I just try it once; and besides, they said it would make me feel really good. Besides, it's not like it's an illegal drug. It's an antidepressant or something like that.* The problem was that it was more than an antidepressant. It was a painkiller, and I became addicted to it. I never thought I would be addicted to anything. Pretty soon I was lying to my parents and sneaking it behind their backs. All that mattered was this stupid drug.

They eventually figured out something was wrong because my grades dropped and we started fighting all the time. They made me see a counselor. I was really mad at them at first, but now I'm so glad it happened that way. If I hadn't gotten help, my life probably would have been ruined by my addiction to a tiny pill.

I've had to make new friends now. That has been the hardest part because your senior year is supposed to be the best, but it has been hard to find a group to fit into. I'm just taking it one day at a time and looking forward to college next year. ❞

♥ *Sunny, 18*

For Julie, the situation was slightly different. She knew she'd probably be the only one not drinking at the party, and she was right. Part of her didn't even want to go, but this seemed better than sitting home alone.

❝ It was really hard being the only one not drinking. Everyone looked like they were having so much fun. But they were also acting really stupid.

I don't need to drink to have fun. Nonetheless, it's hard being the only one who isn't drinking. **)**

♥ *Julie, 17*

Impact on growth and judgment

As a teenager, your body and brain are still developing, and putting illegal substances into your body can affect its growth, as well as your judgment. We know from research and from talking to girls that more will have unprotected sex and/or do more than they had planned sexually as a result of drinking or using drugs.

((I was sixteen, and we were watching our school basketball state championships. We stayed for the weekend with some friends. The first night my friend's friend offered us something to drink. I knew it was alcohol, and it actually tasted good because it was mixed with grape juice or something like that. I didn't even have much to drink, and I was really excited to hang out with Travis from the basketball team. He had something to drink, too. I was just in awe of him. One thing led to another, and before I knew it, we were doing things sexually I had never done before. I didn't want to have sex, and he respected that, but I felt icky the next day. **)**

♥ *Veronica, 16*

As awful as this situation was, Veronica was really lucky. Not only was she underage, but she didn't really know what was in her drink. She's also lucky that the boy respected her and didn't force her to have sex, but she still did things sexually she wished she hadn't done. *The bottom line is this: alcohol impairs judgment and increases risky sexual behavior.*

How do you know whether you're addicted?

Anyone can become addicted to drugs or alcohol, regardless of whether they're rich or poor, get good grades or bad, or have broken or complete families. However, you are more at risk if one of your parents is an alcoholic. It might be hard to tell whether you're addicted, especially if you're stuck in a place of denial, but if you answer yes to any of the following questions, you may well be addicted.

- If you have a problem or get angry, do you turn to this substance?
- Do you drink or do drugs by yourself?
- Do you drink or do drugs every day?
- Do you feel you can't live without alcohol or drugs?
- Has your drug or alcohol use started to affect your grades, work, or extracurricular activities?
- Has it had an impact on your family or friends?

If you have an addiction and need help, try to be honest about it. Talk to your parents or another adult and find a professional to talk to. Be open to the fact that you may need to change your lifestyle beyond breaking your addiction. You may need to make new friends and come up with new strategies for dealing with peer pressure. It's not easy, but if you want help, you can start to turn your life around.

Other ways to have fun

Yes, there are alternatives to getting drunk with your friends. Here are a few ideas girls shared.

- Get dressed up in your favorite genre or costume and go bowling.
- Have your own dance party.
- Have a bonfire and sing songs, talk, or roast marshmallows.
- Girls Night Out! Create your own Do-It-Yourself Spa.

- Are you musical? Pull together your own band or miniconcert.
- Get outdoors . . . go to your favorite park, climbing place, or lie outside and watch the stars.
- Surprise someone with a good deed. Make them their favorite cookies, wash their car, and so on—get the idea?
- Hit all of the tourist spots in your town.
- Hang out at the local coffee shop.

EATING DISORDERS

I don't know one girl, including myself, who has never made or thought a negative comment about her body. It's thoughts like "I'm so fat, "I hate my hair," or "I'm not pretty enough." However, sometimes girls feel these to the extreme in cases like eating disorders. Sometimes girls with a negative body image can't stop obsessing about their weight, and it turns into an eating disorder. There are multiple disorders, but some of the most common are anorexia and bulimia.

The facts about eating disorders:

- According to the Academy for Eating Disorders (www.aedweb.org/), 1 percent of female adolescents suffer from anorexia. In other words, one out of every 100 young women between ten and twenty years old is starving herself—sometimes to death. The academy also adds that at any given time 10 percent or more of late adolescent women report symptoms of eating disorders. Even though these symptoms may not warrant a full diagnosis, they often cause problems.
- Nationwide, a 2007 CDC survey showed that 45.2 percent of high school students were trying to lose weight, and 11.8 percent of

high school students went without eating for twenty-four hours or more to lose weight or to keep from gaining weight.

How to know if you have an eating disorder

" I don't remember how it started exactly, but it became a game to me. Hiding my lack of eating from my parents and my doctor, I was determined to be thin. I would take any extra minute I had to exercise, whether I was waiting for the bus or running up and down the stairs twice in between my classes at school. "

♥ *Melinda, 13*

Only a physician can diagnose you, but here are a few things to consider:

Anorexia nervosa

Anorexics starve themselves excessively and typically lose at least 25 percent of their average body weight.

- Do you think about food all of the time?
- Do you control and limit what you eat?
- Do you think you are fat? Are you obsessed with how much you weigh?
- Do you hide what you eat or don't eat from your family and friends?
- Have you missed your period three consecutive times?
- Are you fearful of becoming fat, even when you are underweight?

On the other hand, bulimics binge eat and follow this by vomiting or laxative use. Typically they are near normal weight, but some might be underweight.

Bulimia nervosa

- Do you obsess about your weight?
- Are you fearful of becoming fat?

- Do you eat high quantities of food in secret?
- Do you make yourself throw up after eating or use laxatives?

This type of behavior is very dangerous. The repeated cycle of throwing up hurts the body and causes multiple health problems.

Many people with eating disorders are more likely to suffer from other problems like depression, loneliness, anxiety, substance abuse, low self-esteem, and obsessions with weight loss.

Even if you don't have a full-blown eating disorder, if you are spending an extraordinary amount of time obsessing about your weight, counting calories, or exercising, it's still not healthy. These extreme habits can put your health and safety at risk. More scary is the fact that they can rapidly spiral out of control and turn into an eating disorder.

Here's the all-important bottom line: it's vital to not keep this a secret and get appropriate treatment for all these problems, and the sooner you get started, the better the outcome.

It's important to know that willpower and determination can't always make anorexia go away. If you think you might be suffering from an eating disorder, it's very important that you seek professional help and support from others.

What can you do if you have an eating disorder?

- Don't be afraid to talk about it.
- Tell a friend, teacher, parent, coach, youth group leader, doctor, counselor, or nutritionist what you're going through.
- Also check out the National Eating Disorders Association's website (www.nationaleatingdisorders.org) for many great resources.
- It's important to get support to change your thoughts and behaviors. Doing so could save your life.

With thorough treatment, most teenagers can be successfully treated for their eating disorders by a child and adolescent psychiatrist. Treatment usually requires a team approach, including individual therapy, family therapy, working with a primary care physician, working with a nutritionist, and taking medication.

❝❝ I was in eighth grade. I lived in a big family with two parents and three younger brothers. Everyone looked up to me. I had good grades and worked really hard at school. One of the guys at school was talking about girls who were too fat. I took a look in the mirror and didn't like what I saw. I thought if I could lose five pounds, then I would look good. Well, five pounds turned into ten pounds, which turned into fifteen pounds. I became obsessed with how I looked and how much I weighed. I would calculate ways I could add extra exercise into my day, and my diet consisted of diet soda and crackers.

Things spun out of control, and my parents took me to see a doctor. This was the first of many hospital visits over the next couple of years, but I was one of the lucky ones. In college, I lost my roommate Samantha to anorexia. She literally starved herself to death.

I still wasn't sure how to deal with my eating disorder, but this was a wake-up call for me. It helped me turn the corner and make progress with the things my nutritionist, doctor, and therapist had been talking about. I still deal with eating issues, but I'm a normal weight now. I know how to get help, and I'm glad I'm alive. ❞❞

> Even if you don't have a full-blown eating disorder, if you are spending an extraordinary amount of time obsessing about your weight, counting calories, or exercising, it's still not healthy.

♥ *Jacquelyn, 20*

Being overweight

❝ ❝ I've always been overweight, or at least as long as I can remember. My whole family is overweight, and it really bugs me. I always feel like people are staring at me, and it's even worse when I have to go somewhere with my parents. Then I really feel the stares. ❞ ❞

♥ *Natasha, 16*

For every girl who struggles with being too thin, many more struggle with being overweight. Childhood and teenage obesity are on the rise. In fact, a 2007 CDC report, at www.cdc.gov, states that 13 percent of high school students are obese. This is tough for many reasons. Girls I've talked to tell me about being teased, feeling self-conscious, or not being able to find clothes they like. Sometimes they feel isolated by other girls or even boys. This is paralyzing and can even lead to depression, as well as serious health problems, but there is hope. Whether you have been overweight your entire life or experienced a significant weight gain more recently, if you want to make a change, it is possible.

What is a perfect weight? I know it's not what we see blasted in front of us on most TV ads. Ideally, you should find out from your physician what the right target weight is for you. It's important, not from a cosmetic perspective, but because your health is at stake.

❝ ❝ When I went for my eighth-grade physical, my doctor told me I was overweight. Those weren't her exact words, but I was so embarrassed. I decided I needed to do something about this. I talked to my mom, and she told me she'd help. I stopped eating the lunches at school and brought my own. I started walking every day, and I cut back on soda and treats and drank more water. In just two months, I had lost ten pounds! That was more than a year ago, and I feel great! ❞ ❞

♥ *Paige, 15*

What can you do if you are overweight?

- Find a doctor you like and talk to him or her about your weight.
- Find out what a good weight for you is and get input on how you can achieve your goals.
- Get to the source of your overeating. What are the underlying causes? Often, an emotional issue needs to be addressed.
- Get a good support system in place. This is key! Surround yourself with people who are positive and who can encourage you. This might be your parents, friends, a nutritionist, a fitness trainer, a teacher, a counselor, and so on.
- Read the success stories of others and stay positive. Remind yourself of your beauty every day.
- Have a strong "Why?"—as in why you want to do this. Is it to look and stay healthy? Do you have another reason?
- Think about your future. What will happen if you don't lose the weight? How will you feel if you do lose the weight?
- Join a program. Local hospitals, fitness clubs, summer camps, and others have programs. It's so much easier when you're not alone.
- Make peace with your body. Love yourself, no matter what— and no matter your weight.

DATING VIOLENCE

Nothing is worse than being abused emotionally, mentally, or physically. If you think this might be happening to you or a friend, read about the warning signs below. Then make sure you read Chapter 2, which also addresses the issue of dating violence.

Know the early warning signs of dating violence. *Does your partner:*

- Try to make the relationship go too fast? Do you feel pressure to have sex or get really serious?

- Act very jealous and possessive? Limit time with your friends?
- Blame you for his or her mistakes or tell you it's your fault for being treated badly?
- Try to control you? Does he or she want to decide what you wear, whom you can talk to, and where you can go?
- Not value your opinion? Does he or she try to limit or eliminate the time you spend with family and friends?
- Try to get you alone when you don't want to be?
- Talk about sex like it's a game?
- Use verbal and emotional violence by yelling, swearing, manipulating, spreading rumors, and so on?
- Put other people down using sexual language?
- Use a lot of guilt trips?
- Use drugs and/or drink too much and then later blame the alcohol and drugs for his or her behavior?
- Try to use drugs or alcohol to influence you?
- Threaten to hurt you physically?
- Have a history of violence or other bad relationships in which he or she has abused a former boyfriend or girlfriend?
- Accept and defend the use of violence by other people?

When you're with your partner, do you:

- Lose your confidence?
- Feel frightened or scared?
- Worry about saying or doing the wrong thing?
- Change your actions or words in order to avoid a fight?

If any of these warning signs hit home and you are starting to feel funny, scared, weird, or uncomfortable, trust yourself and get out of the situation. This could turn into a violent relationship, or you may already be in one.

If you fear for your safety and believe there is no way out, talk to someone you trust, go to the police, or call a hotline such as the National Teen Dating Abuse Helpline at 1-866-331-9474. When you call, you will be able to talk to someone about your situation and get help, including a plan for safety.

Also look out for friends who may be in violent dating situations or relationships. Do any of your friends' relationships show the warning signs listed above? Do your friends show signs that they have been physically hurt in some way? *Keep in mind that your friends may not tell you and may even hide some of the things that are happening.*

Friends (or anyone) in violent relationships may:

- Stop spending time with you, other friends, or family members
- Change their personal style, clothes, or makeup
- Seem to lose their self-confidence or begin to have problems making decisions
- Start having trouble at school with grades
- Quit participating in regular school activities
- Start using or increase their use of alcohol or drugs

If you believe a friend is in an abusive relationship, talk with an adult you trust about the situation so you aren't carrying the burden by yourself. Though you might want to, it's highly unlikely you will be able to "rescue" your friend on your own.

Don't put up with dating violence. No one deserves to be treated this way. You can read more about this at our website, www.girls withdreams.com.

SEXUAL ABUSE

Unfortunately, thousands of young people are sexually abused each year. If this has happened to you, I'm very, very sorry. *Please know you are not alone and whatever happened to you was not your fault. If you are still keeping this secret, it's never too late to get help and heal.* The site www.aacap.org states that 80,000 reports are made each year, even though the actual number of cases is believed to be much higher (since many cases go unreported). According to www.apa.org, any time an adult forces or coerces a child into any type of sexual activity, from fondling to intercourse, this is considered abuse. It isn't just about physical contact. It could include exposing children to pornography or themselves. The abuse can happen from another young person as well. Professionals agree that child sexual abuse is and remains a serious problem.

It is important for all of us to understand and help each other learn these two important facts.

- **No one has the right to touch you.** No one has the right to touch your body in any way that makes you feel uncomfortable. If someone suggests this or tries this, tell them NO. If it's already happened, this isn't your fault and you need to reach out to someone for help.
- **You can be respectful and still disobey adults.** Children are taught to listen to and respect adults. However, this doesn't mean if an adult is trying to get you to do something that makes you feel uncomfortable you have to go along. It's okay to say NO if an adult is putting you into any awkward situation.

Some Facts About Sexual Abuse:

- Anyone is at risk for sexual abuse. It occurs across all cultural, social, and economic backgrounds.
- Surprisingly, the perpetrator is usually a family member or someone you know.
- Young people who have been abused may develop many problems like depression, withdrawal, nightmares, seductiveness, school problems, secretiveness, suicidal behavior, aggression, and others.

Tips for Victims (as found at www.apa.org and www.aacap.org):

- **Get help, even if you're scared.** If you think you are a victim of sexual abuse, find an adult you trust. If that is too hard, many resources online can help. Try going to http://www.childhelpusa.org/ or call 1-800-4-A-CHILD (1-800-422-4453). You can also find resources at the end of this book.
- **Be aware of the negative effects.** The initial or short-term effects of abuse usually occur within two years of when the abuse stops. However, the negative effects of child sexual abuse can affect victims for many years and into adulthood.
- **You can heal.** Victims shared several key things that help them deal with the abuse and start to heal: handling the guilt they feel about the abuse, attending workshops about sexual abuse, reading about it, finding a support group, and meeting with a therapist.
- **Give yourself space and time to recover.** Research has also shown that the passage of time is a key element in getting better.
- **Remember your family.** The support you have from your family, as well as how well your family is functioning, plays a big role in your recovery from the abuse. There are many counseling and services available for families of abused children.

TEEN PREGNANCY

❝ We usually used a condom, but this time we didn't have one. We didn't think it would be a big deal because we hadn't had problems before. Well, about one month later I found out I was pregnant. Joey was so stressed-out he stopped talking to me. How can he be stressed? I'm the one who's pregnant. I have never been so confused and scared. ❞

♥ *Tanya, 16*

The facts about teen pregnancy

- The CDC reports that about one-third of the girls in the United States get pregnant before age twenty.
- Of those pregnancies, one-third will end in spontaneous miscarriage, one-third will end in abortion, and one-third will result in a baby.
- The teen birth rate in the United States rose in 2006 for the first time since 1991.

> Did you know that less than one-third of teens who have babies before the age of eighteen finish high school?

What should you do if you're pregnant?

- Try not to panic. You have a lot of big decisions to make, and you need to give yourself time and space to think about them.
- It's important to get help. Don't try to make this decision alone. Talk to a friend or an adult you trust.
- At our website, find a community agency to help you.
- Whatever you do, don't let this ruin your dreams. Things may need to change a little bit, but you can still have a bright future.
- Most of all, figure out a way to complete school. If you don't have an education, your dreams truly will be ruined. Unfortunately, most girls who do get pregnant don't finish school, which ultimately

means that many of them live in poverty or make less money in their lifetime.

• Listen to other girls' experience at www.youtube.com/girlswithdreams.

❝ I was so confused, so scared about what to do. I wasn't ready to be a mom, and the guy who had gotten me pregnant freaked out and wasn't any help. I felt like my only option was abortion. On the way to the doctor's office, I got this gut feeling, and I just couldn't go through with it. The doctor's office was really great and gave me more referrals to people I could talk to. I eventually decided adoption was what I wanted to do. I was able to pick out her parents and family. It wasn't easy carrying the baby around for nine months and then saying good-bye. ❞

♥ Jackie, 18

❝ I thought if I had a baby, everything would be better. I thought I'd finally have someone to love and to love me back. Sometimes I regret having my baby when I was sixteen. It didn't make things easier, just harder. ❞

♥ Jana, 17

If you've made a decision and feel bad about it, don't keep it a secret. Talk to your friends, your doctors, and other girls who have been through what you are going through.

SEXUALLY TRANSMITTED DISEASES (STDS)

❝ As I sat in the doctor's office wondering where the pain was coming from, I kept thinking in my head, how could I have an STD? We were just fooling around, and we didn't even have sex! Ten minutes later, I found out I would have to wait a few days for lab results. I later found out I had genital herpes. There is no cure for this STD. Why wasn't I more careful? ❞❞

♥ Anita, 17

Many girls think that you can only get an STD if you're having sex, but that isn't true. These are tough personal decisions, and you need to know the facts, information, and resources that are available when you are thinking about your sexuality. It's very confusing! Our society sends so many mixed messages. On the one hand, we hear "don't be sexual," yet starting at the age of three we are bombarded with overly sexual role models from dolls to rock stars to TV.

By the time high school rolls around, random hookups and cuddle parties are promoted as the norm. But what is really normal? What is sex really supposed to be like? What about committed, solid relationships? What about waiting? Again, we need to stop hiding and keeping secrets and start talking openly. It's dangerous to have a "know-it-all" attitude. I know so many girls are afraid to ask questions of their parents. If that is too hard, reach out to books, mentors, and other resources before you make your decisions.

The facts about STDs (as found on www.cdc.gov)

- Teenagers remain at high risk for STD infection. By the twelfth grade, 65 percent of high school students have had sexual intercourse, and one in five has had four or more sexual partners.
- Young people (ages fifteen to twenty-four) have five times the reported chlamydia rate as the general population.
- Most high school students undergoing routine physical examinations do not talk to their health care practitioner about preventing sexually transmitted diseases (STDs) or pregnancy.

If you are sexually active, thinking about STDs is part of the picture.

What is an STD?

Sexually transmitted diseases, or STDs (which used to be called venereal diseases, or VD), are infectious diseases that spread from person to person through intimate contact. Sexually transmitted diseases have become common among teens. Because teens are at high risk for getting certain STDs, it's critical to know about them and how you can protect yourself. See how much you know by taking our quiz on page 237.

What increases your chances of getting an STD?

- **Sexual activity at a young age.** The younger you start having sex, the greater your chances are of becoming infected with an STD.
- **Lots of sexual partners.** If you have sexual contact—not just intercourse but any form of intimate activity—with lots of partners, you are more at risk than those who stay with the same person.
- **Unprotected sex.** Latex condoms are the only form of birth control that reduces your risk of getting an STD. Other birth control methods may help you prevent pregnancy, but they don't protect you against STDs.

❝ My best friend called me crying. 'It was just one time,' she sobbed. 'John didn't have a condom, and we did it without one, and something isn't right. I made a doctor's appointment. Will you go with me?'

I went with her to the appointment. She felt lucky to find out she had a treatable STD because she had feared the worst—AIDS. ❞

♥ *Ryan, 18*

Preventing and treating STDs

Abstaining from all types of sexual contact is the only sure way to completely prevent sexually transmitted diseases. Think about it—it's much easier to prevent STDs than to treat them. If you're going to have sex, you want to know as much information as you can so you can make an informed decision. You'll want to make sure you read the chapter on dating (Chapter 2) and also talk to your doctor, parent, or another adult you trust. If you decide to move forward with sex, the best way to lower your risk of getting an STD is to use a condom.

Teen girls who are thinking about being sexually active should talk to their doctor and get regular gynecological examinations. This is crucial because it gives doctors an opportunity to teach you about STDs and how to guard against them. Second, your doctor can check for STDs while they're still in their initial, most treatable stages.

If you want these exams to help you, you need to talk with your doctor, and let him or her know if you're thinking about having sex or if you've already started. This is true for all types of sex: oral, vaginal, and anal. Even if you're scared or embarrassed, don't let that stop you from seeing a doctor. Whether you think you have an STD or you fear your partner might, waiting can allow a disease to advance and cause more damage.

If you don't have a doctor or prefer not to see your family doctor, you may be able to find a local clinic in your area where you can get an exam confidentially, or you can call the national STD hotline at 1-800-227-8922 for information and referrals. These hotlines are confidential.

Just remember that not all infections in the genitals are caused by STDs. Sometimes you may have symptoms that seem very like those of STDs even though you've never had sex. For example, a yeast infection can easily be confused with an STD.

Quiz

How Much Do You Know About STDs?

1. If untreated, STDs can cause permanent damage   ○ T   ○ F
   such as infertility (the inability to have a baby) and
   even death (in the case of HIV/AIDS).

   This is true. It's important to seek medical attention if you think
   you have an STD.

2. The only way to get an STD is to have sexual   ○ T   ○ F
   intercourse.

   This is false. The main reason STDs spread so rapidly in
   teenagers is misinformation. STDs don't just happen during
   sexual intercourse. A person can get STDs like herpes or genital
   warts through skin-to-skin contact with an infected area or sore.

3. You can't get STDs if you have oral or anal sex.   ○ T   ○ F
   False. This is also untrue because the viruses or bacteria that
   cause STDs can enter the body through tiny cuts or tears in the
   mouth and anus as well as the genitals.

4. You can have an STD and not realize it.   ○ T   ○ F
   This is true. And because of this, STDs also spread easily
   because you can't always tell whether someone has an infection.
   People who don't realize they have an STD are in danger of
   passing on an infection to their sexual partners without even realizing it. Also, many medical exams don't test for major STDs.

SELF-HARMING BEHAVIORS

❝ I began cutting when I was sixteen. I used it to cope with my anger
and to make myself feel better. It was relaxing, and the act of hiding the

cuts and caring for them was a high that I was addicted to.

My alcohol use was also out of hand, and when I cut, it always ended up too deep and resulted in stitches. I stopped counting stitches when I acquired more than fifty, but I didn't stop cutting. I had no desire to, and when people wanted me to, it was like they were trying to take something from me that kept me alive.

I had a wonderful support system in my family and friends. I knew it hurt them to see my behavior, but that did not stop me. I decided to stop cutting when I was twenty-two years old. I'd been in and out of mental institutions for suicidal behavior, which only angered me because I wasn't trying to kill myself. I now realize I very well could have accidentally killed myself because the cuts began to get so deep and careless.

♥ *Abby, 26*

What is it?

Self-injury (also known as self-mutilation, self-harm, or self-abuse) is a growing and dangerous trend among teens that involves deliberately injuring one's own body. It includes things like deliberately:

- Cutting
- Scratching
- Burning
- Punching
- Hair pulling
- Excessive body piercing or tattooing
- Infecting oneself
- Picking at scabs
- Breaking bones

Cutting arms and legs is common. Researchers estimate that at least 2 million people in the United States are self injurers (or 1 percent), as found on www.helpguide.org. Wendy Lader, a psychologist who has coauthored books on self-injury, says the rate is much higher among adolescents and females.

Many self-injurers attempt to conceal the resultant scarring with clothing and, if discovered, often make excuses as to how an injury occurred. A significant number also struggle with eating disorders and alcohol or substance abuse, which only intensifies the threats to their health and quality of life.

Why do people self-injure?

If you've never hurt yourself, it is difficult to understand. Often, it occurs because the person hasn't really learned to express or identify feelings in a healthy way (www.helpguide.org). This behavior is usually deliberate, repetitive, and impulsive. Here is some more information (as found on www.helpguide.org):

- Some who self-injure report physical and/or sexual abuse during their childhoods.
- Many report that during their childhood they were discouraged from expressing feelings, especially anger and sadness.
- Self-injurers say they feel an emptiness inside, over- or understimulated, and unable to share their feelings; they are also lonely, misunderstood, and fearful of close relationships.
- Hurting themselves is not usually a suicide attempt; however, their lack of self-control and addictive nature of their acts might lead them to real suicide attempts. They feel that cutting helps them cope with pain and overwhelming emotions.
- Only a licensed professional can determine the diagnosis for someone who self-injures, as it can be a symptom of several mental illnesses.

Getting help

If you or your friends are engaging in self-injuring behaviors, seek help. Here are some suggestions:

- Talk to someone you trust or call 1-800-DONT CUT (1-800-366-8288. Depending on your situation, your doctor might recommend outpatient therapy, inpatient therapy, or a specialized self-injury hospital program and/or medication. More resources are at http://www.selfinjury.com and http://www.helpguide.org/mental/self_injury.htm.
- Think about your "triggers." What happens before you decide to cut? For example, you may cut when you feel rejected by friends or when you're sad, angry, or disappointed. If you can figure out what usually sets you off, you can start to deal with that problem.
- Find appropriate alternative coping strategies that work for you. It's best to talk about this with a professional. Use contracts, journals, and behavior logs to help you regain self-control.
- Work with a therapist to create a "coping kit." Items in your kit might include a timer, music, puzzle, word game, journal, rubber band, stress ball, gum or candy, encouraging notes to yourself or from others, and ideas of other activities (go for a walk, call a friend, draw). Instead of reaching for a knife, reach for your box of healthy ways to pass time. Once that intense feeling of "I need to feel better now" has passed, it's easier to avoid self-injury.
- Try replacing the word "cut" with "hurt." Truthfully, you do not want to hurt yourself. Using the word "hurt" forces you to realize what you are doing.
- Be realistic. Ask yourself: Should this (whatever just happened that is bothering you) really matter in the big picture? Will it matter in twenty-four hours? If you react by hurting yourself, will it be helpful? Thinking through the situation and using positive self-talk gives you time to decide how to react, as it did for Abby below.

❝ I believe I had to grow up mentally and change all my behaviors to quit cutting. It was difficult to change the way I thought when anger crept inside me, but I changed my friends, changed my drug and alcohol use to minimal, and decided I did not want to cut. It just isn't worth it.

I relapsed when I was twenty-three and cut myself while intoxicated. I couldn't believe how quickly my thoughts went to thinking cutting would help me. I decided no more self-abuse and have not cut in three years. It does not enter my mind when I am angry anymore because I have trained my brain not to think that way. I believe self-injury is an addiction, and to get through it you need the same support as if quitting a drug.

I had many people I would call at any hour to talk to, and I suggest always calling before you act on a thought. One coping mechanism that got me through this addiction was painting. I would paint all night and write angry poetry. Find an outlet that helps you express yourself and stick to it. Also, if you want to cut, wait fifteen minutes. After those fifteen minutes, wait another fifteen minutes. This technique can get you all the way till morning, when you should realize you don't need to cut. Keep a journal with you at all times and write everything in it; it will help you not feel so bottled up.

People love you or they wouldn't be so angry when you are hurting yourself, but you have to decide for yourself that you will not self-injure anymore. Little cuts are not okay because the addiction will pull you in deeper, wanting more. Decide and believe, and you will feel a high that you overcame it. That high, I promise you, is the best high. ❞

❤ *Abby, 26*

DEALING WITH GRIEF AND LOSS

❝ Since second grade I've known something wasn't right with my mom. She's always tried to hide it, but I knew something was wrong, between all the doctors' appointments. Now I'm thirteen, and the cancer has returned for the third time. I'm really tired of it. ❞

❤ *Deidra, 13*

Death. It's something we can't change, but it's one of the hardest things to understand and come to terms with. If you are reading this, I am sorry for your loss. I hope you find the peace you need to move forward.

No one deals with grief, the feeling we have when we experience a loss, the same way. In fact, there is no right or wrong way to grieve. But certain feelings are commonly felt by most individuals. These are known as the five stages of grief, discovered by Elisabeth Kübler-Ross.

1. **Denial** is usually the first response, as in, "I can't believe this happened" or "This didn't really happen."
2. **Anger** is common, as in, "I'm so angry! This isn't fair!"
3. **Bargaining** is another common feeling, as in, "I promise I will never drink alcohol or yell at my mother again if she just gets well" or, "If I had only helped her out, or sat and read with her, or cleaned the house . . ."
4. **Depression** is common, as in, "I'm so sad. I'll never feel better. I'll never feel good again."
5. Finally, there is **acceptance**, as in, "I might not ever be able to understand why this happened, but I know it did happen." At this stage, you are finally able to move forward.

People who are grieving often experience denial first, but these stages don't always happen in the order given above; we may experience the different stages over and over.

My best friend was driving home from work when her car was hit by a drunk driver. This couldn't have happened to Pam. There is no way. They must have the wrong Pam! (Denial)

This isn't fair. I hate my mom's doctors. They don't know what they're doing. Why didn't they get all of the cancer? I will never forgive them. (Anger)

I lost my dad to a heart attack. I was only thirteen, and he was forty-three. If only I had made him eat better or go on walks with me, maybe he wouldn't have had such a bad heart. (Bargaining)

Just go away. I don't want to talk to anyone about Jerry's death. I just want to sleep. I don't feel like doing much of anything. (Depression)

It's been three years since we lost Ariel. I still really miss her and think about her, but I'm doing better. I'm happy most days, and I know Ariel would want it that way. (Acceptance)

How can you deal with the death of a loved one?

A number of actions can help you move through your loss to a place where you feel better. Try any or all of these:

- Remember, it's okay to talk about the person.
- Write a letter to your loved one.
- Visit your loved one at his or her grave.
- Plant a tree or garden in your loved one's memory.
- Finish an important project.

• Assemble pictures to make a collage or create a memorial in the form of a book or pictures.

• Tell or write down stories you love.

• Get your feelings out. Don't be afraid to show how you are feeling. A strong person doesn't hold everything in.

• Find a support group of others who are dealing with grief. Check online or with your school counselor or local hospital.

• Be patient with yourself. It takes time to heal.

❝ The longer you live without loved ones doesn't mean that you're going to get over it and it won't be as hard. I have just learned to live with it. Keep the memories of your loved one close to your heart, because as you grow up, the memories start to fade. Losing someone you love is not the end of your life. It's just a part of your life that you can learn to grow through and live on the legacy they couldn't continue. ❞

♥ *Barbara Jean, 17*

Dealing with illness in someone you love

If someone you love is ill, don't panic. You undoubtedly feel scared and overwhelmed, but think about how many people survive illnesses. Get as much information as you can about what is going on and talk honestly to the people you love. Try to live as normally as possible under the circumstances and stay balanced. This will keep you healthy while you're dealing with this.

Give yourself a break from time to time. It's okay to hang out with your friends. It's okay to watch a movie and try to relax in the moment. You might feel a little guilty, but you need some down-time in order to deal with everything in front of you.

Sometimes kids have more responsibilities when a parent or sibling is ill. If it becomes too much, don't be afraid to say so, and don't be afraid to talk about your feelings—you might be really angry that this is happening. Sometimes it's easy to take it out on the people we love, but try to release it in a positive way.

Finally, try to join a support group. Many hospitals have support groups for families dealing with serious illnesses, and it can make a huge difference to spend time with other people who are going through the same emotions and experiences you are.

Even though your loved one may still be with you, it's important to understand the stages of grief. Depending on how much your parents' lifestyle has changed because of the illness, this is like dealing with grief. The one who is sick is undoubtedly feeling sad, confused, frightened, and maybe even angry as well. Let the illness be a way to unite you in your struggle and grief. Don't let it tear you apart.

Seven Tips Every Girl Needs to Deal with Tough Stuff

Tip One: You Gotta Use Your Gut

Before you take the first hit, cut your skin, get behind the wheel drunk, have sex, skip school, or shoplift that top you can't afford, stop and listen to your gut.

The hard part is that you may not want to always listen to your gut. You might already be doing something that deep down you know you shouldn't be doing. I know that when I was not eating very much, I ignored my gut. But ultimately, if you're going to deal with your problems, you have to be willing to face yourself.

❝ I was having a blast at this party with my friends. We weren't supposed to be drinking, but we were anyway. I had come with two of my girlfriends, and they were ready to go. There was one problem. I didn't have a driver's license, and I really thought that both of them were too drunk to drive. They each insisted they were fine. I knew they weren't; my gut was telling me not to get in the car with them, but part of me was saying, 'We're only driving a couple of miles; we'll be fine.'

I headed out to the car with my friends, but then I couldn't do it, and I couldn't let them do it, either. I grabbed the keys and ran back inside. **"**

♥ *Isobel, 17*

Tip Two: Discover Your Strengths and Use Them

You will need to rely on your strengths to help you overcome the genuinely difficult problems you face.

> Character cannot be developed in ease and quiet. Only through experience of trial and suffering can the soul be strengthened, vision cleared, ambition inspired, and success achieved.
> —Helen Keller

" Losing my mom was the hardest thing I've ever had to deal with, but I got through it by relying on my strengths. Not only was I a really positive person, but I was good at talking to people. At first when my mom died, I pushed people away, but I came to see that I needed to spend time with other people and stay focused on the good things in life to get through this. I know my mom wanted me to be happy. **"**

♥ *Meggan, 15*

Even on your bad days, you matter. You count. Don't let yourself ever believe anything different. Whatever it is you're dealing with, you're not alone! You must realize how important it is to get help, even if you're afraid. Be honest about what is going on, and do your best to uncover the source of your pain. This is the hardest part, but it's essential if you're going to be successful in coming to terms with the tough stuff in your life.

My friend Nicole had her share of tough times as a teen. In her twenties she created a game (www.shiftthegame.com) to remind each of us that we have the ability to control our thoughts. Once you become aware of what you're thinking and believing, you can change your life. In essence, what you believe is what you will experience. This is another great tool you can use to help deal with tough times and to recognize your own strengths and value.

Tip Three: Choose the Right Friends and Respect Them

Take a good, hard look at your friends. Are they the right people to help you get through what you're dealing with? If they are, great. If they aren't, you need to make new friends. *Surround yourself with people you want to be like.*

By the same token, if your friends are dealing with tough stuff, help them if you can, but also realize you can't always be their savior.

❝ I loved Jenny. She was a blast to be around. She had an infectious laugh, and we had a lot of fun together. We loved hanging out so much that we spent almost every extra minute of our days together. But there was another side to Jenny. She liked to party, and I didn't. I didn't think it was a big deal at first, but as I got closer to Jenny, I saw how wrong I was.

I wasn't sure what to say to her. I didn't think she would listen. I decided not to say anything about the drinking because I didn't think I could change her mind. It was hard, but we started to drift apart. She became really close to Kira, and it just made it hard to hang out. I always felt like the odd person out. It took a while for me to deal with this, but I eventually got over it and made other friends. ❞

♥ *Madison, 20*

Tip Four: Be Courageous and Confident

If you're dealing with a tough issue, it's going to take courage to do the three things necessary to overcome it:

- Face yourself honestly.
- Get help.
- Find and accept a new path for yourself.

> The thing you fear most has no power. Your fear of it is what has the power. Facing the truth really will set you free.
> — Oprah Winfrey

Ask yourself, "How does this challenge increase or decrease my confidence?" For example, when you are getting high, are you really being courageous, or are you avoiding the real issue? Does skipping school increase or decrease your confidence in the long run?

Being courageous and confident aren't always easy things to do. Don't feel like you have to tackle this alone. Surround yourself with people who make you feel confident and who are willing to help you when you get off track.

❝ I had a terrible childhood. I was sexually abused by my uncle, and my mother defended him (it was her brother). I never really knew my dad. He left us when I was only two. Then my mom died in a car accident when I was eleven, and I went to live with my other aunt and uncle. I was so angry about everything, I hated being there. They tried to love me, but I pushed them away. My aunt wouldn't accept this and made me see a counselor. I resisted for a while, but eventually I started to face the things that were making me mad. I learned how to deal with my past and how to focus on my future. My life wasn't always perfect, and I made my share of mistakes, but I'm proud to say I'm going to college next year. ❞

♥ *Kendra, 18*

Tip Five: Be Fit and Stay Fit

Most tough issues result from us trying to fix an emotional wound. The truth is that when

> The longer we dwell on misfortunes the greater is their power to harm us.
> —Voltaire

you're fit physically, emotionally, and mentally, you will have a shield for some of the issues you have to deal with. When you exercise, you release endorphins and other stress-reducing chemicals into your body.

Alisa's mom was a great role model. She loved to walk, and she always talked about how it cleared her mind. Alisa ran track. This cleared her mind. Alisa also made sure she took care of herself. She had good friends, and she ate healthy meals.

When her friend died in a car accident, depression hit Alisa. For a while, she was in pretty bad shape. She stopped running and didn't sleep well, but her friends and mom helped her get back on track. Starting to run again and taking care of herself helped her deal with the emotional pain of her friend's death.

Then again, don't underestimate the power of eating properly.

    " I didn't realize how much the food that I was eating was affecting the way I felt. I had heard a talk at school and decided to try some of the things they mentioned. I started eating breakfast (usually cereal). I had a healthy lunch (instead of french fries, I got a deli sandwich). I stopped drinking soda, except occasionally, and I made an effort to eat more fruits and veggies. I couldn't believe how different I felt. I had more energy through the day and could think more clearly. "

♥ *Madeline, 16*

Tip Six: Dream Big

When you're in the middle of dealing with tough stuff, sometimes the last thing you feel like you can do is "dream big."

> Sometimes I've believed as many as six impossible things before breakfast.
> —Lewis Carroll

Some girls who've had tough stuff to deal with their entire lives may never have dreamed. Even if you're one of these girls, ask yourself, "What do I want my life to ultimately look like?" Try to push yourself to think bigger, to look outside your day-to-day life. This will help you get out of your rut and begin to channel yourself in a new direction.

Next, ask yourself, "What are the results of my actions? Do they get me closer to or further from my dreams?"

> Ever since I was a little girl, I loved playing with hair and makeup. I would even put makeup on my dolls when my little sister wouldn't let me practice on her. Now I have a dream of opening up my own salon and spa. My dad thinks I'm crazy, but this is my dream. I don't know how I'm going to do it, but I hope to go to college to figure it out.
>
> ♥ Bailey, 17

Tip Seven: Get Outside of Yourself

Try handling the tough stuff in your life by reaching out to others. There is a whole world out there that needs us! It is by extending ourselves that we often

> Good actions give strength to ourselves and inspire good actions in others.
> —Plato

see we aren't the only ones with problems and that we need others as much as they need us. Just make sure you don't neglect yourself when you're reaching out.

" Our social studies teacher gave us a service project. I decided to volunteer at a local battered women's shelter. We babysat the kids so the moms could go to counseling. This was something really close to my heart. I never told anyone my dad used to beat my mom. Volunteering here was like therapy in many ways. It gave me a chance to give back and be there for other kids, just by showing them someone cared. "

♥ *Danielle, 15*

Think about it . . .

- If you had a magic wand, what would you change in your life? How can you start to make a small change?
- What tough stuff are you dealing with? Is this situation new, or is there a pattern? What is the underlying fear or pain?
- If you've lost your dream of a future, how can you get in touch with it?
- Who are your biggest supporters? If you feel alone and don't have any, whom could you let in?
- Think about summertime. What program could you become involved in? Could you volunteer somewhere?
- Are you setting yourself up for success or failure?
- Are you ready to change? Do you need to make amends? How have you overcome a hardship before? What can you learn from that and apply it to now?

Try it!

- Make sure you are looking at the big picture. Rate yourself on a scale of 1 to 10 (10 being great). How well are you taking care of yourself physically? Mentally? Socially? At school? With family? How do you feel about your score? Pick one area to improve.
- Dump your thoughts into a journal every day.

- Create your own stress shield: eat well, get enough sleep, and exercise every day.
- Don't give up on yourself—ever.
- Reach out to a friend or family member who is having a tough time. It feels good, and that act of kindness will come back to you.
- Create a dream board. Cut out images or words from magazines that symbolize your future and the life you want to create. Get a poster board or use the back of wrapping paper and paste your pictures in a special place to remind you of your big dreams.
- Make a pact with a friend about what you will and won't do.
- Start a Girls with Dreams Friend Circle to help you get through tough times.

8

What's Your Secret?

So, what's your big secret? Are you still hiding? I hope you've figured out that no matter what you've gone through or experienced, you're going to get through it, and you're not alone. Whatever your challenges are, whatever your secret is, there are thousands of other girls with the same challenges and the same

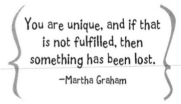

You are unique, and if that is not fulfilled, then something has been lost.

—Martha Graham

secret. Nothing is too embarrassing, shameful, or horrible to share. I hope you can move past your tough times and, yes, even your mistakes, and start creating the life you've always wanted. I hope you can value yourself enough to hold your expectations high for everything you do and every friendship you experience.

I hope you remember the biggest secret of all—the fact is that there's no one else like you in the entire universe. You are beautiful, amazing, and unique! Don't ever forget it! Don't you think that's amazing and something worth celebrating?

A FEW FINAL THINGS TO THINK ABOUT...

- Do you rely on your gut to help you make decisions? Are you listening to that little voice inside of you?
- Have you identified your strengths and are you using them to improve your life and your attitude? Of course, you'll still ask yourself from time to time the age-old question "Am I good enough?" The answer to that is yes. You are good enough! We all doubt ourselves from time to time, but sometimes these doubts can stop us in our tracks. Don't let that happen to you!

> *If you're able to be yourself, then you have no competition. All you have to do is get closer and closer to that essence.*
> —Barbara Cook

- Are you making the right friends, friends who support you? By the same token, are you being a good friend? Be pro-girl: build other girls up instead of tearing them down! Let's set a new standard for how we treat other girls! Contact us to help you start your own Girls with Dreams Friend Circle, and use this as your springboard for success.
- Are you courageous and confident? Whether you use courage to get help or to stand up for yourself, don't wait until it's too late, like other girls you have read about who have died from overdoses, anorexia, or suicide. "Heart" equals "courage." Respect your decisions, your heart, your actions, and your body, and act with courage!
- Are you keeping stress under control by keeping fit? Are you staying fit physically, mentally, and emotionally? Do you get rest, eat well, and exercise? Do you have friends, express your feelings, and stay levelheaded?
- Do you dream big? When you get an idea, do you think about how you can make it a little bigger? Don't stop yourself from being

open to new dreams and directions, and don't worry if you find
your dreams change; that's normal, too. Just having dreams pushes
you in the right direction!

• Do you get outside of yourself? Can you laugh at your own mistakes? Do you help others and work for something bigger than
and beyond yourself? Are you doing your part for our world and
environment? Sometimes we forget how great it feels to give.
We've all heard touching stories of tremendous outreach.

Will you join our movement? Remember to visit us at www.girls
withdreams.com and Facebook. Not only will you get more great
advice, but you will also meet some of
the girls who shared their stories in this
book. If you liked what you read, sign
up for a FREE membership and create
your own profile. You'll get more fun
freebies and secret tips—and besides,
it's a great way to be part of this growing
community of teen girls just like you.

> All of these steps, big
> and small, create ripple
> effects in our communi-
> ties, and they help us
> realize that we are part
> of something greater than
> ourselves.

Finally, I'd love to meet you and bring a Girls With Dreams program to your school. Look at our site for more information.

So what are your secrets for dealing with life's most challenging
problems? Do you have some that you would be willing to share?
We're already thinking about our next book and would love to hear
from you. Contact us at info@girlswithdreams.com.

In the meantime, I hope the tips and stories will remind you that
we are never alone and that we all have things to overcome and
good to share. It is my intention for these stories, ideas, and tips to
ultimately help you live a life that is true for you, so you don't have
to hide anymore, and you can live your best life!

The Final Quiz

The Seven Tips will always be here for you. The big question is, how well are you using them? *Take one final quiz and find out.* On a sheet of paper, write down the Seven Tips. Next to each one, decide on a scale of 1 to 10 how well you are using each strategy in your life. Your score will help you see where you can make improvements. If you have many areas you want to improve, don't overwhelm yourself. Start small and pick one place to start.

For example, if you scored a four on friends, maybe you'd like to improve there. What is one thing you could do this week to move your four to a five? You can also read more great stories, tips and advice, and get more freebies at www.girlswithdreams.com. These secrets belong to you. Use them!

> *Just don't give up trying to do what you really want to do. Where there is love and inspiration, I don't think you can go wrong.*
> —Ella Fitzgerald

Most of all, I hope you will discover that when you are honest about who you are and what you are experiencing, when you live in harmony with your passions, soul, and purpose—watch out world! Just think about what it would be like if all girls were living this way!

For now, start with yourself. With the help of the tips in this book, you will feel marvelous, powerful, radiant, confident, and strong. And you will absolutely make a significant contribution to the world!

Acknowledgments

A thank you is not enough; my gratitude runs deep. This book would not have been possible without the help of many teens, colleagues, friends, and family members. A special thank you to everyone at HCI, especially my editor, Allison Janse. A huge thanks to the countless teenagers who spent time talking with me. Your stories and lives have shown me the real meaning of courage and hope. A thank you is not enough to Kate Gilliam O'Toole, editor and art director at Girls with Dreams. Your belief in girls and my dream, along with your hundreds of selfless contributions, are priceless to me.

A special thanks to the teen advisors who were there in the beginning: Tessie Brady, Lindsay Edwards, Abby Feil, Aubrey Gohl, and Kylie Smith. Thank you as well to teen advisors who helped along the way: Chelsea Eifert, Sarah Henke, Molly Jasper, Jordyn Klackner, Stevie Johnson, and Thu Nguyen.

A special thank you to these contributors for opening up their hearts and sharing their secrets: Rukiya Anthony, Lisa Ashpole, Maddie Baum, Betsy Blanchard, Tessie Brady, Abby Collins, Patty Doyle, Lindsay Edwards, Dani Findlay, Amy Getzlow, Kate Gilliam O'Toole, Aubrey Gohl, Morgan Hamby, Megan Henderson, Sarah Henke, Lee Howard, Audrey Hudlin, Molly Jasper, Stevie Johnson, Alex Little, Emily "Mo" Molinaro, Thu Nguyen, Natalie Noble, Barbara Jean Palmer, Maria Ramirez, Katie Seto, Wendy Sheppard, Katie Siebuhr, Kylie Smith, Jeslyn Trau, Marissa Wegmann, and Elizabeth Whitaker. All of you energize and inspire me more than you know!

A huge thanks to Jan King for not just believing in me, but all women authors. You are amazing, and I'm so grateful for all you have done for me. Thanks to Gail Richards for your encouragement.

Debbie Josendale. I've loved our journey together the last few years. Your friendship, insight, and weekly encouragement means so much.

Thank you to my "Friend Circle," my friends from the Billionaire Girls Club, who I get inspiration from every day. I'm incredibly grateful for your love and cheering: Nicole Casanova, Sarah Endline, Traci Fenton, and Ingrid Vanderveldt.

And thanks to my special friends, family, and colleagues whose support means so much: Jennai Bachus, Kim Butler, Jenna Collins-Reed, Beth Crumbacher, Brian and Tami Gavaletz, Meggan Madden, Aaron Manfull, Monica Schwartz, Nel Shelby, Erik and Jen Silver, Michelle Slaughter, Andy VanVleck, and Mary Williams. Also, my friends from the St. Louis eWomen network chapter, especially Danelle Brown, Donna Gamache, and Karen Hoffman. Plus, I'd like to thank coaches Alecia Huck and Amanda Murphy who provided invaluable help along the way. To other friends whom I may have accidentally missed, I thank you too.

Finally, an enormous thank you to my family, who without them, this book would not be here. My parents gave me hundreds of hours of quiet time and sanity as well as their incredibly unselfish devotion to our family. You lifted us up during the tough times. And my husband, Steve, my best friend, thank you for being there when I needed it the most, bringing out the best in me, and for the countless sacrifices you've made to help me realize my dreams. And Dylan and Skyler, I love you more than words can express and appreciate your daily hugs, giggles, insights, questions, creativity, and limitless energy.

Share Your Secret

Gotta secret? You can share it at the book's official website, www.secretsgirlskeep.com. We would love to hear from you! Here are all of the places you can find us and meet up with girls just like you.

www.girlswithdreams.com is the official website dedicated to teens helping teens create their best life.

www.girlswithdreams.net, here you can create your own profile and meet up with other girls like you who are up to big things.

www.secretsgirlskeep.com, the official website and fan club for this book.

www.facebook.com, we're on too many places here to list them all. Find us by searching with these words: (Secrets Girls Keep, Girls With Dreams, Carrie Silver-Stock).

www.twitter.com/girlswithdreams (Follow us and what we're up to!)

www.youtube.com/girlswithdreams (Check out our cool videos on lots of fun topics)

www.myspace.com/girlswithdreams

www.carriesilverstock.com, Carrie's official site. Find out how to bring Carrie to your school or community.

Just remember: this book and your friends at www.girlswithdreams.com are never far away. While you're busy creating a wonderful life, don't forget to stop by and tell us your secret and how you're doing!

Note to Parents and Professionals Working with Teens

Find out more about how you can use this book to help your daughter or the young women in your life by visiting www.secretsgirlskeep.com. Use this book as a tool during individual or group sessions. Teachers or school professionals might want to consider helping girls start their own Girls with Dreams Friend Circle or use the exercises in this book to facilitate discussions or group activities. Bring Carrie to your school or event. Visit www.carriesilverstock.com to find out about exciting workshops and talks.

References

Introduction
Earth Day Network, "Green Tips," Earth Day Network, http://www.earthday.net/greentips.

Chapter Two
Centers for Disease Control and Prevention, "Understanding Teen Dating Violence Fact Sheet 2008," Centers for Disease Control and Prevention, http://www.cdc.gov/injury.

Chapter Six
Teen Research Unlimited, "Cox Communications Teen Internet safety Survey Wave II," Federal Trade Commission, http://www.ftc.gov/bcp/edu/pubs/consumer/tech/tec14.shtm.

Chapter Seven
Academy For Eating Disorders, "Prevalence of Eating Disorders," Academy For Eating Disorders, http://www.aedweb.org/eating_disorders/prevalence.cfm.

Alabama Coalition Against Dating Violence, "Dating Violence," Alabama Coalition Against Dating Violence, http://www.acadv.org/dating.html.

American Psychological Association, "What is Child Sexual Abuse," American Psychological Association Online, http://www.apa.org/releases/sexabuse/.

Centers for Disease Control and Prevention, "Dating Violence Fact Sheet," Centers for Disease Control and Prevention, http://www.cdc.gov/ncipc/dvp/dating_violence.htm.

Centers for Disease Control and Prevention, "Most Teens Not Provided STD or Pregnancy Prevention Counseling During Check-ups," Centers for Disease Control and Prevention, http://www.cdc.gov/STDConference/2000/media/Teens2000.htm.

Centers for Disease Control and Prevention, "Suicide: Facts at a Glance," Centers for Disease Control and Prevention, http://www.cdc.gov/ViolencePrevention/suicide/index.html.

Centers for Disease Control and Prevention, "Understanding Suicide," Centers for Disease Control and Prevention, http://www.cdc.gov/ViolencePrevention/suicide /index.html.

Cutter, D., Jaffe, J., and Segal, J., "Self-Injury: Types, Causes, and Treatment," Helpguide, http://www.helpguide.org/mental/self_injury.htm.

National Center for Chronic Disease Prevention and Health Promotion, "Trends in the Prevalence of Obesity, Dietary Behaviors, and Weight Control Practices," National Center for Chronic Disease Prevention and Health Promotion, http:// www.cdc.gov/HealthyYouth/yrbs/trends.htm.

National Highway Traffic Safety Administration, "Young Drivers Traffic Safety Fact Sheet (DOT-HS-811-001) Traffic Safety Facts 2007," National Highway Traffic Safety Administration, http://www.nhtsa.dot.gov/portal/site/nhtsa/menuitem. 6a6eaf83cf719ad24ec86e10dba046a0/.

National Institute on Alcohol Abuse and Alcoholism of the National Institutes of Health, "The Facts About Youth and Alcohol," National Institute on Alcohol Abuse and Alcoholism of the National Institutes of Health, http://pubs.niaaa. nih.gov/publications/PSA/Factsheet.htm.

http://www.samhsa.gov.

National Youth Violence Prevention Resource Center, "Youth Dating Violence-Information and Resources," National Youth Violence Prevention Resource Center, http://www.safeyouth.org/scripts/faq/prevdateviol.asp.

Substance Abuse and Mental Health Services Administration, "Youth & Substance Abuse: 5-Year Trends," Substance Abuse and Mental Health Services Administration, http://www.samhsa.gov/SAMHSAnewsLetter/Volume_17_Number_1 /YouthSubstanceAbuse.aspx.

Resources

Books

The Beauty Myth by Naomi Wolf. This timeless book shares Naomi's study of society and explores our culture's image of beauty and how women and girls are affected.

Deal with It! A Whole New Approach to Your Body, Brain, and Life as a gURL by Esther Drill, Heather McDonald, and Rebecca Odes.

The Good Girl Revolution by Wendy Shalit.

The Truth About Rape by Teresa M. Lauer.

Mean Chicks, Cliques, and Dirty Tricks: A Real Girl's Guide to Getting Through the Day with Smarts and Style by Erika V. Shearin Karres.

Sisterhood of the Traveling Pants series by Ann Brashares. A moving series of books about four friends, their families, and the bonds that keep them together and help them through tough times. These books have been turned into two movies.

The Divorce Workbook for Teens: Activities to Help You Move Beyond the Break Up by Lisa M. Schab.

Invisible Girls: The Truth about Sexual Abuse—A Book for Teen Girls, Young Women, and Everyone Who Cares about Them by Patti Feuereisen with Caroline Pincus.

Beyond the Blues: A Workbook to Help Teens Overcome Depression by Lisa M. Schab.

What's Eating You?: A Workbook for Teens With Anorexia, Bulimia, & Other Eating Disorders by Tammy Nelson.

Stopping the Pain: A Workbook for Teens Who Cut & Self-Injure by Lawrence E. Shapiro.

Hotlines

National Domestic Violence Hotline

1-800-799-SAFE (7233) or (TTY) 1-800-787-3224

National Teen Dating Abuse Helpline

Call toll-free at 1-866-331-9474 or (TTY) 1-866-331-8453.

Rape, Abuse, and Incest National Network

1-800-656-HOPE

National Runaway Switchboard

1-800-Runaway

Suicide Hotline

1-800-273-TALK (8255)

Movies

America the Beautiful (2008) is a powerful documentary about America's beauty standards and the impact it has on many levels, from pop culture to eating disorders.

Penelope (2007) is a unique fairy tale coproduced by Reese Witherspoon and starring Christina Ricci that shows the importance of learning to love ourselves for who we are.

American Teen (2008) highlights the ups and downs of teens through the eyes of five real high school seniors.

Akeelah and the Bee (2006) is a touching story about friendship, courage, and Akeelah overcoming her own fears to compete in the National Spelling Bee.

Bend It Like Beckham (2002) is an amazing story of friendship, determination, and courage.

Mean Girls (2004) is a somewhat comical but also serious look at bullies, cliques, and friendships in high school.

Odd Girl Out (2005) is a Lifetime movie based on Rachel Simmons's bestselling book that follows a middle school student struggling with emotional bullying from her friends. Much of what happens is in the cyber world.

Juno (2007) is about Juno, a teenager who faces an unplanned pregnancy and creates a plan to find the perfect parents to adopt her baby.

For a complete list of Carrie's favorite websites, books, and movies please visit www.secretsgirlskeep.com.

Index

A

aacap.org, 231
abuse, 60–62, 79–81, 230–31
  self-, 2, 61, 209–10, 237–41
academic strengths, 5
Academy for Eating Disorders, 222
acceptance, 242
achievement
  alcoholism and, 142
  grades and, 160–62
acne, 34, 36–37
activities
  drugs/alcohol and, 221
  over-involvement in, 164–66
addiction, drugs/alcohol and, 140–43, 221
adults, as confidantes, 2
affirmations for self, 48
AIDS, 235
Al-Anon, 143
Alateen, 143
alcohol, 217–22, 228
alcoholism
  parents and, 140–43
  teens and, 221
Alcott, Louisa May, 157
anger
  alcoholism and, 142
  divorce and, 150
  grief and, 242
Anorexia nervosa, 223
anxiety
  alcoholism and, 142
  pressure and, 165
apa.org, 231
arguing. See fighting
attraction
  to boys, 56
  to girls, 81–86
Austen, Jane, 87

B

Ban Breathnach, Sarah, 5
bargaining, 242
Barrymore, Drew, 25
beauty
  introduction to, 23
  lies about, 25–31
  secrets about, 24–25
  self-care and, 31–40
  self-confidence and, 40–49
Bebo, 191. See also Internet
body image, boys and, 55
Bombeck, Erma, 125
boys
  dating, 56–60 (see also dating)
  dating problems and, 67–81
  friends and, 105–6
  grades and, 161
  insight about, 60–67
  interests and, 57–58
  Internet and, 191–96
  lies about, 29–30
  older, 77–78

questions about dating, 53–56
secrets about, 50–53
breaking up, 76–77
breast development, puberty and, 34
Brown, Bobbi, 40
Buddha, 3
Bulimia nervosa, 223–24
bullies, 110–16, 187–91. See also teasing
bullyingawarenessweek.org, 205
bystanders, of bullying, 112, 113, 188, 190

C

careers, expectations for, 138–39
Carroll, Lewis, 19, 250
CDC. See Centers for Disease Control
Centers for Disease Control, 60, 80, 212, 222,
  226, 232, 234
charity, 166–67
chat rooms, 195–96
child predators, 195
childhelpusa.org, 231
clinginess, dating and, 66–67
cliques, 104–5
clothes. See fashion
college
  grades and, 161
  preparation for, 172–76
Coloroso, Barbara, 115
communication
  divorce and, 148
  Internet and, 197–201
  with parents, 134–35
  with teachers, 160
comparisons, beauty and, 28, 48–49
competition
  beauty and, 48–49
  friends and, 102–4
  rejection and, 170–72
  self and, 254
complaints, 44, 49
confidence. See also dreams
  beauty and, 45–46
  boys and, 90
  challenges and, 248
  dating violence and, 228
  family and, 153–54
  friends and, 121–22
  importance of, 9–12, 254
  Internet and, 203
  school and, 178–79
confusion, divorce and, 147
control, 228
Cook, Barbara, 254
courage
  beauty and, 45–46
  boys and, 90
  challenges and, 248
  family and, 153–54
  friends and, 121–22
  importance of, 9–12, 254
  Internet and, 203
  school and, 178–79
cutting, 2, 61, 209–10, 237–41

cyber bullying, 187–91
cyberspace. See Internet

D
dating. See also boys
    breaking up and, 76–77
    common problems of, 67–81
    finding boyfriends and, 59–60
    interests and, 57–58
    questions about, 53–56
    types of daters, 52–53, 66–67
    violence and, 60–62, 79–81, 227–29
    when to start, 57
denial, 2, 242
depression, 14, 142, 210–11, 214–15, 242
Diaz, Cameron, 17
disabilities, learning, 172
divorce
    parents and, 146–49
    remarriage after, 149–50
downloads, 196–97
dreams
    beauty and, 47
    boys and, 92
    challenges and, 250
    family and, 155
    friends and, 123
    importance of, 15–18, 254–55
    Internet and, 204–5
    school and, 179–80
drinking, 2, 4
driving, 4
drugs, 217–22, 228

E
eating disorders, 1, 2, 27–28, 222–27. See also nutrition
embarrassment
    alcoholism and, 142
    parents and, 143–44
Emerson, Ralph Waldo, 177, 182
emotional violence, 80–81
emotions
    boys and, 91–92
    health and, 14–15, 122
    puberty and, 34
empathy
    parents and, 132–34
    teachers and, 158–59
environmentalism, 21–22, 205
exercise, 13–14
expectations, 137–39

F
Facebook, 191. See also Internet
failure, 3
family
    abuse and, 231
    boys and, 63–64, 67
    challenges with, 125–26
    drugs/alcohol and, 221
    grandparents and, 126
    homosexuality and, 84–85, 126
    parent problems and, 131–50
    secrets about, 126–27
    siblings and, 127–30
fashion, 38–39
favorites, siblings and, 130
fears
    dating violence and, 228
    dreams and, 180

fighting
    dating violence and, 228
    parents and, 131–32, 140
    siblings and, 128–29
file sharing, 196–97
fitness
    beauty and, 46
    boys and, 90–92
    challenges and, 249
    family and, 154
    friends and, 122
    importance of, 12–15, 254
    Internet and, 204
    school and, 179
Fitzgerald, Ella, 256
food. See eating disorders; nutrition
forwards, Internet, 198
friends
    beauty and, 44, 49
    boys and, 67, 89
    boys as, 53–54
    bullies and, 110–16
    challenges and, 247
    challenges with, 100–110
    choosing, 7–9, 120–21
    circles (see Girls with Dreams Friend Circles)
    confidence and, 12
    dating violence and, 229
    depression and, 211
    dreams and, 181
    family and, 152–53
    good friendships and, 98–99
    holding on to, 116–19
    homosexuality and, 83–84
    importance of, 96–97, 254
    Internet and, 191–96, 202–3
    keeping secrets from, 97–98
    school and, 178
    sharing secrets with, 2
    suicide and, 214–15, 216–17
frustration
    alcoholism and, 142
    divorce and, 147
fun, ideas for, 221–22

G
gaming, 196
gengreenlife.com, 205
Giambattista, Lindsay, 186
girls
    attraction to, 81–86
    strengths and, 6
Girls with Dreams Friend Circles, xviii, xix, 8, 12, 19, 22, 117–19, 124, 165, 252, 254–55
Goethe, 121
gossip, 162–64
grades, 160–62
Graham, Martha, 253
grandparents, 126
green movement, 21–22
grief
    dealing with, 241–45
    divorce and, 148–49
    parents and, 145
growth, drugs/alcohol and, 220
guilt, alcoholism and, 142
gut feelings. See instincts

H
hair, caring for, 35–36
Halligan, Ryan Patrick, 188

happiness, boys and, 64–65
healing, abuse and, 231
health, 12–15
height, 25–26
homeschooling, 135–37
homosexuality, 81–86, 126
hook-ups, 1
hormones, 34–35, 63
humor, 19–20
Hyde, Catherine Ryan, 20–21

I
idolizing, dating and, 66–67
image, perfection and, 2
independence, financial, 166–67
insecurities, 1
instincts
    beauty and, 43
    boys and, 86–87
    challenges and, 245–46
    family and, 150–51
    friends and, 119
    importance of, 3–5, 254
    Internet and, 201
    school and, 176
Internet
    boys and, 78
    cyber bullying and, 187–91
    downloads/file sharing and, 196–97
    risks of, 185–87, 197–201
    savviness regarding, 193–94
    secrets about, 184–85
interviewing for jobs, 168–69
intuition. See instincts
involvement, activities and, 164–66

J
jealousy
    boys and, 78–79, 228
    friends and, 102–4
    siblings and, 128
Jeffers, Susan, 23
jobs, 167–69
journaling, xix, 18, 77, 91, 94, 107, 129, 134, 156,
    181, 183, 240, 241, 251
judgment, drugs/alcohol and, 220

K
Keller, Helen, 15, 246
Kent, Corita, 1
Kielburger, Craig, 186
Kingsley, Charles, 96
Kübler-Ross, Elisabeth, 242

L
laughing at self, 19–20
learning disabilities, 172
Locke, John, 13
Lopez, Jennifer, 138
loss
    dealing with, 241–45
    of parent, 145
love, boys and, 69–70, 87–88

M
magazines. See media
makeup, 39–40, 49
media, 4, 73
meganmeierfoundation.org, 188–89
Meier, Megan, 188–89, 205, 206
mental fitness, 14–15, 91–92, 122
mental violence, 80–81
messages, drugs/alcohol and, 218–20

metowe.com, 186
mistakes, friends and, 99
money, 166–69, 180
movies. See media
My Space/Our Planet: Change is Possible, 21
MySpace, 191. See also Internet

N
Nin, Anaïs, 8
nutrition, 14, 26–27, 215

O
online gaming, 196
organization
    college preparation and, 172–76
    grades and, 161–62
    involvement and, 164–65
overweight. See weight

P
parents, challenges with, 131–50
password safety, 189–90
patience, teachers and, 159
Pay it Forward, 20
paying it forward, 20–21
pedophiles, 195
peer pressure, 107–10, 190–91
perfection, 2
periods, puberty and, 34
personal information, on Internet, 197–98
physical fitness, 13–14
physical strengths, 5
physical violence, 81
Plato, 250
popularity, 104–5
pornography, 194–95
possessions, suicide and, 215
predators, sexual, 195
pregnancy, 73, 232–33
pressure, involvement and, 164–66
privacy, Internet, 198
professional help, 86
puberty, 34–35
put-downs, 7, 9, 68, 139–40

Q
Qualls, Ashley, 185

R
rape, 81
recovery, abuse and, 231
rejection
    athletics and, 170–72
    dating and, 66–67
relationships. See boys; dating; friends
relaxation, 15
relief, divorce and, 147
remarriage, 149–50
Remen, Rachel Naomi, 120
research, homosexuality and, 84
resources. See support
respect
    adults and, 230
    beauty and, 44
    boys and, 60–62, 89
    challenges and, 247
    family and, 152–53
    friends and, 120–21
    importance of, 7–9, 254
    Internet and, 202–3
    school and, 178
Roberts, Julia, 50, 123
role models

confidence and, 12
dreams and, 181
routines, beauty, 28–29
rumors, 162–64
ryanpatrickhalligan.org, 188

S
sadness, divorce and, 147
Salk, Jonas, 184
savings, 166–67
school
  challenges with, 170–72
  grades and, 160–62
  homeschooling and, 135–37
  life after, 172–76
  money and, 166–69
  problems at, 6
  secrets about, 157–58
  social concerns and, 162–64
  teachers and, 158–60
secrets
  about beauty, 24–25
  about boys, 50–53
  about cyberspace, 184–85
  about family, 126–27
  about school, 157–58
  about tough subjects, 208–10
  girls and, 1–3
  identification of, 253–56
  keeping from friends, 97–98
  sharing with friends, 2
self
  boys and, 64–65, 93–94
  caring for, 31–40
  challenges and, 250–51
  competition and, 254
  confidence in, 9–12
  dating and, 66–67
  family and, 155–56
  friends and, 98–99, 123
  getting outside of, 18–22, 47–49
  importance of, 255
  Internet and, 205
  laughing at, 19–20
  school and, 180–81
  strength and, 7–9
  suicide and, 215
  view of, 27–28
self-esteem. See self
self-harming behavior, 2, 61, 209–10, 237–41
selfinjury.com, 240
separation, parents and, 146–49
sex
  boundaries regarding, 71–73
  boys and, 55–56
  drugs/alcohol and, 220
  homosexuality and, 81–86
  puberty and, 34
  STDs and, 73, 233–37
  violence and, 61, 228
sexting, 195, 197–98
sexual abuse, 230–31
sexual predators, 195
sexual violence, 81
sexually transmitted diseases. See STDs
shock, divorce and, 147
siblings, 127–30
skin, caring for, 36–37
sleep patterns. See fitness; suicide
social concerns
  Internet and (see Internet)
  school and, 162–64
  strengths and, 5

social network sites, 191. See also Internet
spending, 166–67
spiritual strengths, 5
STDs, 73, 233–37
strengths
  beauty and, 43–44
  boys and, 88–89
  challenges and, 246–47
  family and, 151–52
  friends and, 119–20
  grades and, 161
  identification of, 181
  Internet and, 201–2
  recognizing, 5–7
  school and, 176–77
  self-care and, 32
stress
  controlling, 254
  nutrition and, 14
  pressure and, 164–66
success
  confidence and, 10–11
  secrets and, 1
suicide, 2, 212–17
support. See also Girls with Dreams Friend Circles
  abuse and, 231
  alcoholism and, 142–43
  depression and, 211
  divorce and, 148
  eating disorders and, 224–25
  friends and, 99
  homosexuality and, 83–84, 86
  pregnancy and, 232–33
  pressure and, 165
  self-harming behavior and, 239–41
  STDs and, 236
  suicide and, 214–15
  weight and, 227

T
taylorscloset.org, 186
teachers, 158–60
teasing, 162–64. See also bullies
teen pregnancy, 73, 232–33
teenangels.com, 205
television. See media
texting, 195, 197–98
thenationalcampaign.org, 198
Think Before You Post campaign, 190
Thompson, Dorothy, 207
trust
  alcoholism and, 142
  parents and, 135–37

V
victims
  of abuse, 231
  of bullying, 112, 188
  of violence (see violence)
violence
  dating, 60–62, 79–81, 227–29
  parents and, 140, 144–45
virginity. See sex
Voltaire, 249
volunteering, 20

W
weight, 25–26, 49, 222–27
whateverlife.com, 185
Winfrey, Oprah, 21, 248

Meet Carrie

Photo by Laun Baker

Carrie Silver-Stock, M.S.W., L.C.S.W., founded Girls with Dreams (www.girlswithdreams.com) to create a global movement where girls discover their power, passion, and big dreams. The mission is simple: girls will empower one another to build their best lives while learning how to make a positive impact in their own lives and the world.

She has advocated for and helped young people for more than fifteen years, in numerous settings, from schools to mental health agencies. She is a former radio talk show host, speaker, social worker, author, life coach, and frequent contributor to newspapers and other organizations, including *GLOW* magazine. Silver-Stock has appeared in numerous media outlets, such as ABC Radio, *Guidelines for Mental Health* (cable TV), *Today in St. Louis* (KSDK/NBC), Fox, *On the Road with IV, Women's Media*, CKOM Radio, and the *Working Women's Show*. Her first book, *The Powder Box Secrets*, won several awards, including the prestigious Benjamin Franklin award.

Carrie's favorite activities include spending time with her husband, two boys, and two dogs, and staying active. She especially loves walking, boating, water-skiing and working out.